MICHAEL FIELD, THE POET

broadview editions
series editor: L.W. Conolly

MICHAEL FIELD, THE POET
Published and Manuscript Materials

"Michael Field"
(Katharine Bradley and Edith Cooper)

edited by Marion Thain and Ana Parejo Vadillo

broadview editions

Library and Archives Canada Cataloguing in Publication

Field, Michael
  Michael Field, the poet / edited by Marion Thain and Ana Parejo Vadillo.

(Broadview editions)
Includes bibliographical references.
ISBN 978-1-55111-675-4

  I. Thain, Marion   II. Parejo Vadillo, Ana   III. Title.   IV. Series: Broadview editions

PR4699.F5 A6 2009   821'.8   C2009-901361-4

Broadview Editions
The Broadview Editions series represents the ever-changing canon of literature in English by bringing together texts long regarded as classics with valuable lesser-known works.

Advisory editor for this volume: Martin R. Boyne

Broadview Press is an independent, international publishing house, incorporated in 1985. Broadview believes in shared ownership, both with its employees and with the general public; since the year 2000 Broadview shares have traded publicly on the Toronto Venture Exchange under the symbol BDP.

We welcome comments and suggestions regarding any aspect of our publications— please feel free to contact us at the addresses below or at broadview@broadviewpress.com.

North America
Post Office Box 1243, Peterborough, Ontario, Canada K9J 7H5
2215 Kenmore Avenue, Buffalo, NY, USA 14207
Tel: (705) 743-8990; Fax: (705) 743-8353;
email: customerservice@broadviewpress.com

UK, Ireland, and continental Europe
NBN International, Estover Road, Plymouth UK PL6 7PY
Tel: 44 (0) 1752 202300   Fax: 44 (0) 1752 202330
email: enquiries@nbninternational.com

Australia and New Zealand
NewSouth Books
c/o TL Distribution
15-23 Helles Ave, Moorebank, NSW, 2170
Tel: (02) 8778 9999
Fax: (02) 8778 9944
email: orders@tldistribution.com.au

www.broadviewpress.com

This book is printed on paper containing 100% post-consumer fibre.

Typesetting and assembly: True to Type Inc., Claremont, Canada.

PRINTED IN CANADA

Contents

Acknowledgements

This project was part-funded by an Arts and Humanities Research Council research-leave grant awarded to Marion Thain; we gratefully acknowledge this assistance. We would also like to thank the University of Exeter for providing Ana Parejo Vadillo with a 2005 RA Scheme grant.

For permission to reproduce manuscript materials, we thank: the British Library, London (for material from the following deposits: Add.ms. 45854; Add.ms. 45855; Add.ms. 46776–46804B; Add.ms. 46866; Add.ms. 46867; Add.ms. 58087; Add.ms. 58089); the Bodleian Library, Oxford (for material from the following deposits: Ms.Eng.Lett.c.418; Ms.Eng.Lett.c.419; Ms.Eng.Lett.c.432; Ms.Eng.Lett.e.32; Ms.Eng.Lett.e.33); the Trustees of the National Library of Scotland (for material from the following deposits: Dep. 372, no. 17, no. 18, no. 20); Harvard University and I Tatti (for the Berenson manuscript collection); and the Berg Collection of English and American Literature, The New York Public Library, Astor, Lenox and Tilden Foundations (for the correspondence from John Gray). We also gratefully acknowledge the assistance of library staff at these locations, particularly that of Colin Harris at the Bodleian Library and Ilaria Della Monica at I Tatti.

For copyright permissions we thank Leonie Sturge-Moore and Charmian O'Neil, for the material by Michael Field and Charles Ricketts; the Order of Preachers, for the letters from John Gray to Michael Field; the Dominican Council, for the letters of Michael Field to John Gray; *Villa I Tatti*, for the letters from Bernard Berenson to Michael Field; Nicholas Deakin, for material by Havelock Ellis; Brian Read, for the letter from Arthur Symons; and Harper Collins, for the letters from John Ruskin and Oscar Wilde to Michael Field.

For illustrations, we thank: the Mark Samuel Lasner Collection, University of Delaware, for generous permission to reproduce illustration 1, 4, and 5; the University of Bristol's Special Collections for kind permission to reproduce illustration 2 and 3; the British Library for illustration 6 (Add.ms. 46780 f. 134r); and the Bodleian Library, Oxford, for the cover illustration (Ms.Eng. misc.c.304 f. 22).

Every effort has been made to secure permissions for reproduction where copyrights are still active. If we have failed in any case to trace a copyright holder, we apologize for any apparent negligence and will make the necessary arrangements at the earliest opportunity.

A particular vote of thanks must go to Kelsey Thornton for help with checking particularly troublesome transcriptions. For help with translating Greek and Latin sources we thank: John Hilary; Nial Livingstone; Kyriaki Hadjiafxendi; Yopie Prins; and the Classics scholars at Birmingham University. For help with translating German we thank Martina Lauster. (Any mistakes in these translations are ours and not theirs.) For advice on our proposed selections we thank the following: Sharon Bickle; Joseph Bristow; Hilary Fraser; Michelle Lee; Rachel Morley; Angela Leighton; and Margaret Stetz. We would like to draw the reader's attention to Sharon Bickle's book, *The Fowl and the Pussycat: the Love Letters of Michael Field, 1876-1909*, which was published when we were at final proof stage of this manuscript and we were glad to benefit from this work. We also acknowledge the work of J.G. Paul Delaney, whose editing of both Michael Field and Charles Ricketts has been influential for this volume, and of Ivor Treby, whose Michael Field catalogue has been invaluable. Finally, our thanks must go to Yopie Prins, who first suggested this edition to us.

List of Illustrations

Michael Field: A Brief Chronology

1835 Feb. 1 Emma Harris Bradley (Katharine's elder sister, and Edith's mother) is born to Emma Harris Bradley and Charles Bradley in Birmingham.

1846 Oct. 27 **Katharine Harris Bradley** is born to Emma Harris Bradley and Charles Bradley (their second daughter) in Digbeth, Birmingham.

1848 Feb. 17 Charles Bradley dies, and Katharine is left alone with her mother and sister.

1860 Oct. 27 James Robert Cooper is married to Katharine's sister, now Emma Harris Cooper.

1862 Jan. 12 **Edith Emma Cooper** is born to James and Emma in Kenilworth: Katharine's niece.

1863 March 5 Amy Katharine Cooper is born to James and Emma, Edith's younger sister. Emma becomes an invalid.

1867 July By now Katharine and her mother are living with the Cooper family.

1868 May 30 Katharine's mother dies of cancer.

1868 Oct. 16 Katharine is studying in Paris.

1874 Oct. Katharine goes to Newnham College, Cambridge.

1875 May 10 Katharine's first book, *The New Minnesinger*, is published under the pseudonym Arran Leigh.

1879 Autumn The Cooper family and Katharine move to Ivythorpe, Stoke Bishop, Barton Regis, near Bristol (they move house several times in the Bristol area over the next few years—during these years Katharine and Edith attend Bristol University).

1881 May 21 *Bellerophôn* is published by Arran and Isla Leigh, the first verse-drama on which Katharine and Edith collaborate.

1884 May Publication of *Callirrhoë* and *Fair Rosamund*: two verse-dramas and the first volume to carry the name Michael Field.

1888 April The Cooper family and Katharine move to Blackboro' Lodge, Reigate, Surrey. Katharine and Edith begin the diary of Michael Field.

1889 May 20	Publication of *Long Ago*, the first book of poetry to appear under the name Michael Field.
1889 Aug. 20	Edith's mother (Katharine's sister) dies of cancer.
1893 Oct. 27	One of their dramas, *A Question of Memory*, is staged at the Opera Comique Theatre (Michael Field's only production).
1897 June 24	Edith's father (Katharine's brother-in-law) disappears mountaineering in Zermatt: months later they discover he died in a fall.
1898 Dec. 25	Amy (Edith's younger sister) gets engaged to John Ryan.
1899 May 16	Edith and Katharine move to 'the Paragon' in Richmond, where, after Amy marries, they will live alone together for the first time.
1899 Sept. 25	Amy and John marry and live, at first, in Clifton.
1907	Both Katharine and Edith convert to Catholicism, writing almost exclusively religious verse from now on.
1910 Jan. 22	Amy dies in Dublin.
1913 Dec. 13	Edith dies.
1914 Sept. 26	Katharine dies.

Michael Field's Circle:
A Key to Names

A.W.F. (All Wise Fowl)—nickname for Katharine Bradley.

Archer, William (1856–1924)
Author and critic. He advised on Michael Field's production of
A Question of Memory.

Bell, Amy
Good friend of Katharine Bradley.

Bell, Ernest (1851–1933)
Publisher who published many of Michael Field's plays and
several books of their poetry.

Berenson, Bernhard or Bernard (1865–1959)
A charismatic art critic and connoisseur of Renaissance art, who
was enlisted to tutor the women during their tours of Italian art
galleries, but who then became closely involved with them per-
sonally.

Bottomley, Gordon (1874–1948)
Writer (poet and playwright), who, with his wife, became a good
friend of Michael Field, and an admirer of their work.

Browning, Robert (1818–89)
Well-known poet, and mentor to Michael Field. He was drawn to
the women through the quality of their early work.

Cobbe, Frances Power (1818–1904)
Well-known women's rights writer and campaigner, and antivivi-
sectionist.

Cooper, Amy Katharine (married to John Ryan in 1899)
(1863–1910)
Edith Cooper's sister and Katharine Bradley's niece.

Cooper, Emma Harris (1818–89)
Elder sister of Katharine Bradley, and mother of Edith and Amy
Cooper.

Cooper, James Robert (1818–97)
Brother-in-law of Katharine Bradley, and father of Edith and Amy Cooper.

Costelloe (later Berenson), Mary (1864–1945)
She left her husband for Berenson, whom she married once her husband was dead. She travelled with Berenson, shared his passion for art, and became involved with Bradley and Cooper through him.

"Doctrine"—nickname for Bernhard Berenson.

"Elk"—nickname for Elkin Mathews (1851–1921)
Avant-garde, decadent publisher. With John Lane he published the controversial *Yellow Book*. After dissolving his partnership with Lane, he became one of the most important publishers of poetry in the late nineteenth and early twentieth century.

Ellis, Henry Havelock (1859–1939)
One of the leading sexologists of the age. He was impressed with Michael Field's early poetry (particularly *Long Ago*) and corresponded with the women about it.

Field—nickname for Edith Cooper.

FitzGibbon, Gerald (dates unknown)
Priest at St. Elizabeth's Catholic Church, Vineyard, Richmond. Edith Cooper's confessor.

Goss; Gosscannon—nicknames for Gerald Fitzgibbon.

Gray, John (1866–1934)
The decadent poet turned priest who was thought to be the model for Oscar Wilde's *The Picture of Dorian Gray*, but who converted around 1900 and became a devout Catholic. He was the author of *Silverpoints* (1893) and *Spiritual Poems* (1896).

Gray, John Miller (1850–94)
Curator of the Scottish National Portrait Gallery, but also a literary reviewer for several journals. A trusted friend of Bradley and Cooper, he was valued highly for his comments on their work, as well as for his ability to gain their works coverage in the press.

Grein, J.T. (1862–1935)
Journalist and drama critic, he founded the Independent Theatre Society in 1891 and staged Michael Field's play *A Question of Memory* at the Opera Comique Theatre in 1893.

Henry, Hennie, Heinrich—nicknames for Edith Cooper.
The nurse who fell in love with Cooper in Dresden renamed her Heinrich. After their return to London, Bradley announced that "Henry" had been born.

Kittie—nickname for Amy Cooper.

Lee, Vernon (Violet Paget) (1856–1935)
One of the most important art critics and theorists of the *fin de siècle*, she became famous for her *Studies of the Eighteenth Century in Italy* and for her work on psychological aesthetics with her lover Kit Anstruther-Thomson.

McNabb, Vincent (1868–1943)
A Dominican priest who was in London at the Priory, Haverstock Hill, until his move to Leicester (Hawkesyard Priory) in the middle of 1908. Bradley moved to be near him towards the end of her life.

Meynell, Alice (1847–1922)
Well-known poet and contemporary of Michael Field.

Moore, George (1852–1933)
Well-known novelist and contemporary of Michael Field.

Mud, muddie—"mother": nickname for Edith Cooper's mother (Emma Harris Cooper).

Old Gentleman—nickname for Robert Browning.

Painter—nickname for Charles Ricketts.

Persian Puss, P.P., P.—nicknames for Edith Cooper.

The Puss, little pussie—nicknames for Amy Cooper.

Raffalovich, Marc André (1864–1934)
Russian-born English poet and writer on sexuality. Also a patron

of the arts. He was very close to John Gray, under whose influence he converted to Catholicism.

Ricketts, Charles de Sousy (1866–1931)
Artist, designer, and art writer. Founder of the Vale Press, which published several of Michael Field's books. He also designed beautiful covers for some of them. A very close friend to Bradley and Cooper.

Robinson, A. Mary F. (1857–1944)—Afterwards Darmesteter, afterwards Duclaux.
A successful poet, and contemporary of Michael Field, moved to Paris in the late 1880s after her marriage to James Darmesteter.

"The Roadman"—John Lane (1854–1925)
Avant-garde, decadent publisher, co-founder of the Bodley Head press. With Elkin Mathews he published the controversial *Yellow Book*.

Ruskin, John (1819–1900)
Writer, critic, and philanthropist who was Bradley's first mentor. They fell out over Ruskin's criticism of her ambitions and her work, and had little to do with each other after 1880.

Shannon, Charles (1863–1937)
Painter and lithographer. He collaborated and cohabitated with Charles Ricketts. Also a close friend to the women. He and Ricketts seemed to provide Bradley and Cooper with a partnership they recognised as similar to their own.

Sim, Simorg, Simiorg (a monstrous bird of Persian fable)—nicknames for Katharine Bradley.

Sturge Moore, Thomas (1870–1944)
Writer and artist who became Michael Field's literary executor, a role he took very seriously, publishing selections from the diaries and the poetry.

Symons, Arthur (1865–1945)
Decadent poet and writer; a figure central to late nineteenth-century literature.

V—presumably an icon of the monstrous Simiorg—signature for Katharine Bradley.

Whym Chow; Whymmie (1897–1906)
Bradley and Cooper's beloved Chow dog; one of a number of pets, but perhaps the most significant to the women's life narrative.

Wilde, Oscar (1854–1900)
Well-known playwright and poet, with whom Bradley and Cooper had a few encounters. He was a key member of the literary circle of which they were a part.

Yeats, William Butler (1865–1939)
Well-known poet and dramatist who was interested in Michael Field's work.

Figure 1. Michael Field (Katharine Bradley and Edith Cooper), 1891.

Introduction

> "To reveal art and conceal the artist is art's aim."
>
> Oscar Wilde

Becoming "Michael Field"

Oscar Wilde's playful aphorism illuminates Katharine Bradley and Edith Cooper's decision to enter the public world of letters in 1884 under the joint pseudonym of "Michael Field." It also explains the women's distress when news of the dual and female authorship was leaked to the press. The creative ferment that was "Michael Field" stemmed from an aesthetic programme that proclaimed the primacy of art over life. They thought of the world aesthetically, and consciously made their lives subservient to art—to Michael Field. "This happy union of two in work & aspiration," as Cooper and Bradley defined the entity "Michael Field," was endowed with the power to transfigure the world through the primacy of language, of poetry.[1] Thus, the revelation of their pseudonym, as they wrote to Robert Browning, "would indeed be utter ruin." "[T]he report of lady-authorship will dwarf & enfeeble our work at every turn. [...] [W]e have many things to say the world will not tolerate from a woman's lips. We must be free as dramatists to work out in the open air of nature—exposed to her vicissitudes, witnessing her terrors: we cannot be stifled in drawing-room conventionalities."[2] For Katharine Bradley and her sixteen years younger niece, Edith Cooper, to be "Michael Field" was to be reborn into language, into poetry.

But the sharing of one complete name reflected as much about their aesthetics as about their own literary and personal relationship, of which they often spoke as a "marriage."[3] The women were keen readers of Spinoza and adopted the metaphysical

---

1 EC to Robert Browning (30 May 1884). See "Letters" Section, p. 310.

2 KB to Robert Browning (23 November 1884). See "Letters" Section, p. 311.

3 See, for instance, KB to EC (August 1885). See "Letters" Section, p. 304. Of Robert and Elizabeth Barrett Browning's marriage they observed: "those two poets, man and wife, wrote alone; each wrote, but did not bless or quicken one another at their work; *we are closer married*" (Michael Field, *Works and Days. From the Journal of Michael Field*, ed. T. & D.C. Sturge Moore [London: John Murray, 1933], 16).

monism of his *Foundations of the Moral Life* (1632), the idea that there is one basic substance whose attribute is thought, as the philosophical foundation of their being. As they explained to Browning, quoting verbatim from Spinoza: "if two ~~natures~~ [<] individuals of exactly the same nature [>] are joined together, they make up a single individual, doubly stronger than each alone."[1] On the basis of their decision to create a world of poetry, they began privately to close the gap between the real Katharine Bradley and Edith Cooper and their ideal "Michael Field" with the writing of a journal, aptly entitled *Works and Days*, which the women began in 1888 and continued to write until the end of their lives. This intricate and exceptional text unveils a powerful narrative of how this writing entity became their everyday reality; of how, to paraphrase Wilde's axiom in *The Decay of Lying*, their joint lives came to imitate the art of Michael Field.

From Michael Field's early biographers, Mary Sturgeon and Ursula Bridges, we know that Katharine Harris Bradley was born in Birmingham to a tobacco-manufacturer in 1846 and that her father died when she was only two years old. She had one sister, Emma, eleven years her elder. When Emma married James Robert Cooper they went to live in Kenilworth. It was here that Emma's daughter, Edith Emma Cooper, was born in 1862. The absence of Katharine's father and the persistent frailty of Emma provided the impetus for Katharine and her mother to move to Kenilworth to live with the Coopers around the time of Edith's birth. But Katharine was soon to play a far more central role within her sister's family than she could have expected. When Emma Cooper became a permanent invalid after the birth of her second daughter, Amy (in 1864), Katharine, at the age of eighteen, took the responsibility of caring for her niece Edith. In spite of Emma, who saw with great anxiety and uneasiness her daughter's admiration and affection for her sister (and tried in all sorts of ways to stop it), Bradley and Cooper were soon inseparable.[2]

The women were of independent means and had a good education. Bradley followed the path of many aesthetes and decadents of the later part of the nineteenth century and in 1868 travelled to Paris to pursue her literary interests at the prestigious *Collège de France*. During this period, not only did she learn French language and literature, but she was instructed on subjects such as Latin, the Woman Question, and the history of the

---

1 KB to Robert Browning (23 November 1884). See "Letters" Section, p. 311.

2 See, for example, KB to EC (April 1885). "Letters" Section, p. 300.

Roman Empire. She also fell in love with Alfred Gérente, twenty-five years her elder and the brother of her Parisian companion Eliza. His sudden death weeks after their first meeting meant that she never told him of her love. She returned to England broken-hearted, with the conviction that she would be a spinster for life. Her enthusiasm for literature and writing, however, continued to grow, and in 1874 she attended a summer course in Newnham College, Cambridge, recently founded to promote academic excellence for women. She would later reflect on the importance of her period at Cambridge: "I came to Newnham empty-headed, with vague ambition, vague sentiment—the pulpy lyrics of the N. M. in my brain."[1] A year later, in 1875, Longman published Bradley's first book of poems, *The New Minnesinger and Other Poems*, under the pseudonym of "Arran Leigh."

Bradley completed her education at University College, Bristol, where the family moved in 1879. Aged seventeen, Cooper could now join her aunt. Publicly, and for the next five years, Bradley and Cooper were day students at University College, attending courses on classics and philosophy.[2] Secretly, as Sturgeon says, "they were already dedicated to poetry, and sworn in fellowship." She also notes that it was an era when "Higher Education and Women's Rights and Anti-Vivisection were being indignantly championed, and when 'aesthetic dress' was being very consciously worn—all by the same kind of people. Katharine and Edith were of that kind."[3] The next volume of poems to be published marked the beginning of the women's literary partnership, which was to last for the rest of their lives. *Bellerophôn* (1881) was presented as the work of two people: "Arran and Isla Leigh."[4] Yet there were also pronounced differences between the women: Cooper was passionate about philosophy, Bradley about Greek language and literature. Although they presented themselves in their writing as a seamless whole, the women were in fact very different in appearance and character.

---

1 Entry for 13 February 1891. See "Diaries" Section, p. 245.
2 See Ivor C. Treby, *The Michael Field Catalogue* (n.p.: De Blackland Press, 1998), 29; Mary Sturgeon, *Michael Field* (London: George G. Harrap, 1921), 18.
3 Sturgeon, 21, 20.
4 Yopie Prins notes that this pair of names also blurs genders and "suggests various possible relationships between the two names: a pair of siblings, a parent and child, a married couple," an ambiguity utterly appropriate for an aunt and niece who were also mother and daughter, sisters, lovers ("Greek Maenads, Victorian Spinsters," in *Victorian Sexual Desire*, ed. Richard Dellamora [Chicago and London: U of Chicago P, 1999], 43–81, 55).

Figure 2. Edith Cooper's *Carte de Visite* as "Field," c.1885.

Bradley was robust, forthright, and plumper, while Cooper was less confident in public and more fragile and feminine in appearance. By the time the women began writing together, their relationship was, in Sturgeon's words, a friendship "clearly on the grand scale and in the romantic manner."[1] Textually and sexually the women were becoming closer, an erotic bond developing to supplement and complicate their familial ties.

This budding literary career was positively discouraged by John Ruskin, Bradley's mentor at this stage in her life (1875–80), who at one point bluntly told her to stop writing poetry.[2] She became a "companion" of his Guild of St George[3] for a while, but a series of letters between the two charts the rift that developed around Christmas 1877 over Bradley's acquisition of a pet dog, which inaugurated a new phase of the poets' lives. Ruskin's much quoted letter is a testament to Bradley's increasing disaffection with Victorian culture:

> I don't care how much pain you are in—but that you should be such a fool as coolly to write to me that you had ceased to believe in God—and had found some comfort in a dog—this is deadly. And of course I have at once to put you out of the St. George's Guild—which primarily refuses atheists—not because they are wicked, but because they are fools.[4]

Gradually the two women were finding their way towards a sensual, pagan, and erotic mode of being, which was very far from Ruskin's petty and puritanical doctrine. The term "pagan" had a multiplicity of connotations at this time that accurately signify the various facets of Michael Field's life between 1877 and 1907: the Graeco-Roman non-Christian realm—and its pantheistic religion—that so fascinated the two women, but also those tenets central to Pater's aestheticism (itself so connected to the ancient world) that structured Bradley and Cooper's experience at this time, and the "perverse" sexuality (liberal heterosexuality and any homosexually inclined behaviour) that was connected with this lifestyle. Their commitment to this pagan existence was translated into their everyday life in many ways. For

---

1 Sturgeon, 23.
2 "I *should* like you to give up dreaming, and writing verses as far as you possibly can" (Michael Field, *Works and Days*, 154).
3 Ruskin's philanthropic society. Bradley contributed financially to the Guild but did not live according to its laws.
4 John Ruskin to KB (30 December 1877). See "Letters" Section, p. 308.

example, they erected a Bacchic altar in their garden and often celebrated good reviews of their work by dancing madly like Bacchic satyrs.[1] They were also engaged in building up a large library collection of Dionysian works,

The Faun "Michael Field" was born out of this pagan mode of experience, and came into existence with the publication of the verse-drama *Callirrhoë* in 1884. ("John Cooley"—a combination of Cooper and Bradley—had also been experimented with as the signature for the first draft of *Callirrhoë*.[2]) It was at this time that the women's literary career began in earnest. "Michael Field" was the name under which they were to establish their literary reputation, and which they used for all subsequent publications (except for those dramas, such as *Borgia*, that were published anonymously). Bradley even continued to publish under this name after Cooper's death. The pseudonym came directly from the women's private articulation of their identity. Fond of nicknames, Katharine was known amongst her friends as "Michael" or "Sim," and Edith was "Field" or "Puss." "Michael" seems to have carried connotations of the archangel, while "Field" has a less obvious significance.[3] *Callirrhoë*, which was an instant success, brought the couple to the attention of Robert Browning and secured his enthusiastic support. He took Ruskin's place as their new literary mentor, and this friendship was to last until Browning's death. However, after the generally very successful reception of *Callirrhoë* in 1884, Michael Field's dramatic work was never to be so joyously received again.

It was only for a very short while that Michael Field was thought to be a single male author. During that time the women received some intense personal interest from other writers (such as André Raffalovich and A. Mary F. Robinson) who seemed to be looking for intimacy of a kind only made possible by a belief in their masculinity.[4] Some knew, at this stage, that Michael Field

1 Entry for 10 September 1893. See "Diaries" Section, p. 259.

2 Bod.ms: Ms.Eng.poet.d.74 (a partial draft of the play in manuscript form).

3 Treby argues that the name Field comes from the earlier pseudonym "Arran Leigh," because Field and "lea" have the same meaning, which links Michael Field firmly back to a tradition that contained "Aurora Leigh." In this case, the name is both a means of situating the women within a particular female literary heritage, while also protecting and demarcating the androgynous textual space they want to occupy (*The Michael Field Catalogue*, 30).

4 See A. Mary F. Robinson to "Michael Field Esqre" (16 May 1884) and KB to Robert Browning (23 November 1884). "Letters" Section, pp. 348 and 311.

was a pseudonym, but didn't know the identity of the writer; a game of divination ensued, involving Havelock Ellis, one of the great sexological figures of the age, and whose sister would later design clothes for the women.

Bradley and Cooper left Bristol in 1888 to move, with their remaining family members, to Reigate. Reigate's closeness to London ensured the women's involvement in London's budding literary and artistic world. The British Museum, The National Gallery, literary "at homes," musical soirées, lectures at Bernard's Inn, and visits to the theatre now became common-place.[1] They also became lyric poets with the publication in 1889 of their first volume of verse, *Long Ago*, widely acclaimed as one of the most important lyrical collections of the *fin de siècle*. It was also during this phase of their lives that they travelled in Europe, mainly with the purpose of seeing art of various kinds. In the course of a trip to Dresden, where the women hoped to hear Wagner's opera cycle *The Ring*[2] and to feast their eyes on their favourite painting, Giorgone's *Sleeping Venus*, Cooper suffered an attack of scarlet fever. Her hospital treatment involved cutting off her hair. With her new boyish looks she was renamed "Heinrich" by a female nurse who showered her with mad kisses and hungry embraces. Though "jealous" of the nurse's advances and "stormily tearful," Bradley joyfully celebrated the birth of the androgynous "Henry," as Bradley would address Cooper from now on.[3]

During these trips abroad they were sometimes accompanied by friends, and one, in particular, was much sought out for this purpose: Bernard Berenson, the well-known art critic, was a subject of fascination for the women. They first met him at the Parisian "at home" of the American poet and woman of letters Mrs. Chandler Moulton. Cooper's feelings for the man caught her unaware. Her relationship with Berenson turned out to be as personally tempestuous as it was professionally productive. Painfully recognising that she "should sicken of very passion for him,"[4] their frisson soon turned sour, resulting in a long period of estrangement. Angst-ridden about the future of "Michael Field," Cooper calmed Bradley's anxiety by confiding to her in

---

1   See Ana Parejo Vadillo, *Women Poets and Urban Aestheticism* (Bas-ingstoke: Palgrave, 2005), 163–75.

2   *The Ring* explores a number of incestuous relationships, including the love between Siegfried and his aunt Brünnhilde.

3   Entry for December 1891. See "Diaries" Section, p. 251.

4   Entry for 22 June 1892. See "Diaries" Section, p. 254.

their diary: "I love my art & will not dare to injure it—I love my own Love & could not do violence to her or myself—so let her not fear."[1]

During this time, their friendship with John Miller Gray—the curator of the Scottish National Portrait Gallery—blossomed both in personal and professional terms. Impressed with their first volumes, he was a loyal supporter, and, as a critic and reviewer of the arts he was generous with his advice on their subsequent works. This advice was sought avidly by the women, who both respected his opinion and recognised their own need for input from outside their own tightly knit authorial dyad. It helped a great deal that Gray's criticism was always tactfully given, with sensitivity to the women's foibles. He was, in fact, appointed as their literary executor, until his early death (in 1894) prompted a change of plan. Their success during the 1880s and early 1890s put them in touch with many in the literary world, including George Meredith (who sent them a letter of praise on the publication of *Long Ago* on 13 June 1889), A. Mary F. Robinson, Arthur Symons, Richard Garnett, Lionel Johnson, D.G. Rossetti, Oscar Wilde, Herbert Spencer, and many other influential figures of the age. Their passion for beautiful objects led them to contact book designers, painters, and illustrators. During a visit to the studio of Herbert Horne and Selwyn Image, the designer of many of Michael Field's books during the 1880s and early 1890s in London's Fitzroy Street, they could not resist this comment: "Here lives Herbert Horne, editor of the <u>Century Guild Hobby Horse</u>, here Selwyn Image has his studio, & other artists & artmen dwell in unity."[2] Michael and Field were keen to meet other kindred spirits living and working as one, such as Berenson and his lover (later his wife), Mary Costelloe, or the artists Charles Ricketts and Charles Shannon, who gradually became fixtures in the women's lives. The women's devotion to each other and to their work meant that Michael Field flourished, publishing prolifically. This does not, however, mean that their books were well received. The two great sadnesses for Michael Field at this time were their bad literary reviews and the death of Cooper's father in 1897 in a mountaineering incident. The staging of their drama *A Question of Memory* in 1893 was the only time in their lives any of their plays was performed,[3] and while the process introduced

---

1 Entry for 1892. See "Diaries" Section, p. 256.
2 Entry for 5 March 1890. See "Diaries" Section, p. 237.
3 This was once again performed, this time in New York by the Airmid Theatre, in 2008.

Figure 3. Katharine Bradley with Whym Chow, c.1897-1906.

the women to a whole new world of contacts and critics—some of whom spent a good deal of time and energy helping them—nothing could have prepared them for the negative reviews they received after the audience found the play's scenario too gruesome to comprehend.

The close friendship formed during this period with Ricketts and Shannon was to last for twenty years. The poets contributed to the artists' journal *The Dial*, and Ricketts published four of the poets' plays at his own Vale Press (many of Michael Field's books were published privately) and decorated nearly all of their subsequent books. Indeed, their friendship with Ricketts and Shannon was based around a shared love of handsome objects. Bradley and Cooper showered Ricketts with gifts, while he made finely wrought jewellery for them (now held in the Fitzwilliam Museum, Cambridge). It was at the suggestion of Charles Ricketts that, in 1899, Bradley and Cooper moved from Reigate to a small Georgian house at 1, The Paragon, Richmond (the first house they were to occupy without other members of their family), and inhabited it with Whym Chow, their pet dog, who was to become an obsessively important figure in the next phase of Bradley and Cooper's life.

In 1907, the women entered into the Roman Catholic Church. This conversion was undoubtedly partly the result of Cooper's ill-health, but the women insist that the primary cause was the death of the beloved Whym Chow in 1906 (it is on this occasion that Cooper writes that it was "the worst loss of my life—yes, worse than that of beloved Mother or the tragic father"[1]). Their conversion distanced them from many of their old friends (even Ricketts and Shannon) but opened up a whole array of new ecclesiastical personalities in their lives and important new literary opportunities with spiritual advisers such as John Gray (himself a Decadent poet turned priest).

In February 1911 it was discovered that Cooper had cancer; she died on 13 December 1913. Bradley also died of cancer just under a year later on 26 September 1914. The last few years of their lives were spent reading and learning about theological doctrine, and writing continuously. *Poems of Adoration*, Cooper's last work, was published in 1912. Bradley's companion volume of religious lyrics, *Mystic Trees* (also her last work), emerged in print the following year. Both appeared under the joint pseudonym and the two were designed to be bound together by a strap to form one complete work. Sensitive to criticism as the women

---

1 Entry for 28 January 1906. See "Diaries" Section, p. 281.

were, it would have hurt them enormously to read the entry on their work that appeared in the *Cambridge History of English Literature* just after their deaths, in 1916. The author writes of the "curious fancy" of two women writing in collaboration under one masculine name, and the assessment of their work is damning.[1]

Although Michael Field was first celebrated as a dramatist, it is the lyric poetry that has left the stronger legacy, and so that is what we represent in this book. The story of the formation of Michael Field as a playwright must be left for another occasion.

Poetic Beginnings

Like other women of her generation, Bradley began her poetic career ostensibly within the nineteenth-century female poetic tradition.[2] As Bradley's pseudonym suggests, the model for *The New Minnesinger and Other Poems* (1875) was *Aurora Leigh* (1857), Elizabeth Barrett Browning's fictional narrative poem about a woman poet. It is notable, for example, that the poem that gives the title to the volume, "The New Minnesinger," is, among other things, a defence of women's rights to a poetic career and to the title of poet. But, if the volume invoked Barrett Browning by name, Bradley's poetry evoked the democratic poetics of Walt Whitman's *Leaves of Grass* (1855). The quotation that introduced the title poem, "Think of womanhood; and thou to be a woman," was lines taken from Whitman's "Think of the Soul."[3] By aligning "The New Minnesinger" with Whitman's poetics, Bradley was not simply defending women's authority as poets; she was also effectively declaring that a more democratic fellowship between the sexes ("[S]he must be / Full woman: lifted to a free / And fellow-life with man" [12]) would bring about a "free-growing womanhood" (13).

Yet, what is striking about the volume is not its overt emphasis on "woman's speech" (12) or its firm support for a feminist nineteenth-century poetics, but its engagement with nineteenth-century German poetry, since one third of the volume is dedicated to translations from the works of Schiller, Heine, and

---

1 *Cambridge History of English Literature*, ed. A.W.Ward and A.R.Waller (Cambridge: Cambridge UP, 1916), Vol. 13: *The Nineteenth Century*, 181.

2 See for example Alice Meynell, *Preludes* (London: H.S. King & Co.), also published in 1875.

3 Walt Whitman, "Think of the Soul," in *Leaves of Grass* (New York, 1855).

Goethe. Most significant is the book's chosen title. A "Min-nesinger" was a German knight, poet, and singer of *Minne* (Middle High German for courtly love). This lyrical tradition, exemplified most notably in the legend of the poet Tannhäuser, was popular among Romantic German poets (especially Heine), and was famously retold by Richard Wagner in his 1845 opera of that title.[1] Wagner's interpretation of the legend, whose key theme is the struggle between sacred and profane love (and redemption through love), fascinated aesthetic writers such as A.C. Swinburne and William Morris, who reworked the tale in works such as "Laus Veneris" (1866) and *The Earthly Paradise* (1866). By invoking therefore the Tannhäuser tradition, "The New Minnesinger" explicitly presented "Leigh" as a "new" woman poet aesthetically affiliated to the medieval tradition of courtly love.

Love is, undoubtedly, the central theme of Bradley's volume, with poems about her sacred (and secret) platonic love for Alfred Gérente;[2] about her profane love for her niece Edith Cooper; and her own devotion to Christianity (the last third of the volume is called "Devotional Poetry"). It is no accident that Bradley's introductory poem to *The New Minnesinger* is "To E.C.," [Edith Cooper]. "My deep need of thy love, its mast'ring power," "Leigh" writes, "I scarce can fathom, thou will never know; / My lighter passions into rhythm may glow; / This is forever voiceless" (vii). Foreshadowing the marriage of passion and rhythm in Bradley and Cooper's later work, the volume reveals Bradley's outward movement towards the poetics of passion of the "art for art's sake" movement; the homoerotic discourse of Whitman's *Leaves of Grass*;[3] the sensual poetics of D.G. Rossetti's *Poems* (1870); and, most significantly, the intensity of the moment found in Walter Pater's *Studies in the History of the Renaissance* (1873).

---

1   The legend tells the story of Tannhäuser, who was initially in love with Elizabeth. But after finding the Venusburg (the home of Venus), he diverted his attention to worshipping the goddess. When he left Venus-burg, he became filled with remorse and decided to travel to Rome to seek absolution from Pope Urban IV. The Pope told him that just as his pilgrim's staff would never blossom, he could never be forgiven. However, shortly after he left the Pope's staff flourished.

2   The sequence entitled "Songs" tells the story of her platonic love for the Frenchman.

3   A forgery of 1872 (Washington) edition of *Leaves of Grass* appeared in London compiled by John Camden Hotten in 1873.

What changes took place as soon as Bradley and Cooper started to write together? *Bellerophôn*, published in 1881, was both Cooper's first book of poems (she was only 19) and their first joint book of verse. While the women's pseudonyms, "Arran and Isla Leigh," continued to invoke the fictional persona of Aurora Leigh, the volume's content and form signalled a radical departure from Bradley's earlier work. Though badly received by their contemporaries,[1] *Bellerophôn* interests modern scholars because it outlines, quite distinctly, the two poetic directions that Bradley and Cooper's writings were to take under the name of "Michael Field": drama and lyric poetry. The volume is divided into two discrete sections: "Bellerophôn" and "Poems." The title poem, "Bellerophôn" (an exploration of the adventures of the beautiful Greek hero), was the women's first attempt at a strange and quintessentially nineteenth-century genre: historical closet-drama, the form that came to dominate most of Michael Field's dramatic work. (Other writers who contributed to this fascinating but still little studied genre include Swinburne, Amy Levy, A. Mary F. Robinson, and Robert Browning.) The second half of the book is a series of poems on a variety of Greek myths and romantic subjects. What unifies these two sections is their affiliation to Victorian and Aesthetic Hellenism, most notably Pater's suggestion that Greek mythology (the foundation of the Romantic imagination) was a part of the modern spirit.[2] The poem "Apollo's Written Grief"(158–170), for example, whose title is taken from Shelley's closet-drama *Prometheus Unbound* (1819), is an exploration of the Greek myth through Shelley's romantic lens. Equally interesting is Bradley and Cooper's use of Titian's painting "Adônis and Aphrodîtê" (131–32), which draws on Hellenism to write about the world of art—a passion that both women would cultivate throughout their lives both privately and publicly as "Michael Field."

Bradley and Cooper's ultimate re-invention as "Michael

---

1 With the exception of a review in *The Academy*, the volume met with a "resounding silence" (Virginia Blain, "'Michael Field, the Two-Headed Nightingale': Lesbian Text as Palimpsest," *Women's History Review* 5.2 [1996]: 244). The reviewer mocked the author's "trumpery pedantry" and argued that the volume had no merits "either in conception or execution." [Anon], "Review of Bellerophôn," *The Academy* (10 September 1881): 196.

2 See, for example, "Postscript (Romanticism)," in Harold Bloom, ed., *Selected Writings of Walter Pater* (New York: Meridian Books, 1974), 208–23.

Field" marked the beginning of a new and more productive writing career, which was no longer linked to the feminist poetics of Barrett Browning. Now a male poet, Michael Field was positioned within a newer and younger generation of modern poets who, in rejecting the Victorian tradition, adopted the Bohemian *ethos* and *modus vivendi* of the art for art's sake movement.

The poetic publication of the poet Michel Field was concentrated in two distinct periods: 1889–98 and 1906–14. The first corresponds to Michael Field's engagement with a modern, pagan aestheticism, with titles such as *Long Ago* (1889), *Sight and Song* (1892), and *Underneath the Bough* (1893 and 1898).[1] The second coincides with the women's conversion to Roman Catholicism and includes the volumes *Wild Honey* (1908), *Poems of Adoration* (1912), *Mystic Trees* (1913), *Whym Chow: Flame of Love* (1914), and *Dedicated* (1914). However, *Dedicated* corresponds thematically to the earlier, pagan, phase. Though it was partly written in the early 1900s, it was only published after Cooper's death in 1914.

Aesthetic Field

Holbrook Jackson has argued that the "native" "impulsion" of the literature of the 1890s "came directly from the Pre-Raphaelites, and more particularly from the poetry of Dante Gabriel Rossetti and Swinburne." But he adds that "the chief influences came from France, and partially for that reason the English decadents always remained spiritual foreigners in our midst; they were the product not of England but of cosmopolitan London."[2] These two tendencies, and their theorisation by Walter Pater, are particularly important to understand Michael Field's aesthetic phase, as their early poetry was characteristic of the period's intense debates about the sensual nature of poetics, a response to some of the key issues that arose out of understanding sensuality as a new epistemological category, and a significant example of the European tendencies of cosmopolitan London. Moreover, what unites Michael Field's work during this period is the women's modern appreciation of history and past epochs. Whether in the

---

1 In the preface to the American edition of *Underneath the Bough* (1898), Michael Field recognised their forward-looking modernity by noting that "For some years my work has been done for 'the younger generation'—not yet knocking at the door, but waited with welcome."

2 Holbrook Jackson, *The Eighteen Nineties* (Harmondsworth: Penguin, 1950), 57.

context of Greek literature (*Long Ago*), or in the rehearsal of the sense of pleasure occasioned by various historical paintings (*Sight and Song*) or in the modernisation of Elizabethan lyrics (*Underneath the Bough*),[1] it was their aesthetical, not historical, appreciation of history that marked their contemporariness.

To examine those tendencies we must go back to the 1880s and to the birth of Michael Field, the poet. The emphasis on current studies on decadence and the 1890s has, to a certain extent, obscured the workings of the earlier decade, a most creative period in the production and cultivation of aestheticism. Not only were some of aestheticism's key texts published during this decade (see, for example, John Addington Symonds's *A Problem in Greek Ethics* [1883] and Walter Pater's *Marius the Epicurean* [1885]), but also the impressive number of poetic volumes produced during these years (by both male and female writers) shows the decade's centrality in any discussion about aestheticist poetry. These include, to name but a few, A.C. Swinburne's *Studies in Song* (1880); Dante Gabriel Rossetti's *Poems, a New Edition* (1881) and *Ballads and Sonnets* (1881); Christina Rossetti's *A Pageant and Other Poems* (1881); Oscar Wilde's *Poems* (1881); Amy Levy's *Xantippe and Other Verse* (1881); A. Mary F. Robinson's *The Crowned Hippolytus* (1881) and *An Italian Garden* (1886); Katharine Tynan's *Louise de la Vallière and Other Poems* (1885); and William Ernest Henley's *A Book of Verse* (1888). Consider, in particular, the number of volumes published in 1889 alone: Marc André Raffalovich's *It is Thyself*; Arthur Symons's *Days and Nights*; Margaret Veley's *A Marriage of Shadows and Other Poems*; Graham R. Thomson's *The Bird-Bride: A Volume of Ballads and Sonnets*; Amy Levy's *A London Plane-Tree*; Mathilde Blind's *The Ascent of Man*; W.B. Yeats's *The Wandering of Oisin and Other Poems*; and, of course, Michael Field's first volume of poetry, *Long Ago*, a recreation of Sappho's lyric fragments.

Michael Field's diaries reveal their intimate knowledge of these works and writers. But more particularly, *Long Ago* displays their connection with the pagan homoerotic philhellenism of authors such as Symonds, Robinson, and Levy through the volume's affiliation with Greek literature and its homoerotic discourse. If, as Holbrook Jackson suggests, this was "a time when people went about frankly and cheerfully endeavouring to solve

---

1   See Joseph Bristow, "Michael Field's Lyric Aestheticism: *Underneath the Bough*," in *Michael Field and Their World*, ed. Margaret Stetz and Cheryl A. Wilson (Aylesham, UK: Rivendale Press, 2007), 49–62.

the question of 'How to Live,'"[1] Michael Field's reply was to live as Sappho did, so long ago. The volume was sparked by Pater's theorisation of modern poetry in two key pieces, "Aesthetic Poetry" and "Dante Gabriel Rossetti," both republished by Pater in his infamous 1889 collection of essays *Appreciations; with an Essay on Style*.[2] "'[A]esthetic' poetry," Pater claimed, "is neither a mere reproduction of Greek or medieval poetry, nor only an idealisation of modern life and sentiment." "It is a finer ideal," he continued, "extracted from what in relation to any actual world is already an ideal. Like some strange second flowering after date, it renews on a more delicate type the poetry of a past age, but must not be confounded with it."[3] Pater's definition of aesthetic poetry defines quite precisely *Long Ago*, a volume that was not a "mere reproduction of Greek" poetry, but a "finer ideal," a "strange second flowering" of Sappho's words that "renew[ed] on a more delicate type the poetry of a past age." In doing so, Bradley and Cooper created a volume that was read by their contemporaries just as the Greeks read Sappho.

Sight and Song (1892), by contrast, engaged not with an aesthetic sentiment but with the seizing of sensation. The writing of the book and the bound object showed the poets' indebtedness to the cosmopolitan aesthetics of the period—for example, to Verlaine's recreations of Watteau's paintings in *Fêtes galantes* (1869), to Flaubert's realism, and to Gautier's *l'art pour l'art* philosophy. However, the thinking behind the book's composition lies in Pater's famous last lines: "art comes to you professing frankly to give nothing but the highest quality to your moments as they pass, and simply for those moments' sake."[4] Pater's explanation of that statement appears in his essay "Dante Gabriel Rossetti."

---

1   Holbrook, 27.
2   "Aesthetic poetry" was another version of his 1868 review of Morris's poems, which he had published in another format in 1873 as the "Conclusion" to *The Renaissance*. Because the *Spectator* reviewer had linked it to degeneracy, Pater removed it from the second (1890) edition. In their diary Michael Field noted, "He has struck out the *Essay on Aesthetic Poetry* in *Appreciations* because it gave offence to some pious person—he is getting hopelessly prudish in literature and defers to the moral weaknesses of everybody. Deplorable!" (*Works and Days*, 119). "Dante Gabriel Rossetti" was first published in 1883 in the second edition of T.H. Ward, *The English Poets* (London: Macmillan).
3   Pater, "Aesthetic Poetry," in Bloom, 190.
4   Walter Pater, "Conclusion," in *The Renaissance. Studies in Art and Poetry*, ed. Donald H. Hill (Berkeley: U of California P, 1980), 190.

Here he argues that "For Rossetti [...] the first condition of the poetic way of seeing and presenting things is particularisation."[1] Or as he had previously stated in the "Preface" to *The Renaissance*: "What is this song or picture ... to *me*?"[2] In *Sight and Song*, Michael Field explores and challenges the individualisation of "sight" and its translation into "song." Unlike Rossetti's "poems *for* pictures" (see his *Poems* [1870; rpt. 1881]), their double subjectivity and interest in the art object for its own sake complicated the impressionistic tendencies of the period by suggesting that an intellectualisation and objectification of the aesthetic would lead to a refinement of sensations. More recently, Isobel Armstrong has singled out the black and white quality of some of these poems, defining them as "noir poems."[3] These poems replicate the effect of art photographs, bought and collected by art connoisseurs to complement the Continental art tourism industry of the late nineteenth century.

Underneath the Bough (of which three different editions were published, two in 1893 and the third, the American version, in 1898) corresponds to another key aspect of "aesthetic poetry": pagan spirit. Pater writes: "[o]ne characteristic of the pagan spirit the aesthetic poetry has, which is on its surface—the continual suggestion, pensive or passionate, of the shortness of life." Ecstasy and death, Dionysus and Thanatos, are central to the women's volume, which exemplifies Pater's dictum that aesthetic poetry heightens "the sense of death and the desire of beauty: the desire of beauty quickened by the sense of death."[4] This pagan spirit was not new of course in Michael Field's work. It appears in *Long Ago* and also in *Sight and Song* in their treatment of Fauns, Venus, and other Greek mythological characters. However, what is different in *Underneath the Bough* is that the volume's pagan spirit is predicated on the two central principles of Greek culture, the Apollonian and the Dionysian, as defined by Nietzsche in *The Birth of Tragedy* (1872). The Apollonian, represented by the sun-god, signifies light and form and the principle of oneness. The Dionysian is represented by drunkenness and ecstasy: it is that which annihilates one's individual character, enabling him or her to "merge" with the world. Indeed, the volume celebrates both the dissolved individualism of Michael

---

1 Pater, "Dante Gabriel Rossetti," in Bloom, 200.
2 Pater, "Preface," in *The Renaissance*, xix–xx.
3 Isobel Armstrong, *Victorian Glassworlds. Glass Culture and the Imagination 1830–1880* (Oxford: Oxford UP, 2008), 353.
4 Pater, "Aesthetic Poetry," in Bloom, 198.

Field and, in parallel, the Dionysian revellers "Michael" and "Field," as they dance around Apollo (see "Invocation," *Underneath the Bough*).

The Field of Catholic Poetics

Leon Chai writes that "[f]rom its beginnings, Aestheticism had been preoccupied with the question of sanctity" and that "[a]fter earlier affirmations of the sacredness of life (e.g., Rossetti's *House of Life*)" it shifted "to an emphasis upon liturgy and ritual" in works such as Pater's *Marius the Epicurean*.[1] Pater's account of the aesthetic awakening of a young man in ancient Rome from paganism and stoicism to Christianity became emblematic (or at least one of the key narratives) of the movement. Whether understood as a spiritual awakening (the case of Alice Meynell[2]); as aestheticism's literary evolution from impressionism ("truth to the senses") to symbolism ("truth to the soul");[3] or a shift from "Hellenism" to "Christianity" (the case of Oscar Wilde), there is no doubt that the last few years of the nineteenth century were marked by a Roman Catholic craze that swept the circles of late-Victorian London. Aesthetes and decadents were attracted to Roman Catholicism (and not to ascetic Protestantism) because it offered a sense of rejuvenation to a movement deeply castigated by the trials of Oscar Wilde. Indeed, the church became a refuge for homosexual writers such as Wilde and John Gray because its ceremonies (for example, the celebration of the body of Christ) "could yield a sensuous *frisson* through initiation into a hitherto-unsuspected realm of beauty and symbolism."[4]

To discuss Michael Field's shift to Catholic poetics, it might be helpful to begin with *Whym Chow: Flame of Love*, which though published by Bradley after Cooper's death in 1914 was composed (mostly by Cooper) in 1906. This is perhaps the most daring and imaginative collection of poems in Michael Field's entire oeuvre, conceived as a result of a deep spiritual crisis in the poets' lives brought on by their grief for the loss of their dog. The volume embodies the symbolic communion of the sacred and the profane in Michael Field's art and life at a crucial turning point

---

1 Leon Chai, *Aestheticism: The Religion of Art in Post-Romantic Literature* (New York: Columbia UP, 1990), 129.

2 Meynell converted to Catholicism just before the publication of *Preludes*.

3 See Arthur Symons, "The Decadent Movement in Literature," *Harper's New Monthly Magazine* 87.522 (November 1893): 859.

4 Chai, 129.

in their lives. Here, "Love" represents Pater's "gem-like flame"; their unremitting reliance on Greek love; and, as in mystic literature, their newly found faith in God. The volume is thus both sacrilegious and holy. Typologically and poetically, this is their closest volume to *Long Ago*. Not only are its poems also printed in gold and black, but literally and symbolically "Whym Chow," their "Flame of Love," is the connection between their Bacchant and Christian days. The beautiful flame-like colour of the volume's sensuous, tactile cover (created by Pissarro's Ergany Press), which is made of exquisite velvety ruby suede, signals the volume's central topic: passion. As if singing about Christ's Passion, the poems in *Whym Chow* glorify the tragic suffering of their beloved dog because it allows the poets to transcend their pagan existence as Catholic converts. Like Oscar Wilde's *De Profundis* (conceived as a love letter to Lord Alfred Douglas and exploring their lives and Wilde's conversion to Catholicism), *Whym Chow* delves into the whole nature of the women's relationship. Thus, while the volume sanctifies their dog and speaks of the "consummation" of his Passion it also symbolically presents a transcendent recreation of their family narrative: "Michael," "Field," and Chow, reborn as the Holy Trinity.

If during their aesthetic days Michael and Field had been radically modern in their sensuous exploration of pleasure, Whym Chow's death transformed them into ardent "modernist Catholics," a Christian movement that believed in the adaptation of the church to modern doctrines.[1] Michael Field's religious development from the Hellenic to the Christian is recorded in *Wild Honey* (1908), a volume that overtly engages with the symbolist Catholicism of Maurice Maeterlinck's *The Life of The Bee* (1901).[2] Lord Alfred Douglas, Wilde's lover and ultimately the cause of his imprisonment and later conversion to Catholicism, read the book in manuscript and eagerly recommended it for

---

1 On Catholic modernism, Michael Field, and John Gray, see Jerusha McCormack, *The Man Who Was Dorian Gray* (Basingstoke: Palgrave, 2000).

2 The cover of *Wild Honey* (decorated with bees and honeycombs) is a homage to Maeterlinck's *The Life of The Bee* (see Marion Thain, *"Michael Field": Poetry, Aestheticism and the Fin de Siècle* [Cambridge: Cambridge UP, 2007], 153–55). In this volume, Maeterlinck rejects Schopenhauer's pessimism in favour of a Christian optimism by suggesting that it is possible for an individual to change his or her direction in life.

publication to T. Fisher Unwin. The irony was deeply felt by Edith Cooper, who wrote thus in their diary:

> We have been abjuring the nineties, & all their spirit, in the Church John Gray of <u>Silverpoints</u> has raised for the Divine Presence, beautiful, austere, consecrated—& Alfred Douglas' is the voice that calls to the world to receive us as we come forth of the Church.[1]

At first glance the volume's title, *Wild Honey*, seems to connote a return to the pagan aestheticism of *Long Ago*, most notably to the bridal song "Not the Honey, nor the Bee."[2] But its introductory poem, "Wild was the honey thou did'st eat," with its allusion to St. John the Baptist and the coming of Christ, reveals a radical shift in Michael Field's poetics. Thus, though the volume continues to celebrate the decadent spirit of their earlier work in poems such as the Wildean "A Violet Bank" or "From Baudelaire," it also begins to display their association with Christian observances (consider, for example, "Absence," "Whym Chow," or "Good Friday"). More particularly, the volume negotiates between the erotic and the sacred. As was to be expected, aesthetes such as Berenson preferred the Greek sections, whereas the women's confessor, Father Prior, was shocked by their profane religious imagery. As Bradley put it, "And out of all this what hot cheeks for the religious !! poems in Wild Honey. Is there nothing to erase them?—all, save the envoi. With lay hands they touch the things on the altar, they offend."[3]

The women's conversion to Catholicism signalled a disavowal of their pagan spirit and led them to reconcile their art with their Catholic life. And as their relationship to the world of aestheticism and decadence changed, so did their relation to poetry itself, which from now on revealed a more spiritual purpose. Poetry became a form of prayer, and this implied a more personal endeavour (hence the two individual volumes, Cooper's *Poems of Adoration* and Bradley's *Mystic Trees*). Cooper explains that if "'Wild Honey' [was] the turning-point from Paganism to the gt. [great] 'Ecce, Agnus Dei' vision of St. John the Baptist," *Poems of Adoration* was "the first-fruits of our Catholic life."[4] Thus, in

---

1 Entry for 7 May 1907. See "Diaries" Section, p. 283.
2 See "Poetry" Section, p. 59.
3 K.B. to John Gray (March 1908). See "Letters" Section, p. 344.
4 "Behold, the Lamb of God." Entry for 13 January 1913. See "Diaries" Section, p. 292.

Poems of Adoration, the sensuousness of language is reconfigured to mean "God," the Word of God. Though Bradley's first reaction to Cooper's definitive turn to Christian poetics was ambivalent (as she wrote to Mary Berenson, "I do myself prefer the faun perhaps"),[1] "Michael" nonetheless followed Henry's steps with her own vision of religious poetics in *Mystic Trees*. While both texts sought an identification of their art and their life with religion, Bradley's volume revealed a more humanistic approach to Christian theology. In the body of Christ, Bradley found a deeper communion and spiritual closeness with her fellow poet: an understanding of the suffering and pain of "Love's" dying body, her beloved "Henry."

But to examine these volumes in isolation is to miss an important part of the *fin-de-siècle* period. They must be read in the context of Catholic poets such as Francis Thompson (see *The Hound of Heaven*) and Alice Meynell (whom the women approached after their conversion) or the conversion narratives of John Gray, Oscar Wilde, and Walter Pater. Holbrook Jackson convincingly writes that "white" (and not yellow) was the colour that dominated the *fin de siècle*. He argues that the "decadents adored innocence, and the frequent use of the idea of whiteness, with its correlatives, silver, moonlight, starlight, ivory, alabaster and marble, was perhaps more than half-conscious symbolism. It had also a dash of the debauchee's love of virginity."[2] He contends that the origin of white decadence lies in "White Nights," Pater's chapter in *Marius the Epicurean*. The title is taken from a quotation from an old German mystic who stated that the mystery of the so-called "white things" was an afterthought—"the doubles, or seconds of real things, and themselves but half-real, half material."[3] Jackson signals Alice Meynell's "The Shepherdess" as a prime example of this white, Catholic decadence. But we must also add here the name of Michael Field in poems such as "Relics" (*Adoration*), "The White Passion-Flower" (*Mystic Trees*), or "Trinity" (*Whym Chow*), poems in which "white" becomes the afterthought of their pagan lives.

After a life devoted to "song," *Dedicated* (1914), the last book of verse published by Michael Field, is a fitting conclusion to the women's poetic career. Published in the same year as the heretical *Whym Chow*, Bradley celebrated the life of her fellow by publishing Cooper's most outrageously pagan and explicitly erotic

---

1 K.B. to Mary Berenson (June [?]1912). See "Letters" Section, p. 332.
2 Jackson, 139.
3 Jackson, 140.

poems. "Michael" herself finished the collection with the poem "Fellowship," "singing" "in the old accents" blasphemously to "my Glory, my Delight." "O Love, with pagan might," she wrote, "White in our steeds, and white too in our armour let us ride, / Immortal, white, triumphing."[1]

Contemporary Reception

After the women's deaths, their work was dismissed in the modernist rejection of everything "Victorian," even while much of the poetry of that era seems strongly and covertly indebted to *fin-de-siècle* poets such as Michael Field. Their friends and literary companions, however, did not forget them, as works by Mary Sturgeon, Thomas Sturge Moore, Emily Fortey, and Charles Ricketts clearly show. Yet we have to wait until the 1970s before Michael Field's work is really taken up critically. At this point, a revival of decadent literature meant that the first contemporary critical accounts of Michael Field's work began to be produced. Key figures such as J.G. Paul Delaney and Henri Locard (as well as Kenneth R. Ireland and Jan McDonald) laid the foundations for the larger-scale revival of interest after 1995. What triggered the recent resurgence of interest in the poets was not, however, their relationship with decadence, or with the *fin de siècle* more generally, but their location within a community of "Victorian women poets" whose work was being exhumed as part of a feminist reconsideration of the nineteenth century. A great many poets were reintroduced to the twentieth century through this process of revival, and some have fared better than others. Michael Field is one of those whose place in the literary canon now seems assured, and a fast-growing body of critical work on Bradley and Cooper's poetry, particularly, demands attention from the whole scholarly community. Yet Michael Field's importance goes far beyond the women's place in a gender-defined trajectory of poetry across the nineteenth century. Critics are now using Michael Field's work to rewrite the narratives of many different themes within *fin-de-siècle* culture: whether in relation to *ekphrasis*, the revival of Sappho and classical literature, aestheticism, Catholic conversion, or dual authorship (to mention but a few).

Along with this journey of critical reassessment has gone the process of bringing Michael Field's work back into print. On the back of an earlier renewed interest in decadence, Kelsey Thorn-

---

1 See "Poetry" section, p. 217.

ton and Ian Small published a facsimile edition of both *Sight and Song* and *Underneath the Bough* in 1993. A more widespread re-appearance of the women's work came a bit later, however, with the impressive anthologies of Victorian women's poetry that were published in the mid-1990s, for example, Jennifer Breen's 1994 Everyman edition of *Victorian Women Poets 1830–1901*; Angela Leighton and Margaret Reynolds's 1995 edition of *Victorian Women Poets*; Isobel Armstrong and Joseph Bristow's 1996 edition of *Nineteenth-Century Women Poets*; and the two Longman collections (*Victorian Women Poets*, by Tess Cosslett, in 1996, and *Victorian Women Poets: A New Annotated Anthology*, by Virginia Blain, in 2000). It is largely the poetry that has been published in a printed format, but some dramas, as well as some of the poetry volumes, are available in on-line resources such as Chadwyck-Healey's *Literature Online*, and the complete manuscript diaries and correspondence held in the British Library collection of Michael Field materials is available on microfilm.[1]

What we are able to do in this anthology, however, is quite different from anything else thus far attempted. We are able here to bring together a huge quantity of Michael Field's published and unpublished writing and represent it, for the first time, in one accessible volume. This selection is both a significant milestone in the process of re-integrating Michael Field into the poetic canon, as well as a unique opportunity to represent in print for a twenty-first-century audience such a large collection of published and unpublished material that will change the way we see the *fin-de-siècle* period.

The simple answer to the question "What did Michael Field write?" is—everything. But although the oeuvre is wide-ranging there are clearly focal points. Bradley and Cooper thought of themselves first and foremost as dramatists, although they constantly wrote poetry, and poetry seems to have become their main concern later in life. Primarily it was verse that excited them, whether verse drama or the lyric poem. Yet their thirty manuscript volumes of diaries, intended for publication, show them to be just as talented in this area, and they provide some of the wittiest and most vibrant writing in the genre. Some prose essays too were published in journals, as were other occasional prose pieces. The present collection focuses primarily, however, on the published lyric poetry, supported by unpublished material from the diaries and letters that gives it an aesthetic and historical context.

---

1   Published by Adam Matthews.

This configuration reflects both the current critical interest in Michael Field's lyric work and also the practical considerations of a selection such as this. The dramas are present within this volume only insofar as some of the work published as lyric poetry also appeared as lyrical inserts within the drama,[1] but because of space constraints, the republication of dramas in their complete format must take place elsewhere.

The nature of Bradley and Cooper's collaboration—the way in which they wrote—is, however, much more difficult to describe. This collaboration has been the subject of a great deal of discussion in recent critical literature, which, although we won't rehearse it in full here, requires some attention. Bradley and Cooper's conception of their joint authorship, and the male pseudonym, is clearly stated in the correspondence with Browning included in this volume (pp. 306-13) and is reiterated in dialogue with other interlocutors also. The collaborative authoring of the diaries is open to inspection—at least to the extent of showing "who holds the pen"—in our transcription, which identifies the work of each hand. We know from Bradley and Cooper's own descriptions that poetry and drama were often written through a process where each woman took sections to write independently but then edited the other's work. This process, combined with lots of discussion, seems to be how the texts were produced (the letters between the two women give a clear sense of this pattern). The issue of joint authorship was initially discussed by feminist critics such as Lillian Faderman (in 1981) in terms of "Romantic Friendship": a close bond of shared interests that was a quasi-substitute for marriage.

Angela Leighton's 1992 study offered a very different picture of the two women and paved the way for a new appreciation of the poets, pointing to a rather different conception of their relationship. Following this new direction, recent scholars have tended to invoke a Sapphic discourse to describe the literary and erotic components of the text, and, using this, they have interrogated the more theoretical aspects of the dual literary subject. These studies have focused almost exclusively on Michael Field's poetry because it is within this genre that co-authorship is much more problematic and unusual, defying readers' expectations about the solitary musing of the inspired mind (collaboration is much more common in dramatic writing, where a production

---

1 See, for example, "Ah, Eros doth not always smite" (in *Underneath the Bough*, p. 116), a song from their 1884 drama *Callirrhoë*.

will always be an essentially collaborative process). If the lyric is dual authored then its very premise is questioned. Bradley and Cooper's passionate devotion to each other in life is mirrored, they claim, in their unity in art. "Michael Field" is the unified lyric "I" and they are its two halves. Such issues have been explored particularly thoroughly by critics such as Holly Laird and Yopie Prins, who, in their very different ways, have asked how this particular lyric "field" might operate. These questions are often addressed by critics in relation to Michael Field's first book of poems, *Long Ago*, in which the Sapphic fragments are used as inspiration for Bradley and Cooper's poems, which seem to aspire to complete them. This example of triple authorship focuses the questions of dual authorship even more interestingly.

Yet these proclamations of romantic unity should not, some critics have convincingly argued, be taken at face value. Virginia Blain's pioneering work on disunity within the Michael Field partnership has shown the distance between the myth propagated by the authors and the real, personal tensions that underlie it. This recognition of just how deliberately crafted the persona of Michael Field actually was, is hugely important. Various critics have studied Michael Field's utilisation and manipulation of conventional images of gender and desire, and, along with collaboration, this has been the other major theme of the critical oeuvre. Chris White and Martha Vicinus, particularly, have written insightfully on the multitude of erotic discourses figured knowingly in the poetry.

Sight and Song was the next volume to take the critics' interest because of its fascinating negotiation between the poetic subject and the painting that inspired each poem. Brooke Cameron, Jill Ehnenn, Nicholas Frankel, Hilary Fraser, Krysta Lysack, Julia Saville, Ana Parejo Vadillo, and Julie Wise have all tackled the gendered dynamics of the gaze, in distinct but equally fascinating ways, drawing on a rich, and gendered, nineteenth-century tradition of art criticism.

Over the past five years, two further trajectories of critical study have emerged as central to our understanding of Michael Field. *Underneath the Bough* (the third book of poetry) has begun to receive critical attention, but in this case less in relation to issues of gender, and more in relation to aestheticism and the genealogy of the text. Essays by Robert P. Fletcher and Joseph Bristow both see individual poems as enmeshed within much larger narratives, historical and textual, that inform both their creation and our reading of them. While this concentration on

Long Ago, *Sight and Song*, and *Underneath the Bough* suggests an exclusion of the later poetry, the past few years have also seen a reappraisal of Michael Field's twentieth-century poetry, written after the Catholic conversion and concerned almost entirely with religious themes and motifs. Hilary Fraser, Frederick Roden, Marion Thain, and Ruth Vanita have all explored this work, pursuing the legacy of the earlier euphoric paganism into its newly configured devotional guise, arguing for the interest of this rather neglected and disparaged part of the poetic oeuvre. Thain's 2007 monograph studies Michael Field's poetic oeuvre as a whole, arguing that it is a self-reflexive study in the ideals of aestheticism.

While the poetry has been the subject of a rapidly growing body of critical work, there are still relatively few critical studies of the dramas. More numerous than the volumes of poetry, it was for their dramatic work that Michael Field was originally celebrated. Work on this area includes essays by Vickie L. Taft and Ana Parejo Vadillo.

Similarly, alongside the reconsideration of Michael Field's poetry has come a new interest in their life-writing, particularly those thirty volumes of manuscript diaries held in the British Library. While Mary Sturgeon's 1921 biography interprets the diaries from personal knowledge of many of the people and events described, Emma Donoghue's 1998 biography is a lively and critical interpretation of the diaries. Rachel Morley and María DeGuzmán are two of the few critics making Bradley and Cooper's life-writing their primary subject of study. Margaret Stetz and Cheryl Wilson's edited collection of essays on *Michael Field and their World* (2007) contains much of this new work on their lives, relations with contemporaries, and influential legacies.

Selection Principles

In our selection of material for this book we have tried to find a balance between what is most representative of the poetic oeuvre, and what is of most literary value. We have selected only from the published poetry of Michael Field because it is our aim to show the writers as public literary figures and to allow assessment of them within those terms. The unpublished (and frequently unfinished) poetry has been painstakingly catalogued by Ivor C. Treby, and we refer readers to his *Michael Field Catalogue* for further details. The diaries were, of course, unpublished, but Bradley and Cooper clearly had plans for them to be made public, and they left instructions to their executor to publish them (see Sturge Moore's *Works and Days*). The letters too were frequently as much a part of a public formation of aesthetic identity formation as they were a part of the private sphere.

We have given selections here from every book of poetry published by Bradley and Cooper under the name Michael Field, and also selections from one volume of their unpublished poetry produced after the women's deaths: Emily Fortey's *The Wattlefold*. This final volume reflects the plans Bradley and Cooper laid down before their deaths for a projected volume and so still qualifies to be represented here as part of the Michael Field oeuvre. It is this desire to map that self-defined oeuvre, as well as space constraints, that has dictated that Bradley and Cooper's early work, published under other pseudonyms prior to the Michael Field signature, is not included here. The principles of selection led us to try to balance a representation of the range of different styles apparent within each Michael Field book as well as a focus on the poetry that is most successful (often that which has aroused recent critical interest).

There is much to intrigue, amuse, and enlighten in the diaries; and our selections here aim to cover the temporal span of the work and to represent key moments of content (whether interpersonal, professional or cultural) and high points of the craft of diary writing. With literally thousands of letters surviving, representing the correspondence between Michael Field and their various interlocutors is necessarily a highly selective task. However, because the mass of correspondence, although huge, is to a large extent grouped around a few key mentors and friends, the organisation of this section is therefore able to reflect in microcosm the overall picture of Bradley and Cooper's epistolary communication. The pieces chosen to represent each relationship are selected to give an example of the characteristic tone of the exchange, or to represent key moments within it. The relationships themselves span the full temporal trajectory of Michael Field's career. Representing the ways in which Michael Field's publications were received by the critics is an important part of the historical context this volume aims to build for the author, albeit in a small way. We regret that space does not permit us to include a review for every volume of poetry published, but we can provide pieces representative of the mixed response the poets received.

Clearly, given Bradley and Cooper's prolific production of text of all kinds, there is much that is excluded here. In seeking to achieve a representative balance across the volume as a whole we have sometimes been forced to leave out works of merit or interest in favour of pieces that, although perhaps of less value in today's eyes, are crucial to conveying the range and scope of Michael Field's work. While we know that some readers will bemoan the absence of pieces they find significant, we hope this will be balanced by an understanding that some of the pieces included, while of less interest today, will allow for the ongoing process of re-evaluation of the work and perhaps open up avenues for the critics of tomorrow. In order that this volume be of use to as many future readers as possible, we have tried, as far as we can in limited space, not to close down options as to what kind of a poet Michael Field might be.

Principles of Transcription and Editorial Policy

In our transcription from manuscript sources we have attempted to balance the imperative to capture the spirit and texture of the letters and diary entries, with the desire to render them intelligible to the reader.[1] We have also been aware of the need to establish a set of protocols to ensure, as far as possible, that we do not close down possible meanings where the original text is ambiguous. We do not aim to impose a definitive interpretation on these texts, but rather to represent them in a way that will continue to be useful to developing and changing scholarly needs. The study of this oeuvre is still at a relatively early stage, and we have no doubt that scholars will discover more and refine our understanding of the writers over time.

To this end we have notated deletions and insertions in letters and diary entries. Often these changes simply correct trivial mistakes, but sometimes they indicate the mood of the writer and the tenor of the letter, as well as alternative possible lines of thought. A cleaned-up version of the text would bear no relation to the experience of reading a letter covered in marginal insertions, deletions, and other indications of the letter's expressive qualities. We have tried to avoid inserting extra punctuation and have done so only when the text is otherwise impossible to parse. Whenever

---

1   This latter concern has led us to represent the "+" within the manuscripts by an ampersand ("&"), because the plus sign always signifies "and" in the material we have transcribed, but it is much more difficult for the reader to parse the plus symbol. The ampersand translates much more readily to give the reader the correct meaning.

we have added punctuation we have done so within square brackets. Square brackets are used only to enclose editorial additions and always signal editorial comment. This means that, for the sake of clarity, on the rare occasion when the writer of a manuscript source uses square brackets, we have represented them with curved brackets. Bradley and Cooper used dashes copiously throughout their manuscript writing, in preference to other punctuation marks. To be faithful to the experience of reading the text we have reproduced all of these as they were.

In a letter there are many possible ways of breaking up the text that cannot be represented purely by the formal structures of sentences and paragraphs. Quite frequently writers will start a new line with a dash, as if the new thought is not so much a new paragraph but a comment appended to the previous paragraph, or the start of a list of points, each beginning with a left-justified dash. Occasionally the letter writer draws a vertical line between two sentences rather than starting a new line; and sometimes a pronounced space is introduced between sentences. Usually such markers are used in letters that also use conventional paragraph breaks, but seem to indicate a desire to show something stronger than a new sentence, but less decisive than the beginning of a new paragraph. Such nuances are important to understanding the connections between thoughts expressed in the letters and, in certain instances, may become to future scholars more important than the current editors can know, so (when they are not simply a pragmatic response to the physical constraints of the letter space) we have retained such expressive qualities of the manuscript material as far as possible rather than attempting a faux-definitive version, which, although easier to read, would have sacrificed too much of the manuscript's potential.

In this edition we have assumed a common knowledge of the Bible and Greek mythology (except in *Long Ago*, where we have provided a good number of notes because not only is this the first poetic text reproduced, but also the density of classical allusion makes it difficult to read without this information readily accessible). Similarly, we have not footnoted words easily found in the concise/shorter OED. What we have footnoted are personal references that would otherwise be obscure, and mythological or other references that could not be easily traced by the reader.

Note on Transcription Policy

[<] [>] surrounds text inserted by the author later into a line.

[?] when directly preceding a word, shows we are not certain of the transcription.

[illegible] denotes an illegible word.

[illegible, deleted] denotes an illegible word that has been deleted by the author.

[...] indicates where the editors have cut passages from the middle of a section of text.

Poetry

Figure 4. Book cover of *Long Ago*, 1889.

1. From *Long Ago* (1889)

[Until the publication of *Long Ago* in 1889, Michael Field's fame rested with their dramas, with titles such as *Callirrhoë* and *Fair Rosamund* (both published in 1884); *The Father's Tragedy, William Rufus*, and *Loyalty or Love?* (all published in 1885); *Brutus Ultor* (1886) and *Canute the Great* and *The Cup of Water* (both 1887). But, inspired by a new 1885 English edition of Sappho's poetry—Henry Wharton's *Sappho: Memoir, Text, Selected Renderings, and a Literal Translation*—the women turned their hand to lyric poetry.[1]

Long Ago, like Wharton's edition, adopts Theodor Bergk's influential reconstruction of the Sapphic fragments in *Poetae Lyrici Graeci*, volume 3 (Leipzig, 1882). Conceived as an "extension of Sappho's fragments into lyrics," the volume is a lyrical sequence of sixty-eight poems, each introduced by a Greek epigraph by Sappho. The epigraph is then translated into English to be woven into, responded to, and elaborated on by Michael Field. The result was a strikingly innovative lyrical collection of bilingual poems (the Greek fragments in gold, the English text in black) by a new voice: Michael Field. The book came out on 23 May 1889; a month later, all 100 copies had been sold.

This method of artwork (the use of poetic translations from Greek poetry) was part of a new trend among late-Victorian poets who found in Greek poetry new ways with which to re-invigorate the lyric. Consider for example A. Mary F. Robinson's *The Crowned Hippolytus* (1881) and Amy Levy's *Medea* (1881), both translations from Euripides, or John Addington Symonds's *Studies of the Greek Poets* (1873). Moreover, by drawing on the well-known associations between hellenism and homoeroticism, philhellenist poets such as Robinson, Symonds, or A. C. Swinburne were able to find new metres and a new erotic language with which to modernise nineteenth-century poetry. Indeed, as Yopie Prins has demonstrated in her monumental *Victorian Sappho* (1999), a wide range of late nineteenth-century poets, both male and female, turned to Sappho's poetry in their search for new lyric possiblities. What is new about *Long Ago*, however, is the way in which Michel Field's lyrics engaged with Sappho's. Like a palimpsest, Sappho's voice from "long ago" becomes alive in Michael Field's text. In the process, Sappho is not just celebrated as a revered lyric poet who sings of sensuality, of homo-

---

1 Henry Thornton Wharton, *Sappho: Memoir, Text, Selected Renderings and A Literal Translation* (London: David Stott, 1885).

sexual and heterosexual love: she lives on as the aesthetic poet Michael Field. This complex multiplicity of the lyric voice, both male and female, single and double, homosexual and heterosexual, is one of the most distinguishing features of the collection. But what situates *Long Ago* as one of the key texts of the *fin-de-siècle* period is its emphasis on the links between the modern and the ancient: indeed, for Michael Field, only the truly modern poet can revive the antique world.

Robert Browning, who called them his "two dear Greek women," recognized, as Prins puts it, "the erotic subtext of their poetry."[1] And, after reading the poems in draft, he "prophesied they would make their mark" (see "Diaries" Section, p. 233). When asked if he would write a preface to the volume, he noted that they did not need his mentoring; Bradley proudly noted in *Works and Days*: "We must remember we are Michael Field. Again he said.—Wait fifty years" (see "Diaries" Section, p. 233). When the volume came out it was hailed by critics such as John Miller Gray as "one of the most exquisite lyrical productions of the latter half of the nineteenth century" (see "Reviews" Section, p. 361).

Recent criticism of the volume has focused on the importance of the text to understand late-Victorian aestheticism and decadence (particularly in relation to Swinburne's "Anactoria"). Its homoerotic subtext has attracted attention from critics such as Prins, Chris White, Angela Leighton, and Martha Vicinus. As Prins usefully puts it, "How shall we read these poems written by two women writing as a man writing as Sappho? [...] Their volume [...] proves to be a complex performance of the Sapphic signature: simultaneously single and double, masculine and feminine, Michael Field's Sappho is a name that opens itself to multiple readings."[2]]

Source: *Long Ago*, by Michael Field (London: George Bell and Sons, York Street, Covent Garden, 1889).

---

1 Yopie Prins, "Sappho Doubled: Michael Field," *Yale Journal of Criticism* 8 (1995): 167.
2 Prins, "Sappho Doubled," 165.

[EPIGRAPH]

πάλαι πότα [1]

'Ηράμαν μὲν ἔγω σέθεν, ῎Ατθι, πάλαι πότα [2]

"A great while since, a long, long time ago"

PREFACE

When, more than a year ago, I wrote to a literary friend of my attempt to express in English verse the passionate pleasure Dr. Wharton's book had brought to me, he replied: "That is a delightfully audacious thought—the extension of Sappho's fragments into lyrics. I can scarcely conceive anything more audacious."

In simple truth all worship that is not idolatry must be audacious; for it involves the blissful apprehension of an ideal; it means in the very phrase of Sappho—

'Έγων δ' ἐμαύτᾳ
τοῦτο σύνοιδα [3]

Devoutly as the fiery-bosomed Greek turned in her anguish to Aphrodite, praying her to accomplish her heart's desires, I have turned to the one woman who has dared to speak unfalteringly of the fearful mastery of love, and again and again the dumb prayer has risen from my heart—

σὺ δ' αὔτα
σύμμαχος ἔσσο [4]

---

1 "Long Ago"
2 "I loved thee once, Atthis, long ago." Wharton, fragment 33. Translations from the Greek are taken from Wharton's *Sappho: Memoir, Text, Selected Renderings, and a Literal Translation.* When possible, we have used Wharton's research on Sappho's life and work to contextualise Michael Field's rendering of the poet.
3 "And this I feel in myself." Wharton, fragment 15. In the first edition of *Long Ago*, Sappho's original Greek text was reproduced in an orange-gold ink, which was chosen by the women to highlight the golden beauty of Sappho's poetry.
4 "Be thyself my ally." Wharton, fragment 1.

I

Αὐτὰρ ὀραῖαι στεφανηπλόκευν·[1]

They plaited garlands in their time;
They knew the joy of youth's sweet prime,
    Quick breath and rapture:
Theirs was the violet-weaving bliss,
And theirs the white, wreathed brow to kiss,
    Kiss, and recapture.

They plaited garlands, even these;
They learnt Love's golden mysteries
    Of young Apollo;[2]
The lyre unloosed their souls; they lay
Under the trembling leaves at play,
    Bright dreams to follow.

They plaited garlands—heavenly twine!
They crowned the cup, they drank the wine
    Of youth's deep pleasure.
Now, lingering for the lyreless god—
Oh yet, once in their time, they trod
    A choric measure.[3]

II

'Οφθάλμοις δὲ μέλαις νύκτος ἄωρος [4]

Come, dark-eyed Sleep, thou child of Night,
    Give me thy dreams, thy lies;
Lead through the horny portal white
    The pleasure day denies.

---

1 "But in their time they plaited garlands." Wharton, fragment 73.
    According to Wharton, this fragment is "quoted by the Scholiast on
    Aristophanes' *Thesmophoriazusae* 401, to show that plaiting wreaths was
    a sign of being in love."
2 Apollo was the god of musical and artistic inspiration.
3 Choric, i.e., pertaining to a chorus or choral song in lyric poetry.
    Michael Field playfully links it to prosody and the metrical unit, which
    is of course measured in feet. Hence "trod."
4 "And dark-eyed Sleep, child of Night." Wharton, fragment 57.

O bring the kiss I could not take
   From lips that would not give;
Bring me the heart I could not break,
   The bliss for which I live.

I care not if I slumber blest
   By fond delusion; nay,
Put me on Phaon's lips to rest,[1]
   And cheat the cruel day!

III

Μήτ'ᵉμοι μέλι μήτε μέλισσα· [2]

Oh, not the honey, nor the bee!
Yet who can drain the flowers
As I? Less mad, Persephone
Spoiled the Sicilian bowers
Than I for scent and splendour rove
The rosy oleander grove,
Or lost in myrtle nook unveil
Thoughts that make Aphrodite pale.

Honey nor bee! the tingling quest
Must that too be denied?
Deep in thy bosom I would rest,
O golden blossom wide!
O poppy-wreath, O violet-crown,
I fling your fiery circlets down;
The joys o'er which bees murmur deep
Your Sappho's senses may not steep.

Honey! clear, soothing, nectarous, sweet,
On which my heart would feed,
Give me, O Love, the golden meat,

---

1 According to the legend, Sappho fell in love with Phaon, a man
   endowed with extraordinary beauty, who rejected her.
2 "Neither honey nor bee for me." Wharton, fragment 113. This song is
   an Epitalamia, or Bridal Song. According to Wharton, these "seem to be
   the words of the bride." The proverb refers "to those who wish for good
   unmixed with evil."

And stay my life's long greed—
The food in which the gods delight
That glistens tempting in my sight!
Phaon, thy lips withhold from me
The bliss of honey and of bee.

VI

Πάρθενον ἀδύφωνον [1]

Erinna,[2] thou art ever fair,
Not as the young spring flowers,
We who have laurel in our hair—
Eternal youth is ours.
The roses that Pieria's dew
Hath washed can ne'er decline;
On Orpheus' tomb at first they grew,
And there the Sacred Nine,[3]
'Mid quivering moonlight, seek the groves
Guarding the minstrel's tomb;
Each for the poet that she loves
Plucks an immortal bloom.
Soon as my girl's sweet voice she caught,
Thither Euterpe[4] sped,
And, singing too, a garland wrought
To crown Erinna's head.

---

1   "A sweet-voiced maiden." Wharton, fragment 61.
2   Sappho cultivated a literary salon at Mitylene, where many maidens
    studied music and poetry under her guidance. Around her gathered cul-
    tivated poetesses such as the celebrated and gifted Erinna of Telos and
    Damophyla of Pamphylia. Among her friends were Atthis, Telesippa, and
    Megara. Her pupils included Anagora of Miletus, Gongyla of Colophon,
    Euneica of Salamis, Mnasidica, Gyrina, Andromeda, Gorgo, Anactoria,
    and Dica, many of whom are directly addressed or referred to in her
    poetry.
3   Presumably the Muses.
4   Muse of Lyric Poetry.

XI

Ἄβρα δηῦτε παχήᾳ σπόλᾳ ἀλλόμαν [1]

Dreamless from happy sleep I woke,
On me the piercing sunlight broke,
I drank the laughter of the breeze
Divine, O Cypris,[2] from thy seas,
Then lithely in thick robe I sprang;
To me it seemed my body sang—

"Death is an evil." Phaon bent
Above his nets, magnificent.
"The wise immortals never die."
Phaon grew conscious I stood by;
And, oh! to bury in thy wave,
Lethe, one day, the glance he gave!

XIV

Τὸ μέλημα τοὐμόν· [3]

Atthis, my darling, thou did'st stray
A few feet to the rushy bed,
When a great fear and passion shook
My heart lest haply thou wert dead;
It grew so still about the brook,
As if a soul were drawn away.

Anon thy clear eyes, silver-blue,
Shone through the tamarisk-branches fine;
To pluck me iris thou had'st sprung
Through galingale and celandine;
Away, away, the flowers I flung
And thee down to my breast I drew.

My darling! Nay, our very breath
Nor light nor darkness shall divide;
Queen Dawn shall find us on one bed,

---

1   "Then delicately in thick robe I sprang." Wharton, fragment 55.
2   The goddess Aphrodite was also known as Cypris.
3   "My darling." Wharton, fragment 126.

Nor must thou flutter from my side
An instant, lest I feel the dread,
Atthis, the immanence of death.

XVI

Δεῦτέ νυν ἄβραι Χάριτες, καλλίκομοί τε Μοῖσαι [1]

Delicate Graces, come,
And charm my days,
With purest loveliness and smiles
And gracious ways;
For what were life without the spell
And mirth that in your presence dwell,
When with linked arms, fresh-blushing, ye
Stray from the Cyprian deity!

Ye fair-haired Muses, come,
And bless my days,
With holy ecstasy and might
Of deathless lays;
For what were life without the glow,
The joy that crownèd poets know,
When ye descend your mountain ground,
And wake the cithara's full sound!

XVII

Πλήρης μὲν ἐφαίνετ' ἀ σελάννα,
αἰ δ' ὡς περὶ βῶμον ἐστάθησαν· [2]

A. Παρθενία, παρθενία, ποῖ με λίποισ' οἴχη;
B. Οὐκέτι ἥξω πρὸς σέ, οὐκέτι ἥξω· [3]

The moon rose full: the women stood
As though within a sacred wood

---

1 "Come now, delicate Graces and fair-haired Muses." Wharton, fragment 60.
2 "The moon rose full, and the women stood as though around an altar." Wharton, fragment 53.
3 "A. Maidenhood, maidenhood, whither art thou gone from me?
  B. Never again will I come to thee, never again." Wharton, fragment 109.

Around an altar—thus with awe
The perfect, virgin orb they saw
Supreme above them; and its light
Fell on their limbs and garments white.
Then with pale, lifted brows they stirred
Their fearful steps at Sappho's word,
And in a circle moved around,
Responsive to her music's sound,
That through the silent air stole on,
Until their breathless dread was gone,
And they could dance with lightsome feet,
And lift the song with voices sweet.
Then once again the silence came:
Their lips were blanched as if with shame
That they in maidenhood were bold
Its sacred worship to unfold;
And Sappho touched the lyre alone,
Until she made the bright strings moan.
She called to Artemis[1] aloud—
Alas, the moon was wrapt in cloud!—
"Oh, whither art thou gone from me?
Come back again, virginity!
For maidenhood still do I long,
The freedom and the joyance strong
Of that most blessèd, secret state
That makes the tenderest maiden great.
O moon, be fair to me as these,
And my regretful passion ease;
Restore to me my only good,
My maidenhood, my maidenhood!"
She sang: and through the clouded night
An answer came of cruel might—
"To thee I never come again."
O Sappho, bitter was thy pain!
Then did thy heavy steps retire,
And leave, moon-bathed, the virgin quire.

---

1 Twin of Apollo, Artemis was the goddess of the wilderness and the
   hunt. She often appeared depicted with the crescent of the moon above
   her forehead. She was a virgin goddess.

XX

Ταῖσι [δὲ] ψῦχρος μὲν ἔγεντο θῦμος,
παρ δ' ἴεισι τὰ πτέρα ...[1]

I sang to women gathered round;
   Forth from my own heart-springs
Welled out the passion; of the pain
I sang if the beloved in vain
   Is sighed for—when
They stood untouched, as at the sound
   Of unfamiliar things,
Oh, then my heart turned cold, and then
   I dropt my wings.

Trembling I seek thy holy ground,
   Apollo, lord of kings;
Thou hast the darts that kill. Oh, free
The senseless world of apathy,
   Pierce it!—for when
In poet's strain no joy is found,
His call no answer brings,
Oh, then my heart turns cold, and then
   I drop my wings.

All flocks are Pan's; the groves resound
   To Orpheus' golden strings;
As swan that, secret, shrills the note
Triumphant from Apollo's throat,
   My muse, from men
Her holy raptures would confound,
   Turns to the woods and springs,
Whene'er my heart grows cold, and when
   I drop my wings.

Or by the white cliff's cypress mound,
   My music wildly rings;
I watch the hoar sails on the track
Of moonlight; they are turning back;
   Night falls; and when

---

1   "But their heart turned cold and they dropt their wings." Wharton,
fragment 16.

By maiden-arms to be enwound
   Ashore the fisher flings,
Oh, then my heart turns cold, and then
   I drop my wings.

XXI

Βροδοπάχεες ἄγναι Χάριτες, δεῦτε Δίος κόραι· [1]

   Ye rosy-armed, pure Graces, come,
     Daughters of Zeus, be near!
   Oh, wherefore have my lips been dumb
     So long in silence drear?

   And why have I so cheerless been,
     So sorrowful and wild?
   It was because ye were not seen,
     Because ye had not smiled.

   Although his prayer the Muses bless,
     The poet doth require
   That ye, in frolic gentleness,
     Should stand beside his lyre.

   Ne'er will be mortal ear delight,
     Nor care-vex'd spirit ease;
   Except he sing with ye in sight,
     Rose-flushed among the trees.

---

1 "Come, rosy-armed pure Graces, daughters of Zeus." Wharton, fragment 65. Quoting Philostratus, Wharton notes that "Sappho loves the rose, and always crowns it with some praise, likening to it the beauty of her maidens; she likens it also to the arms of the graces, when she describes their elbows bare."

XXV

Ah for Adonis! So
The virgins cry in woe:
Ah, for the spring, the spring,
And all fleet blossoming—
The delicate and slight
Anemones, rose-bright,
With buds flushed in and out,
Like Aphrodite's pout
When she is soft and coy;
Ah for the mortal boy,
Who would not hold her dear,
And now is dying here!

Ah for Adonis! Show,
Ye virgins, what ye know!
The white narcissi breathe
Between the grass, and sheathe
Their fragrance as they die;
From the low bushes nigh,
Mimosa's golden dust
A little later must
Be squandered on decay:
And can the fair youth stay,
When every lovely bloom
Goes to obscuring doom?

Ah for Adonis! No,
He must to Hades go:
A goddess may not keep
Safe from the mortal sleep
Those limbs and those young eyes;
Nor can her frantic cries
Recall one transient grace
Secure Immortals trace

---

1   "Ah for Adonis!" Wharton, fragment 63. According to Wharton, this is
    from Marius Plotius, and it appears to be the refrain of the ode to
    Adonis. Wharton reproduced this translation by Michael Field in his
    1895 re-edition of *Sappho*.

In things of earthly mould.
Ungirt and sable-stoled
She wanders through the glades,
And tears her heavenly braids.

Ah for Adonis! Throw
All flowers that quickly grow
And perish on his bed!
He will come back, though dead,
When spring returns, and fill
Cythera's arms until
He must again depart,
Again her bosom smart.
O virgins, joy is sent,
And soon with sorrow blent;
All we have loved is made
To re-appear, and fade.

XXVIII

... Ἔγω δὲ κήν' ὅτ-
τω τις ἔραται· [1]

Love, fatal creature, bitter-sweet,
For my Alcæus[2] I entreat.
Should I not plead? To wasting fires
    A secret prey I live,
Yet, Eros, that which he desires
    I cannot give.

Who shall deliver him? Lo, I,
For love of whom he soon will die,
Weep through the starry night oppressed
    That he should love in vain.
Ah, can another mortal breast
    Learn Sappho's pain!

---

1 "But that which one desires I ...." Wharton, fragment 13.
2 A poet and Sappho's older contemporary, who was believed to be one of her lovers.

When once his feet to me did stray,
He would forget the homeward way;
And when he gazed I turned to greet
     The grace within his eyes;
With love it is such joy to meet
     In any guise.

To him, O heavenly Muses, come!
He cannot live if he be dumb.
Leave me awhile. O let him feel
     His heart set free in song;
Hasten, for ye alone can heal
     A lover's wrong.

XXX

Πόλυ πάκτιδος ἀδυμελεστέρα, χρύσω χρυσοτέρα [1]

Thine elder that I am, thou must not cling
To me, nor mournful for my love entreat:
And yet, Alcæus, as the sudden spring
Is love, yea, and to veiled Demetia sweet.

Sweeter than tone of harp, more gold than gold
Is thy young voice to me; yet, ah, the pain
To learn I am beloved now I am old,
Who, in my youth, loved, as thou must, in vain.

XXXIII

Ταῖς κάλαις ὔμμιν [τὸ] νόημα τῶμον
     οὐ διάμειπτον· [2]

Maids, not to you my mind doth change;
Men I defy, allure, estrange,
Prostrate, make bond or free:
Soft as the stream beneath the plane

---

1 "Far sweeter of tone than harp, more golden than gold." Wharton, frag-
ments 122, 123.
2 "To you, fair maids, my mind changes not." Wharton, fragment 14.

To you I sing my love's refrain;
Between us is no thought of pain,
      Peril, satiety.

Soon doth a lover's patience tire,
But ye to manifold desire
Can yield response, ye know
When for long, museful days I pine,
The presage at my heart divine;
To you I never breathe a sign
Of inward want or woe.

When injuries my spirit bruise,
Allaying virtue ye infuse
With unobtrusive skill:
And if care frets ye come to me
As fresh as nymph from stream or tree,
And with your soft vitality
      My weary bosom fill.

XXXIV

Οὔ τι μοι ὔμμες. [1]

"Sing to us, Sappho!" cried the crowd,
   And to my lyre I sprang;
Apollo seized me, and aloud
   Tumultuous I sang.
I did not think of who would hear;
I knew not there were men who jeer;
Nor dreamed I there were mortals born
To make the poet's heart forlorn.

There is a gift the crowd can bring,
   A rapture, a content;
Pierian[2] roses scarcely fling
   So ravishing a scent

---

1 "Ye are nought to me." Wharton, fragment 23.
2 Pertaining to Pieria, Macedonia, where the Muses were worshipped. It
   also refers to the Muses and to poetry.

As that with which the air is stirred
When hearts of heavenly things have heard—
Sigh, and let forth the odour steal
Of that which in themselves they feel.

But now no subtle incense rose;
    I heard a hostile sound
And looked—oh, scornfuller than those
    'Mong men I ne'er have found.
I paused: the whistling air was stilled;
Then through my chords the godhead thrilled,
And the quelled creatures knew their kind
Ephemeral through foolish mind.

They saw their ghosts in Hades' grove
    A dismal, flitting band;
They felt they were shut out from love
    And honour in their land;
For never in the Muses' strain
Of them memorial would remain;
And spell-bound they received the curse
Of the great King's derided verse.

XXXV

Ἀλλα, μὴ μεγαλύνεο δακτυλίω πέρι· [1]

Come, Gorgo, put the rug in place,
    And passionate recline;
I love to see thee in thy grace,
    Dark, virulent, divine.
But wherefore thus thy proud eyes fix
    Upon a jewelled band?
Art thou so glad the sardonyx
    Becomes thy shapely hand?

Bethink thee! 'Tis for such as thou
    Zeus leaves his lofty seat;
'Tis at thy beauty's bidding how
    Man's mortal life shall fleet;

---

1   "Foolish woman, pride not thyself on a ring." Wharton, fragment 35.

Those fairest hands—dost thou forget
   Their power to thrill and cling?
O foolish woman, dost thou set
   Thy pride upon a ring?

XXXVI

Διὸς παῖς ὁ χρυσός, κεῖνον οὐ σῆς οὐδὲ κὶς δάπτει, [1]

Yea, gold is son of Zeus: no rust
   Its timeless light can stain;
The worm that brings man's flesh to dust
   Assaults its strength in vain:
More gold than gold the love I sing,
A hard, inviolable thing.

Men say the passions should grow old
   With waning years; my heart
Is incorruptible as gold,
   'Tis my immortal part:
Nor is there any god can lay
On love the finger of decay.

XLIV

Οὔ' τι μοι ὔμμες· [2]

Nought to me! So I choose to say:
We meet, old friends, about the bay;
The golden pulse grows on the shore—
Are not all things as heretofore
Now we have cast our love away?

Men throng us; thou art nought to me,
Therefore, indifferent, I can see
Within thine eyes the bright'ning grace
That once thou gavest face to face;
'Tis natural they welcome thee!

---

1   "Gold is son of Zeus, no moth nor worm devours it." Wharton,
   fragment 142.
2   "Ye are nought to me." Wharton, fragment 23.

Nought to me, like the silver ring,
Thy mislaid, worthless gift. Last spring,
As any careless girl, I lost
The pin, yet, by the tears it cost,
It should have been worth cherishing.

Nought, nought! and yet if thou dost pass
I grow as summer-coloured grass,
And if I wrap my chiton round,
I know thine ear hath caught the sound,
Although thou heedest not, alas!

Nought to me! Wherefore dost thou throw
On me that glittering glance, as though,
Friend, I had ever done thee wrong,
When the crowd asks me for the song,
"Atthis, I loved thee long ago?"

LII

Ἔγων δ' ἐμαύτᾳ
τοῦτο σύνοιδα·[1]

Climbing the hill a coil of snakes
Impedes Tiresias' path;[2] he breaks
His staff across them—idle thrust
That lays the female in the dust,
But dooms the prophet to forego
His manhood, and, as woman, know
The unfamiliar, sovereign guise
Of passion he had dared despise.

---

1 "And this I feel in myself." Wharton, fragment 15.
2 According to the Greek legend, one day Tiresias went walking in the
   woods and saw two snakes copulating. When he hit them with a staff he
   was changed into a woman. Seven years later, as s/he was walking in the
   same area, s/he saw again two snakes copulating. He struck them with
   his staff and was changed back into the male sex. The poem recreates
   the famous account of the origin of Tiresias' blindness and prophetic
   powers: the moment when he is asked by Zeus and his wife, Hera, to
   judge who has most pleasure in sex, women or men.

Ah, not in the Erinnys' ground
Experience so dire were found
As that to the enchanter known
When womanhood was round him thrown:
He trembled at the quickening change,
He trembled at his vision's range,
His finer sense for bliss and dole,
His receptivity of soul;
But when love came, and, loving back,
He learnt the pleasure men must lack,
It seemed that he had broken free
Almost from his mortality.

Seven years he lives as woman, then
Resumes his cruder part 'mong men,
Till him indignant Hera becks
To judge betwixt the joys of sex,
For the great Queen in wrath has heard
By her presumptuous lord averred
That, when he sought her in his brave,
Young godhead, higher bliss he gave
Than the unutterable lure
Of her veiled glances could procure
For him, as balmy-limbed and proud
She drew him to Olympia's cloud.

"In marriage who hath more delight?"
She asks; then quivers and grows white,
As sacrilegious lips reveal
What woman in herself must feel—
And passes an avenging hand
Across his subtle eyelids bland.

Deep-bosomed Queen, fain would'st thou hide
The mystic raptures of the bride!
When man's strong nature draweth nigh
'Tis as the lightning to the sky,
The blast to idle sail, the thrill
Of springtide when the saplings fill.
Though fragrant breath the sun receives
From the young rose's softening leaves,
Her plaited petals once undone
The rose herself receives the sun.

Tiresias, ere the goddess smite,
Look on me with unblinded sight,
That I may learn if thou hast part
In womanhood's secluded heart:
Medea's penetrative charm
Own'st thou to succour and disarm,
Hast thou her passion inly great
Heroes to mould and subjugate?
Can'st thou divine how sweet to bring
Apollo to thy blossoming
As Daphne; or, as just a child
Gathering a bunch of tulips wild,
To feel the flowery hill-side rent
Convulsive for thy ravishment?

Thou need'st not to unlock thine eyes,
Thy slow, ironic smile replies:
Thou hast been woman, and although
The twining snakes with second blow
Of golden staff thou did'st assail,
And, crushing at a stroke the male,
Had'st virtue from thy doom to break,
And lost virility re-take—
Thou hast been woman, and her deep,
Magnetic mystery dost keep;
Thou hast been woman, and can'st see
Therefore into futurity:
It is not that Zeus gave thee power
To look beyond the transient hour,
For thou hast trod the regions dun,
Where life and death are each begun;
Thy spirit from the gods set free
Hath communed with Necessity.
Tilphusa's[1] fountain thou may'st quaff
And die, but still thy golden staff
Will guide thee with perceptive hand
Among the Shades to understand
The terrors of remorse and dread,
And prophesy among the dead.

---

1 Tiresias died drinking from the spring of Tilphusa.

LVII

Αὖτα δὲ σὺ Καλλιόπα·[1]

A. Παρθενία, παρθενία, ποῖ με λίποισ' οἴχῃ;
B. Οὐκέτι ἥξω πρὸς σέ, οὐκέτι ἥξω.[2]

My shell is mute; Apollo doth refuse
My prayers; I turn to thee, O mother muse,
    Who fled'st the buoyant brood
    Of crested Helicon,[3]
In secret by a mortal to be wooed,
Yet still, august, keepest thy golden snood:
My maidenhood, my maidenhood is gone.

Clio,[4] ah! thou thyself did'st find it sweet
To feel thy lover's heart against thee beat,
    To let Œagrus[5] teach
    Love's tender, human ways,
No more with thy two arms to strive to reach
The sky, to hear a trembling man beseech,
And give him favour, prompting, and dispraise.

'Twas sweet to clasp thy child, nor did'st thou shrink
To bear him to thy virgin haunts to drink
    Of Aganippe's spring.
    Alas, what ailed thee then?
While delicate girl-muses in a ring
Sang softly to thy babe thou could'st not sing—
Thy maidenhood would never come again.

Mute thou did'st hide him 'mid the devious bowers,
Till he stopped playing with the purple flowers
    One April, and began
    To hum a happy prate

---

1 "And thou thyself, Calliope." Wharton, fragment 82.

2 "A. Maidenhood, maidenhood, whither art thou gone from me?
    B. Never again will I come to thee, never again." Wharton, fragment 109.

3 Helicon is a mountain in the region of Thespiai, Greece, and represents
    poetical inspiration. Two springs sacred to the Muses were located there:
    the Aganippe and the Hippocrene.

4 Muse of heroic poetry and history.

5 King of Thrace and allegedly the lover of Calliope.

That through the little, bosky hollows ran,
And brought the shepherd and the husbandman,
The doe and stag, the lioness and her mate.

But when a Mænad, breathing quick beneath
Her nebris, watched the child with sharpened teeth,
  Did'st feel the poet's fate
  Down Hebrus[1] to be hurled?
Mother, did'st thou forbode how for her great,
Her lyrical enchanters lies in wait
The execrating, fascinated world?

Regret not, glorious lady of the style,
That thou did'st learn how nations travail, while
  Thy heart throbbed with a king's,
  And from Antissa's tomb[2]
The fate and falling of all lovely things;
Thy scroll unwraps the ages; Moira[3] brings
To thee the tattered tissue of her loom.

Yet sometimes, sitting by the sacred well,
Thou call'st to mind the heart-delighting spell
  Apollo cast on thee
  In thy strong, virgin days,
When thou wert close to sunshine and to tree;
What ails thee in thyself, Calliope?[4]
With thee no more the hamadryad plays:

The blowing Hours of thy still form afraid
Bring thee no more the branch, the vine, the blade;
  They love the hands that smite
  The full-stringed barbiton
That we may never touch again aright:
No living creature may we more delight;
Our maidenhood, our maidenhood is gone.

---

1   The name of a river.
2   Antissa is an ancient town on the island of Lesbos.
3   A single goddess of fate in Greek mythology.
4   Muse of epic poetry.

LXI

χελίνη [1]

There is laughter soft and free
'Neath the pines of Thessaly,
Thrilling echoes, thrilling cries
Of pursuit, delight, surprise;
Dryope[2] beneath the trees
With the Hamadryades
Plays upon the mountain-side:
Now they meet, and now they hide.

On the hot and sandy ground,
Crumbling still as still they bound,
Crouches, basks a tortoise; all
But the mortal maiden fall
Back in trepidation; she
Takes the creature on her knee,
Strokes the ardent shell, and lays
Even her cheek against its blaze,

Till she calms her playmates' fear;
Suddenly beside her ear
Flashes forth a tongue; the beast
Changes, and with shape released
Grows into a serpent bright,
Covetous, subduing, tight
Round her body backward bent
In forlorn astonishment.

With their convoluted strain
His upreaching coils attain
Full ascendency—her breast
By their passion is compressed
Till her breath in terror fails;
'Mid the flicker of the scales,
Half she seems to hear, half sees
How each frighted comrade flees.

---

1 "A tortoise." Wharton, fragment 169.
2 Daughter of Dryops and a playmate of the Hamadryades or Nymphes,
   who taught her to sing. Once she was seen by Apollo, who metamor-
   phosed into a tortoise to gain possession of her.

And alone beneath the pine,
With the serpent's heavy twine
On her form, she almost dies:
But a magic from his eyes
Keeps her living, and entranced
At the wonder that has chanced,
As she feels a god within
Fiery looks that thrill and win.

'Tis Apollo in disguise
Holds possession of his prize.
Thus he binds in fetters dire
Those for whom he knows desire;
Mortal loves or poets—all
He must dominate, enthrall
By the rapture of his sway,
Which shall either bless or slay.

So she shudders with a joy
Which no childish fears alloy,
For the spell is round her now
Which has made old prophets bow
Tremulous and wild. An hour
Must she glow beneath his power,
Then a dryad shy and strange
Through the firs thereafter range.

For she joins the troop of those
Dedicate to joy and woes,
Whom by stricture of his love
Leto's son has raised above
Other mortals, who, endowed
With existence unallowed
To their fellows, wander free
Girt with earth's own mystery.

LXIII

Ἄγε δη χέλυ δῖά μοι
φωνάεσσα γένοιο· [1]

Grow vocal to me, O my shell divine!
    I cannot rest;
Not so doth Cypris pine
To raise her love to her undinted breast
When sun first warms the earth, as I require
To roll the heavy death from my recumbent lyre.

O whilom tireless voice, why art thou dumb?
    To-day I stood
Watching the Mænads come
From a dark fissure in the ilex-wood
Forth to the golden poplars and the light;
My tingling senses leapt to join that concourse bright.

Passed is the crowd, passed with his buoyant flute
    The Evian King:
My plectrum still is mute
Of beauty, of the halcyon's nest, of spring;
Though deep within a vital madness teems,
And I am tossed with fierce, disjointed, wizard dreams.

Apollo, Dionysus passes by,
    Adonis wakes,
Zephyr and Chloris sigh:
To me, alas, my lyre no music makes,
Though tortured, fluttering toward the strings I reach,
Mad as for Anactoria's lovely laugh and speech.

For thou—where, in some balmy, western isle
    Each day doth bring
Seed-sowing, harvest smile,
And twilight drop of fruit for garnering,
Where north wind never blows—dost dwell apart,
Keeping a gentle people free from grief of heart.

---

1 "Come now, divine shell, become vocal for me." Wharton, fragment 45.

Sun-god, return! Break from thine old-world bower,
    Thy garden set
With the narcissus-flower
And purple daphne! To thy chariot get,
Glorious arise as on thy day of birth,
And spread illuminating order through the earth.

I scan the rocks: O sudden mountain-rill,
    That sure hast heard
His footsteps on the hill,
Leaping from crag to crag to bring me word—
Lapse quiet at my feet; I hear along
My lyre the journeying tumult of an unbreathed song.

LXV

πολυΐδριδι [1]

Prometheus fashioned man,
    Then ruthful, pitying
His creature when the snowy storms began
To numb, the frost to harass and to cling,

Toward the sun's golden wheel
    He clomb, and, as the blaze
Burned past, taught of Athene, sprang to steal
A scintillating fragment from the rays.

With wisdom-guided torch
    Dipped in the heavenly flame
Back he returned to each unlighted porch,
And filled the homes with joy where'er he came.

Zeus marked the flickering brand,
    And earthward bent to urge
Two countervailing evils through the land:
One was the fever with its fiery scourge;

One was Pandora's face,
    Her smiles and luring feet—

---

1   "Of much knowledge." Wharton, fragment 166.

"Woman," he said, "shall scorch man's petty race,
And fill his senses with insidious heat."

But, Phaon, tremble thou
  Whom beauty cannot fire,
Who livest with no rage upon thy brow,
Unstricken by complaint or by desire.

Remember what thou art,
  Think of the wrath above,
Scathless to stand is not a mortal's part:
O fool, accept the furious curse of love!

LXVIII

"Οπταις ἄμμε. [1]

Thou burnest us; thy torches' flashing spires,
    Eros, we hail!
Thou burnest us, Immortal, but the fires
    Thou kindlest fail:
      We die,
And thine effulgent braziers pale.

Ah, Phaon, thou who hast abandoned me,
    Thou who dost smile
To think deserted Lesbos rings with thee,
    A little while
      Gone by
There will be muteness in thine isle.

Even as a god who finds his temple-flame
    Sunken, unfed,
Who, loving not the priestess, loves the fame
    Bright altars spread,
      Wilt sigh
To find thy lyric glory dead?

---

1 "Thou burnest us." Wharton, fragment 115.

Or will Damophyla, the lovely-haired,
    My music learn,
Singing how Sappho of thy love despaired,
    Till thou dost burn,
       While I,
Eros! am quenched within my urn?

Μνάσασθαί τινά φαμι καὶ ὕστερον ἄμμεων· [1]

O free me, for I take the leap,
Apollo, from thy snowy steep![2]
Song did'st thou give me, and there fell
O'er Hellas an enchanter's spell;
I heard young lovers catch the strain:
For me there is the hoary main;
I would not hear my words again.

Ah, lord of speech, well dost thou know
The incommunicable woe
Finds not in lyric cry release,
Finds but in Hades' bosom peace;
And therefore on thy temple-ground
Thou pointest lovers to the mound
Set high above the billows' sound.

Though in unfathomed seas I sink,
Men will remember me, I think,
Remember me, my King, as thine;
And must I take a shape divine
As thine immortal, let me be
A dumb sea-bird with breast love-free,
And feel the waves fall over me.

---

1 "Men I think will remember us even hereafter." Wharton, fragment 32.
2 According to the legend, Sappho, in love with Phaon, arrived at the
    Temple of Apollo dressed in bridal garments. After having sung a hymn
    to the God, she threw herself from the Leucadian rock, falling into the
    sea never to rise again. In his account of this incident, Wharton argues
    that the myth lacks a sound historical basis and that there is enough evi-
    dence to suggest that she was buried in an Aeolic grave.

2. From *Sight and Song* (1892)

[Published by the decadent publishers Elkin Mathews and John Lane, *Sight and Song* is arguably Michael Field's most ambitious book of poems. The volume is a compendium of thirty-one poems that "translated" into poetry the pictures the poets had seen in their strolls around various art galleries and museums both in London and in Continental Europe, most notably the National Gallery, the Louvre, the Accademia of Venice, the Uffizi, the Campo Santo at Pisa, the Accademia of Florence, the Städel'sche Institut at Frankfurt, the Dresden Gallery, Hampton Court, the Accademia àt Bologna, the Grand Duke's Palace at Weimar, the Ducal Palace at Venice, and Lord Dudley's Collection.

The collection sprang out of Michael Field's deep engagement with art. Passionate about painting, the women attended lectures on art and art criticism at the British Museum and other institutions in London and regularly visited museums, galleries, and exhibitions both in England and abroad. These visits were fully documented in their diary: there are literally hundreds of pages in *Works and Days* with annotations and descriptions of paintings; criticism on artists and art periods; and drafts of poems on pictures. Such was their passion for art that they began to collect photographic reproductions of works of art by historical figures as well as by contemporary artists. These, then considered luxury items, they gave each other as presents. Some were framed and proudly hung in their study and bedroom as *objets d'art*.

Written by devoted students of art history and criticism, *Sight and Song* was an impressive experiment ·in visual aesthetics that aimed to "sing what certain colours and pictures sing in themselves." The theoretical and lyrical origins of the volume were in Ruskin's revival in the third volume of his *Modern Painters* (1856) of the "ut pictura poesis" tradition (the notion that poetry and painting are analogous forms of art), and in Dante Gabriel Rossetti's *Poems* (1870), a book of verse that included several sonnets for pictures Rossetti wrote during the late 1860s. The volume, however, was deeply rooted in the revolutionary aesthetics of the *fin-de-siècle* period. Drafted during the late 1880s and early 1890s, *Sight and Song* was indebted to their friendship with the art critic Bernard Berenson and to Walter Pater's *The Renaissance* (especially the essay on "Leonardo da Vinci" and the volume's infamous "Conclusion"), where he expounded a theory of "art for art's sake" directly related to impressionism and the subjective contemplation and enjoyment of an artwork.

During the 1880s and 1890s, London was at the height of aestheticism, and in *Sight and Song* (the first nineteenth-century book of verse dedicated wholly to poems on pictures), Michael Field addressed questions about impressionism, the human world of sensoria, gender, and the painted lyric in a post-Pre-Raphaelite photographic age. As they claimed in the Preface, their aim was "to express not so much what these pictures are to the poet, but rather what poetry they objectively incarnate," thus proposing a novel method of artwork based on a new visual relation between the viewer and the object of art.

"We have written the queerest little book in the world. Our teeth clatter with fear," they wrote in their Diary.[1] Keenly aware of their daring experimentalism, they had such high expections for the volume that even before the publication of *Sight and Song* they were already researching for a second volume of poems on pictures. These plans were discontinued, however, after the lukewarm response *Sight and Song* received in the press. On the whole, while the lyrics themselves were highly praised by critics and poets alike, Michael Field's theory of the aesthetic was deemed highly controversial and flawed. W.B. Yeats described the collection as a "guide book" to a series of paintings, and Berenson claimed that they "ha[d] confused the material of poetry, which is feeling with colour & outline the materials of painting" (see "Diaries" section, p. 225). In his review for the Academy, John Miller Gray praised many of the poems but noted "it was a bold experiment to publish a whole book of poems upon pictures." By contrast, their friend Alice Trusted described "*L'Indifférent*" as "irresistible," and Arthur Symons referred to the same poem as "the delightful" *L'Indifférent* (see "Letters" Section, p. 351). Curiously enough, despite Yeats's reservations about the volume, he wrote some time later his own "La Gioconda" sonnet, much in the same vein as Michael Field's "Leonardo da Vinci's *La Gioconda*."

Thanks to new research on the visual culture of the nineteenth century, British aestheticism, late-Victorian sexuality, and psychological aesthetics, today critics are beginning to recognize the powerful lyrics of *Sight and Song*.]

Source: *Sight and Song*, by Michael Field (London: Elkin Mathews and John Lane, 1892).

---

1 *Works and Days*, British Library. Add.ms. 46780 f. 89v.

ὅσ᾽ ἂν λέγωμεν πάνθ᾽ ὁρῶντα λέξομεν. [1]

SOPHOCLES, *Oedipus Coloneus*

'I see and sing, by my own eyes inspired.'

KEATS, *Ode to Psyche*

PREFACE

The aim of this little volume is, as far as may be, to translate into verse what the lines and colours of certain chosen pictures sing in themselves; to express not so much what these pictures are to the poet, but rather what poetry they objectively incarnate. Such an attempt demands patient, continuous sight as pure as the gazer can refine it of theory, fancies, or his mere subjective enjoyment.

'Il faut, par un effort d'esprit, se transporter dans les personnages et non les attirer à soi.'[2] For *personnages* substitute *peintures*, and this sentence from Gustave Flaubert's 'Correspondence' resumes the method of art-study from which these poems arose.

Not even 'le grand Gustave' could ultimately illude himself as a formative power in his work—not after the pain of a lifetime directed to no other end. Yet the effort to see things from their own centre, by suppressing the habitual centralisation of the visible in ourselves, is a process by which we eliminate our idiosyncrasies and obtain an impression clearer, less passive, more intimate.

When such effort has been made, honestly and with persist-

---

1 "In all that I speak there shall be sight." (*The Tragedies of Sophocles*, ed. R.C. Jebb [Cambridge UP, 1904], line 75.)

2 In a letter to George Sand dated 15 December 1866, Flaubert wrote: "Je crois que le grand art est scientifique et impersonnel. Il faut, par un effort d'esprit, se transporter dans les personnages, et non les attirer à soi." ("I think that all great art is scientific and impersonal. By an effort of wit, one must transport oneself to the characters and not draw them towards onself.")

ence, even then the inevitable force of individuality must still have play and a temperament mould the purified impression:—

> 'When your eyes have done their part,
> Thought must length it in the heart.'

M.F.

February 15, 1892.

L'INDIFFÉRENT
WATTEAU[1]
The Louvre

He dances on a toe
As light as Mercury's:
Sweet herald, give thy message! No,
He dances on; the world is his,
The sunshine and his wingy hat;
His eyes are round
Beneath the brim:
To merely dance where he is found
Is fate to him
And he was born for that.

He dances in a cloak
Of vermeil and of blue:
Gay youngster, underneath the oak,
Come, laugh and love! In vain we woo;
He is a human butterfly;—
No soul, no kiss,
No glance nor joy!
Though old enough for manhood's bliss,
He is a boy,
Who dances and must die.

---

1 Eighteenth-century French rococo painter, famous for his "Fêtes Galantes" (romanticised scenes depicting elegant women and men at play in an outdoor setting) and for his interest in the theatre and ballet. "L'Indifférent" ("The Indifferent") is a portrait of a male dancer.

VENUS, MERCURY AND CUPID

CORREGGIO

The National Gallery

Here we have the lovely masque
    Of a Venus, in the braid
Of bright oak-boughs, come to ask
    Hermes will he give a task
To the little lad beside her,
Who half hides and half doth guide her.

Can there be indeed good cause
    Cupid should learn other art
Than his mother's gracious laws?
    Hermes—Oh, the magic straws
In his hat!—as one that pineth,
To the pretty babe inclineth.

Oh, the poignant hour serene,
    When sweet Love that is a child,
When sweet Cupid comes between
    Troubled lovers as a screen,
And the scolding and beseeching
Are just turned to infant-teaching.

LA GIOCONDA

LEONARDO DA VINCI

The Louvre

Historic, side-long, implicating eyes;
A smile of velvet's lustre on the cheek;
Calm lips the smile leads upward; hand that lies
Glowing and soft, the patience in its rest
Of cruelty that waits and doth not seek
For prey; a dusky forehead and a breast
Where twilight touches ripeness amorously:
Behind her, crystal rocks, a sea and skies
Of evanescent blue on cloud and creek;
Landscape that shines suppressive of its zest
For those vicissitudes by which men die.

THE FAUN'S PUNISHMENT[1]

CORREGGIO

The Louvre

What has the tortured, old Faun been doing?
　　　What was his impious sin,
That the Maenads have ceased from pursuing
　　　Cattle, with leaps and din,
　　　To compass him round,
　　　On woodland ground,
　　　With cords and faces dire,—
　　　Cords fastened with strain,
　　　Faces hate-stretched?
　　　Why have they fetched
Snakes from the grass, with swift tongues of fire,
And a reed from the stream-sodden plain?

Beneath the sun's and the oak-leaves' flicker,
　　　They settle near—ah, near!
One blows her reed, as dry as a wicker,
　　　Into the old Faun's ear;
　　　The scream of the wind,
　　　With flood combined,
　　　Rolls on his simple sense:
　　　It is anguish heard,
　　　For quietness splits
　　　Within; and fits
Of gale and surge are a fierce offence
To him who knows but the breeze or bird.

One sits with fanciful eyes beside him;
　　　Malice and wonder mix
In her glance at the victim—woe betide him,
　　　When once her snakes transfix
　　　His side! Ere they dart,
　　　With backward start
　　　She waits their rigid pause;
　　　And with comely stoop

1　The "Faun" was an important figure in Michael Field's conception of
　the lyric and the aesthetic. Linked to Bacchus or Dionysus, the Faun
　represented the wild lyrical nature of being. "Faun" was the nickname of
　Bernard Berenson. "Henry" or "Field" was also a "Faun."

One maid, elate
With horror, hate
And triumph, up from his ankle draws
The skin away in a clinging loop.

Before the women a boy-faun dances,
Grapes and stem at his chin,—
Mouth of red the red grape-bunch enhances
Ere it is sucked within
By the juicy lips,
Free as the tips
Of tendrils in their curve;
And his flaccid cheek,
Mid mirthful heaves
And ripples, weaves
A guiltless smile that might almost serve
For the vines themselves in vintage-week.

What meaning is here, or what mystery,
What fate, and for what crime?
Why so fearful this silvan history
Of a far summer-time?
There was no ill-will
That day until
With fun the grey-beard shook
At the Maenads' torn,
Spread hair, their brave,
Tumultuous wave
Dancing; and women will never brook
Mirth at their folly, O doomed, old Faun!

THE BIRTH OF VENUS
SANDRO BOTTICELLI
The Uffizi

Frills of brimming wavelets lap
Round a shell that is a boat;
Roses fly like birds and float
Down the crisp air; garments flap:
Midmost of the breeze, with locks
In possession of the wind,
Coiling hair in loosened shocks,

Sways a girl who seeks to bind
New-born beauty with a tress
Gold about her nakedness.

And her chilled, wan body sweet
Greets the ruffled cloak of rose,
Daisy-stitched, that Flora throws
Toward her ere she set her feet
On the green verge of the world:
Flora, with the corn-flower dressed,
Round her neck a rose-spray curled
Flowerless, wild-rose at her breast,
To her goddess hastes to bring
The wide chiton of the spring.

While from ocean, breathing hard,
With sole pressure toward the bay,—
Olive raiment, pinions grey
By clipt rose-stems thinly starred,
Zephyrus and Boreas pass,
One in wonder, one desire:
And the cool sea's dawnlit mass
Boreas' foot has lifted higher,
As he blows the shell to land,
Where the reed invades the sand.

She who treads the rocking shell—
Tearful shadow in her eyes
Of reluctant sympathies,
On her mouth a pause, a spell,
Candour far too lone to speak
And no knowledge on her brows;
Virgin stranger, come to seek
Covert of strong orange-boughs
By the sea-wind scarcely moved,—
She is Love that hath not loved.

SPRING

SANDRO BOTTICELLI

The Accademia of Florence

Venus is sad among the wanton powers,
That make delicious tempest in the hours
Of April or are reckless with their flowers:
    Through umbrageous orange-trees
    Sweeps, mid azure swirl, the Breeze,
    That with clipping arms would seize
    Eôs, wind-inspired and mad,
    In wind-tightened muslin clad,
    With one tress for stormy wreath
    And a bine between her teeth.
    Flora foots it near in frilled,
    Vagrant skirt, with roses filled;
    Pinks and gentians spot her robe
    And the curled acanthus-lobe
    Edges intricate her sleeve;
    Rosy briars a girdle weave,
    Blooms are brooches in her hair:
    Though a vision debonair,
    Thriftless, venturesome, a grace
    Disingenuous lights her face;
    Curst she is, uncertain-lipped,
    Riggishly her dress is whipped
By little gusts fantastic. Will she deign
To toss her double-roses, or refrain?

These riot by the left side of the queen;
Before her face another group is seen:
In ordered and harmonic nobleness,
Three maidens circle o'er the turf—each dress
Blown round the tiptoe shape in lovely folds
Of air-invaded white; one comrade holds
Her fellow's hand on high, the foremost links
Their other hands in chain that lifts and sinks.
Their auburn tresses ripple, coil or sweep;
Gems, amulets and fine ball-fringes keep
Their raiment from austereness. With reserve
The dancers in a garland slowly curve.
They are the Graces in their virgin youth;
And does it touch their Deity with ruth

That they must fade when Eros speeds his dart?
Is this the grief and forethought of her heart?

For she is sad, although fresh myrtles near
Her figure chequer with their leaves the drear,
Grey chinks that through the orange-trees appear:
    Clothed in spring-time's white and red,
    She is tender with some dread,
    As she turns a musing head
    Sideways mid her veil demure;
    Her wide eyes have no allure,
    Dark and heavy with their pain.
    She would bless, and yet in vain
    Is her troubled blessing: Love,
    Blind and tyrannous above,
    Shoots his childish flame to mar
    Those without defect, who are
    Yet unspent and cold with peace;
    While, her sorrow to increase,
    Hermes, leader of her troop—
    His short cutlass on the loop
    Of a crimson cloak, his eye
    Clear in its fatality—
    Rather seems the guide of ghosts
    To the dead, Plutonian coasts,
Than herald of Spring's immature, gay band:
He plucks a ripened orange with his hand.

The tumult and the mystery of earth,
When woods are bleak and flowers have sudden birth,
When love is cruel, follow to their end
The God that teaches Shadows to descend,
But pauses now awhile, with solemn lip
And left hand laid victorious on his hip.
The triumph of the year without avail
Is blown to Hades by blue Zephyr's gale.
Across the seedling herbage coltsfoot grows
Between the tulip, heartsease, strawberry-rose,
Fringed pinks and dull grape-hyacinth. Alas,
At play together, through the speckled grass
Trip Youth and April: Venus, looking on,
Beholds the mead with all the dancers gone.

A PORTRAIT

BARTOLOMMEO VENETO

The Städel'sche Institut at Frankfurt

A crystal, flawless beauty on the brows
    Where neither love nor time has conquered space
    On which to live; her leftward smile endows
    The gazer with no tidings from the face;
About the clear mounds of the lip it winds with silvery pace
    And in the umber eyes it is a light
Chill as a glowworm's when the moon embrowns an August
    night.

She saw her beauty often in the glass,
    Sharp on the dazzling surface, and she knew
    The haughty custom of her grace must pass:
    Though more persistent in all charm it grew
As with a desperate joy her hair across her throat she drew
    In crinkled locks stiff as dead, yellow snakes ...
Until at last within her soul the resolution wakes

She will be painted, she who is so strong
    In loveliness, so fugitive in years:
    Forth to the field she goes and questions long
    Which flowers to choose of those the summer bears;
She plucks a violet larkspur,—then a columbine appears
    Of perfect yellow,—daisies choicely wide;
These simple things with finest touch she gathers in her pride.

Next on her head, veiled with well-bleachen white
    And bound across the brow with azure-blue,
    She sets the box-tree leaf and coils it tight
    In spiky wreath of green, immortal hue;
Then, to the prompting of her strange, emphatic insight true,
    She bares one breast, half-freeing it of robe,
And hangs green-water gem and cord beside the naked globe.

So was she painted and for centuries
    Has held the fading field-flowers in her hand
    Austerely as a sign. O fearful eyes
    And soft lips of the courtesan who planned
To give her fragile shapeliness to art, whose reason spanned
    Her doom, who bade her beauty in its cold
And vacant eminence persist for all men to behold!

She had no memories save of herself
And her slow-fostered graces, naught to say
Of love in gift or boon; her cruel pelf
Had left her with no hopes that grow and stay;
She found default in everything that happened night or day,
Yet stooped in calm to passion's dizziest strife
And gave to art a fair, blank form, unverified by life.

Thus has she conquered death: her eyes are fresh,
Clear as her frontlet jewel, firm in shade
And definite as on the linen mesh
Of her white hood the box-tree's sombre braid,
That glitters leaf by leaf and with the year's waste will not fade.
The small, close mouth, leaving no room for breath,
In perfect, still pollution smiles—Lo, she has conquered death!

SAINT SEBASTIAN[1]
CORREGGIO
The Dresden Gallery

Bound by thy hands, but with respect unto thine eyes how
  free—
Fixed on Madonna, seeing all that they were born to see!
    The Child thine upward face hath sighted,
        Still and delighted;
Oh, bliss when with mute rites two souls are plighted!

As the young aspen-leaves rejoice, though to the stem held tight,
In the soft visit of the air, the current of the light,
    Thou hast the peril of a captive's chances,
        Thy spirit dances,
Caught in the play of Heaven's divine advances.

While cherubs straggle on the clouds of luminous, curled fire,
The Babe looks through them, far below, on thee with soft desire.
    Most clear of bond must they be reckoned—
        No joy is second
To theirs whose eyes by other eyes are beckoned.

---

1   Saint Sebastian was a Roman martyr. In the nineteenth century many
    associated him with masculinity, masochism, and homosexuality.

Though arrows rain on breast and throat they have no power
   to hurt,
While thy tenacious face they fail an instant to avert.
      Oh might my eyes, so without measure,
            Feed on their treasure,
The world with thong and dart might do its pleasure!

VENUS AND MARS

SANDRO BOTTICELLI
The National Gallery

         She is a fate, although
         She lies upon the grass,
         While satyrs shout *Ho, ho!*
         At what she brings to pass;
         And nature is as free
         Before her strange, young face
         As if it knew that she
         Were in her sovereign place,
         With shading trees above.
The little powers of earth on woolly hips
Are gay as children round a nurse they love;
         Nor do they watch her lips.

         A cushion, crimson-rose,
         Beneath her elbow heaves;
         Her head, erect in pose
         Against the laurel-leaves,
         Is looped with citron hair
         That cunning plaits adorn.
         Beside her instep bare
         And dress of crimpled lawn
         Fine blades of herbage rise;
The level field that circles her retreat
Is one grey-lighted green the early sky's
         Fresh blue inclines to meet.

         Her swathing robe is bound
         With gold that is not new:
         She rears from off the ground
         As if her body grew
         Triumphant as a stem

That hath received the rains,
Hath softly sunk with them,
And in an hour regains
Its height and settledness.
Yet are her eyes alert; they search and weigh
The god, supine, who fell from her caress
When love had had its sway.

He lies in perfect death
Of sleep that has no spasm;
It seems his very breath
Is lifted from a chasm,
So sunk he lies. His hair
In russet heaps is spread;
Thus couches in its lair
A creature that is dead:
But, see, his nostrils scent
New joy and tighten palpitating nerves,
Although his naked limbs, their fury spent,
Are fallen in wearied curves.

Athwart his figure twist
Some wreathy folds of white,
Crossed by the languid wrist
And loose palm of his right,
Wan hand; the other drops
Its fingers down beside
The coat of mail that props
His shoulder; crimson-dyed,
His cloak winds under him;
One leg is stretched, one raised in arching lines:
Thus, opposite the queen, his body slim
And muscular reclines.

An impish satyr blows
The mottled conch in vain
Beside his ear that knows
No whine of the sea-strain;
Another tugs his spear,
One hides within his casque
Soft horns and jaunty leer;
While one presumes to bask
Within his breastplate void

And rolls its tongue in open-hearted zest:
Above the sleeper, their dim wings annoyed,
       The wasps have made a nest.

      O tragic forms, the man,
      The woman—he asleep,
      She lone and sadder than
      The dawn, too wise to weep
      Illusion that to her
      Is empire, to the earth
      Necessity and stir
      Of sweet, predestined mirth!
      Ironical she sees,
Without regret, the work her kiss has done
And lives a cold enchantress doomed to please
      Her victims one by one.

A FÊTE CHAMPÊTRE[1]
ANTOINE WATTEAU
The Dresden Gallery

A lovely, animated group
That picnic on a marble seat,
Where flaky boughs of beeches droop,
Where gowns in woodland sunlight glance,
Where shines each coy, lit countenance;
While sweetness rules the air, most sweet
      Because the day
Is deep within the year that shall decay:

They group themselves around their queen,
This lady in the yellow dress,
With bluest knots of ribbon seen
Upon her breast and yellow hair;
But the reared face proclaims *Beware!*
To him who twangs his viol less
      To speak his joy
Than her soon-flattered choiceness to annoy.

---

1   Literally, a rural festival.

Beside her knee a damsel sits,
In petticoat across whose stripes
Of delicate decision flits
The wind that shows them blue and white
And primrose round a bodice tight—
As grey as is the peach that ripes:
        Her hair was spun
For Zephyrus among the threads to run.

She on love's varying theme is launched—
Ah, youth!—behind her, roses lie,
The latest, artless roses, blanched
Around a hectic centre. Two
Protesting lovers near her sue
And quarrel, Cupid knows not why:
        Withdrawn and tart,
One gallant stands in reverie apart.

Proud of his silk and velvet, each
Plum-tinted, of his pose that spurns
The company, his eyes impeach
A Venus on an ivied bank,
Who rests her rigorous, chill flank
Against a water-jet and turns
        Her face from those
Who wanton in the coloured autumn's close.

Ironical he views her shape of stone
And the harsh ivy and grey mound;
Then sneers to think she treats her own
Enchanted couples with contempt,
As though her bosom were exempt
From any care, while tints profound
        Touch the full trees
And there are warning notes in every breeze.

The coldness of mere pleasure when
Its hours are over cuts his heart:
That Love should rule the earth and men
For but a season year by year
And then must straightway disappear,
Even as the summer weeks depart,
        Has thrilled his brain
With icy anger and censorious pain.

Alas, the arbour-foliage now,
As cornfields when they lately stood
Awaiting harvest, bough on bough
Is saffron. Yonder to the left
A straggling rose-bush is bereft
Of the last roses of the wood;
      For one or two
Still flicker where the balmy dozens grew.

On the autumnal grass the pairs
Of lovers couch themselves and raise
A facile merriment that dares
Surprise the vagueness of the sun
October to a veil has spun
About the heads and forest-ways—
      Delicious light
Of gold so pure it half-refines to white.

Yet Venus from this world of love,
Of haze and warmth has turned: as yet
None feels it save the trees above,
The roses in their soft decline
And one ill-humoured libertine.
Soon shall all hearts forget
      The vows they swore
And the leaves strew the glade's untrodden floor.

SAINT SEBASTIAN
ANTONELLO DA MESSINA
The Dresden Gallery

Young Sebastian stands beside a lofty tree,
Rigid by the rigid trunk that branchlessly
    Lifts its column on the blue
    Of a heaven that takes
      Hyacinthine hue
    From a storm that wellnigh breaks.

Shadiness and thunder dout the zenith's light,
Yet a wide horizon still extends as bright
    As the lapis-lazuli;
    Poignant sunshine streams

Over land and sky,
With tempestuous, sunken beams.

He who was a soldier late is standing now
Stript and fastened to the tree that has no bough,
   In the centre of a court,
   That is bound by walls
      Fancifully wrought,
   Over which the daylight falls.

Arch and chimney rise aloft into the air:
On the balconies are hung forth carpets rare
   Of an Eastern, vivid red;
   Idle women lean
      Where the rugs are spread,
   Each with an indifferent mien.

On the marble of the courtyard, fast asleep,
Lies a brutish churl, his body in a heap;
   Two hard-hearted comrades prate
   Where a portal shows
      Distance blue and great,
   Stretching onward in repose.

And between the shafts of sandy-coloured tone
Slips a mother with her child: but all alone
   Stays Sebastian in his grief.
   What soul pities him!
      Who shall bring relief
   From the darts that pierce each limb?

Naked, almost firm as sculpture, is his form,
Nobly set below the burthen of the storm;
   Shadow, circling chin and cheek,
   Their ellipse defines,
      Then the shade grows weak
   And his face with noonday shines—

Shines as olive marble that reflects the mere
Radiance it receives upon a surface clear;
   For we see no blessedness
   On his visage pale,
      Turned in its distress
   Toward the heaven, without avail.

Massive is his mouth; the upper lip is set
In a pained, protesting curve: his eyes have met
    God within the darkening sky
    And dispute His will,
      Dark, remorselessly
    Fervent to dispute it still.

The whole brow is hidden by the chestnut hair,
That behind the back flows down in locks and there
    Changes to a deeper grain.
    Though his feet were strong,
      They are swoln with strain,
    For he has been standing long.

Captive, stricken through by darts, yet armed with
  power
That resents the coming on of its last hour,
    Sound in muscle is the boy,
    Whom his manhood fills
      With an acrid joy,
    Whom its violent pressure thrills.

But this force implanted in him must be lost
And its natural validity be crossed
    By a chill, disabling fate;
    He must stand at peace
      While his hopes abate,
    While his youth and vigour cease.

At his feet a mighty pillar lies reversed;
So the virtue of his sex is shattered, cursed:
    Here is martyrdom and not
    In the arrows' sting;
      This the bitter lot
    His soul is questioning.

He, with body fresh for use, for pleasure fit,
With its energies and needs together knit
    In an able exigence,
    Must endure the strife,
      Final and intense,
    Of necessity with life.

Yet throughout this bold rebellion of the saint
Noonday's brilliant air has carried no complaint.
   Lo, across the solitude
   Of the storm two white,
    Little clouds obtrude
Storm-accentuating light!

A PEN-DRAWING OF LEDA[1]

SODOMA

The Grand Duke's Palace at Weimar

'Tis Leda lovely, wild and free,
  Drawing her gracious Swan down through the grass to see
  Certain round eggs without a speck:
One hand plunged in the reeds and one dinting the downy neck,
  Although his hectoring bill
  Gapes toward her tresses,
She draws the fondled creature to her will.

  She joys to bend in the live light
Her glistening body toward her love, how much more bright!
  Though on her breast the sunshine lies
And spreads its affluence on the wide curves of her waist and
  thighs,
   To her meek, smitten gaze
   Where her hand presses
The Swan's white neck sink Heaven's concentred rays.

MARRIAGE OF BACCHUS AND ARIADNE

TINTORETTO

The Ducal Palace at Venice

  Dark sea-water round a shape
  Hung about the loins with grape,

---

1 In Greek mythology, Zeus took the form of a swan and slept with Leda.
In the nineteenth century many artists used this erotic motif to explore
sexuality. Another version of this myth is W. B. Yeats's 1924 poem "Leda
and the Swan," which is often associated with modernist poetry. Inter-
estingly, while in Yeats's poem Leda is overcome by Zeus, in Michael
Field's Leda leads Zeus as she walks "lovely, wild and free."

Hair the vine itself, in braids
On the brow—thus Bacchus wades
Through the water to the shore.
Strange to deck with hill-side store
Limbs that push against the tide;
Strange to gird a wave-washed side
Foam should spring at and entwine—
Strange to burthen it with vine.

He has left the trellised isle,
Left the harvest vat awhile,
Left the Maenads of his troop,
Left his Fauns' midsummer group
And his leopards far behind,
By lone Dia's[1] coast to find
Her whom Theseus dared to mock.
Queenly on the samphire rock
Ariadne sits, one hand
Stretching forth at Love's command.

Love is poised above the twain,
Zealous to assuage the pain
In that stately woman's breast;
Love has set a starry crest
On the once dishonoured head;
Love entreats the hand to wed,
Gently loosening out the cold
Fingers toward that hoop of gold
Bacchus, tremblingly content
To be patient, doth present.

In his eyes there is the pain
Shy, dumb passions can attain
In the valley, on the skirt
Of lone mountains, pine-begirt;
Yearning pleasure such as pleads
In dark wine that no one heeds
Till the feast is ranged and lit.
But his mouth—what gifts in it!
Though the round lips do not dare
Aught to proffer, save a prayer.

---

1 A small Greek island.

Is he not a mendicant
Who has almost died of want?
Through far countries he has roved,
Blessing, blessing, unbeloved;
Therefore is he come in weed
Of a mortal bowed by need,
With the bunches of the grape
As sole glory round his shape:
For there is no god that can
Taste of pleasure save as man.

THE SLEEPING VENUS
GIORGIONE
The Dresden Gallery

Here is Venus by our homes
And resting on the verdant swell
Of a soft country flanked with mountain domes:
She has left her archèd shell,
Has left the barren wave that foams,
Amid earth's fruitful tilths to dwell.
    Nobly lighted while she sleeps
    As sward-lands or the corn-field sweeps,
    Pure as are the things that man
    Needs for life and using can
    Never violate nor spot—
    Thus she slumbers in no grot,
    But on open ground,
    With the great hill-sides around.

And her body has the curves,
The same extensive smoothness seen
In yonder breadths of pasture, in the swerves
Of the grassy mountain-green
That for her propping pillow serves:
There is a sympathy between
    Her and Earth of largest reach,
    For the sex that forms them each
    Is a bond, a holiness,
    That unconsciously must bless
    And unite them, as they lie
    Shameless underneath the sky

A long, opal cloud
Doth in noontide haze enshroud.

O'er her head her right arm bends;
And from the elbow raised aloft
Down to the crossing knees a line descends
Unimpeachable and soft
As the adjacent slope that ends
In chequered plain of hedge and croft.
Circular as lovely knolls,
Up to which a landscape rolls
With desirous sway, each breast
Rises from the level chest,
One in contour, one in round—
Either exquisite, low mound
Firm in shape and given
To the August warmth of heaven.

With bold freedom of incline,
With an uttermost repose,
From hip to herbage-cushioned foot the line
Of her left leg stretching shows
Against the turf direct and fine,
Dissimilar in grace to those
Little bays that in and out
By the ankle wind about;
Or that shallow bend, the right
Curled-up knee has brought to sight
Underneath its bossy rise,
Where the loveliest shadow lies!
Charmèd umbrage rests
On her neck and by her breasts.

Her left arm remains beside
The plastic body's lower heaves,
Controlled by them, as when a river-side
With its sandy margin weaves
Deflections in a lenient tide;
Her hand the thigh's tense surface leaves,
Falling inward. Not even sleep
Dare invalidate the deep,
Universal pleasure sex
Must unto itself annex—

Even the stillest sleep; at peace,
More profound with rest's increase,
She enjoys the good
Of delicious womanhood.

Cheek and eyebrow touch the fold
Of the raised arm that frames her hair,
Her braided hair in colour like to old
Copper glinting here and there:
While through her skin of olive-gold
The scarce carnations mount and share
Faultlessly the oval space
Of her temperate, grave face.
Eyelids underneath the day
Wrinkle as full buds that stay,
Through the tranquil, summer hours,
Closed although they might be flowers;
The red lips shut in
Gracious secrets that begin.

On white drapery she sleeps,
That fold by fold is stained with shade;
Her mantle's ruddy pomegranate in heaps
For a cushion she has laid
Beneath her; and the glow that steeps
Its grain of richer depth is made
By an overswelling bank,
Tufted with dun grasses rank.
From this hillock's outer heaves
One small bush defines its leaves
Broadly on the sober blue
The pale cloud-bank rises to,
Whilst it sinks in bland
Sunshine on the distant land.

Near her resting-place are spread,
In deep or greener-lighted brown,
Wolds, that half-withered by the heat o'erhead,
Press up to a little town
Of castle, archway, roof and shed,
Then slope in grave continuance down:
On their border, in a group,
Trees of brooding foliage droop

Sidelong; and a single tree
Springs with bright simplicity,
Central from the sunlit plain.
Of a blue no flowers attain,
On the fair, vague sky
Adamantine summits lie.

And her resting is so strong
That while we gaze it seems as though
She had lain thus the solemn glebes among
In the ages far ago
And would continue, till the long,
Last evening of Earth's summer glow
In communion with the sweet
Life that ripens at her feet:
We can never fear that she
From Italian fields will flee,
For she does not come from far,
She is of the things that are;
And she will not pass
While the sun strikes on the grass.

L'EMBARQUEMENT POUR CYTHÈRE[1]

ANTOINE WATTEAU

The Louvre

Why starts this company so fair arrayed
    In pomegranate brocade,
Blue shoulder-cloak and barley-coloured dress
    Of flaunting shepherdess,
From shelter of the full-leaved, summer trees?
        What vague unease
Draws them in couples to a burnished boat?
    And wherefore from its prow,
Borne upward on a spiral, amber swirl
Of incense-light, themselves half-rose, half-pearl,
        So languorously doth float
    This flock of Loves that in degree
Fling their own hues as raiment on the sea;
    While one from brandished censer

---

1   *The Embarkation for Cythera*, a mythical island of love.

Flings wide a flame and smoke
       Diffusive to provoke
The heavens to consummation and to spread
       Refluence intenser
       Of sun and cool
   And tempting azure on that bed
Of splendour, that delicious, variant pool?
       I see it now!
       'Tis Venus' rose-veiled barque
And that great company ere dark
Must to Cythera, so the Loves prevail,
       Adventurously sail.

O happy youth, that thus by Venus' guile
       Is summoned to her fabulous,
       Her crystal-burnished isle!
       Her virile votaries are not slack
In ceremonious worship: bravely clad
In coats of flickering velvet, crimson-greys
Of corn-field gold, they leap to give her praise,
They grasp long staves, they joy as they were mad,
Drawing their dainty Beauties by the waist
       To that warm water-track.
What terror holds these noble damsels back?
       Alack, what strange distaste
       Works in their hearts that thus
They sigh estranged?   What pressure of what ill
       Turns their vague sweetness chill?
       Why should they in debate,
       Beneath the nodding, summer trees,
   Dissentient dally and defer their fate?
       Methinks none sees
       The statue of a Venus set
   Mid some fair trellis, in a lovely fret
       Of rose; her marble mien,
Secret, imperial, blank, no joy discovers
       In these uncertain lovers
       That parley and grow pale:
       Not one of them but is afraid to sail,
Save this firm-tripping dame who chooses
       The voyage as a queen,
Conscious of what she wins and what she loses.
       Her petticoat of fine-creased white

And, oh, her barley-coloured gown,
    What miracles of silver-brown
They work amid the blues and puces!
    As, full of whimsical delight
To mark a sister's half-abashed surrender,
    Full proudly she doth bend her
Arched, amorous eyelids to commend her,
        Gripping more tight
Her slender stave, that she may seem
Prompt to descend toward that dead, heated stream.

    Her lover's face we lack,
      Bent from us; yet we feel
      How fervid his appeal,
As raised on tip-toe he his lofty dame addresses.
    Fine streaks of light across his raiment steal;
      For, though his cap is black,
    When blossoms of japonica are spread
    In sunshine, whiter-smiling red
Was never seen than glistens on his sleeve.
    And how his furs flash to relieve
His lady's train of chrome!
Ah me, how long must these fond gallants blind
    The fears and waive the light distresses
      Of the coy girls who stay behind,
        Nor yet consent to roam
Toward that soft, vermeil country far, so very far from home!

    First of the twain is seen
A pale-tressed dame, couched on the grass, her bodice lambent
    green,
    Her frilling skirt of salmon and primrose
And green of many a flower before it blows
      Who, pettish in remorse,
    Awhile her lover's urgent hand refuses,
    Then rises buoyant on its welcome force.
      But, see, this third
      Sweet lady is not stirred,
    Though at her side a man
Half-kneels. Why is he pleading in her ear,
      With eyes so near
      That Paradise of light,
Where angles of the yellow, open fan

And gown the sunken pink
Of dying roses rim her bosom's white?
Her eyelids are full-drooped, but under
    The lids is wonder;
      And, at her skirt,
Ah, woe! in pilgrim hood and shirt
Dressed whimsical, a cunning Cupid-lad:
    Soon shall the naked urchin be
Plunged in the depths of that cerulean sea
Where life runs warm, delicious, limpid, free.

So pause the nearer groups: to the land's rim
      Presses a dim
Confluence of hopes and angry amities:
'Forth to the fairy water, come; thine hand ...
Nay then, by force; it is a god's command
And I by rape will bring thee to thy bliss.
What, sweet, so slow!'—'But ere I leave the land
Give me more vows; oh, bind thee to me fast;
    Speak, speak! I do not crave thy kiss.
To-morrow ...'—'Love, the tide is rising swift;
Shall we not talk aboard? Your skirts are wet;
    If once I lift
You in!'—'Nay, nay, I cannot so forget
    The statue in the shade,
    The fountain-trickle by the leafy grot.
Might not this mad embarking be delayed
An instant?'—'Dearest, would you cast your lot
    In that dull countryside,
      Where men abide
    Who must be buried? Note the swell
Of colour 'gainst the coast.'—'Then as you please.
How strange a story we shall have to tell!'

      Two rowers wait; one shoves
      The boat from shore, her cry
From luscious mouth, her bosom lifted high
      Incite; and one doth wait,
    With lip that hath full time to laugh
      And hand on oar,
    Conclusion of the soft debate.
Sudden the foremost of the fulgent Loves
      Seizes a staff

From wanton hand; a thousand flambeaux pour
Their plumy smoke upon the kindled breeze
That wafts these silken loiterers to submerging seas.

Now are they gone: a change is in the light,
  The iridescent ranges wane,
The waters spread: ere fall of night
The red-prowed shallop will have passed from sight
  And the stone Venus by herself remain
Ironical above that wide, embrowning plain.

3. From *Underneath the Bough* (1893; first edition)

[Published in 1893, *Underneath the Bough*, like *Long Ago*, was set within a context of ancient erotic lyricism. The title, and the epigraph, come from The *Rubáiyát of Omar Khayyám*, which was enjoying a renewed popularity in the late nineteenth century after Edward FitzGerald's 1859 translation.[1] The quotation from the *Rubáiyát* that Bradley and Cooper use as an epigraph sets up two important contexts for their volume. One is a context of pleasure: the book of verses together with the wine and bread make this a picnic of sensual delights. More importantly, it also points towards the ideal of shared song that was at the heart of Michael Field's aesthetic. "A girl" is the poem that most explicitly articulates Bradley and Cooper's dual authorship within the text. This poem is really only half a poem, which the author declares awaits the contribution of her co-author before it can be finished. This too, of course, is a love poem, from one woman to the other, showing how their souls are "knit" as closely as their collaborative text, and it is this that a contemporaneous reviewer thinks will be of "peculiar interest" to most readers.[2] "It was deep April, and the morn" is another explicit statement of the women's core identity as "poets and lovers evermore." While their authorial duality often structures their poetry at this time, there is some evidence of the trinity beginning to become an important symbol. In "Twain cannot mingle: we went hand in hand" we see a natural, Pagan trinity that will later in their lives take on a newly religious meaning.

Yet it is not just the ancient Persian context of the *Rubáiyát* that is important here. Indeed, this volume shows more clearly than any other the wide range of influences operative in Michael Field's work. A poem such as "An Invitation" expresses clearly the more general importance of literary heritage to *Underneath the Bough*. This poem is written as an invitation from Bradley to Cooper to "come and sing" with her. Bradley imagines the two of them together in a sun-filled room, intertwined on the settee. Bradley boasts of having books "of long ago / And to-day" that

---

1 *Rubáiyát of Omar Khayyám*, trans. and versified by Edward FitzGerald (London: Bernard Quaritch, 1859). The volume went through many editions, with Edmund J. Sullivan (born 1869) adding illustrations to the 1913 edition (published by Methuen).

2 See the review in the *Athenaeum* reproduced in the "Reviews" Section, p. 367-70.

she will only access if she hears the words through the music of Cooper's voice. Bradley begins by privileging Elizabethan sources, but she goes on to cite French literature, Latin works, and Greek authors. This poem lays out very clearly the connection between the women's erotic relationship and the relationship they configure between past and present literature. In *Underneath the Bough*, this connection is enabled by "song," and, more precisely, "singing together," which encodes a transaction that is both erotic and historical.

Early on in the volume, it is established that desire is the lifeforce that drives the women's poetry, and that "Love" in its manifold forms dominates much of the book. Sometimes the poems address a female beloved ("Say, if a gallant rose my bower doth scale") and sometimes a male lover ("Ah me, if I grew sweet to a man"). Some of these love poems are clearly autobiographical, such as "A gray mob-cap and a girl's," which recalls the time after Cooper's illness in Germany, with her short curls evidence of the shorn hair of the invalid. Several other poems also allude to this incident that, through the threat of loss, seems to have served to crystallize the women's love for each other. Death, as the dark twin of desire, is a powerful corollary theme in the volume and ensures a philosophical depth to the meditation on love that pervades it.

This volume also allows the reader to reflect on Bradley and Cooper's sense of narrative within the volume of lyrics, and how they construct their collections. *Underneath the Bough* is distinctive within Michael Field's oeuvre for appearing in three different editions over the course of five years: each one with a quite different and distinct narrative structure. The first edition, published in 150 copies by George Bell and Sons, in 1893, contained 126 poems.[1] The second edition was published just a little later in the same year, again by George Bell, but it was not a limited edition. This "revised and decreased" edition contained 72 poems in total. The third edition is the American edition of 1898, containing 100 poems and moving back towards the structure of the first edition (but with some substantial cuts, and with the addition of 30 new pieces). Mary Sturgeon explains how it was not long after the appearance of the first edition that the poets received more

---

1 This figure includes the 124 poems listed in the original tables of contents, the "Invocation" that forms the epigraph to the volume, and one poem that appears in the volume but was missed out of the original table of contents (this title, "A Death-Bed," is added to the table of contents of book two in our present edition).

probing criticism from friends and "confessed their repentance for the defective work by immediately cutting the book to the extent of one-half." However, "repenting at leisure of their hasty repentance," writes Sturgeon, "they brought out yet another edition, and reinstated many of the poems which they had rejected from number two."[1] The return to the structure and contents of the first volume in 1898 suggests that ultimately this was, indeed, the version that satisfied the poets. Moreover, many of the poems that critics currently recognise as among the best in the volume appear in the first edition, but not in the second ("An invitation," "Love's sour leisure," "I would not be a fugitive," to name a few). It is for these reasons that the first edition is used as the copy text for this selection. Robert Fletcher has written insightfully on the structure of this first edition, and he finds in it a simultaneous presentation of several different tales of desire: maternal and erotic, homosexual and heterosexual. He sees the narrative of the book as a deliberate attempt to work the two tales into an ambiguous whole, revealing "a desire to tell and not to tell...."[2]]

Source: *Underneath the Bough: A Book of Verses by Michael Field*, 1st ed. (London: George Bell and Sons, 1893).

[EPIGRAPH]

"A Book of Verses underneath the Bough,
A Jug of Wine, a Loaf of Bread, and thou
Beside me singing in the Wilderness.
Oh, Wilderness were Paradise enow!"

INVOCATION

Thee, Apollo, in a ring
We encompass, carolling
Of the flowers, fruits and creatures
That thy features

---

1 Mary Sturgeon, *Michael Field* (London: Harrap and Co., 1921), 65–66.
2 Robert P. Fletcher, "'I Leave a Page Half-Writ': Narrative Discoherence in Michael Field's *Underneath the Bough*," in *Women's Poetry, Late Romantic to Late Victorian*, ed. Isobel Armstrong and Virginia Blain (Houndmills, Basingstoke: Macmillan, 1999): 164–82; 167.

Do express, and by thy side
Live their life half-deified:
Grasshoppers that round thee spring
From their mirth no minute sparing;
Hawk and griffin arrow-eyed;
Cock the gracious day declaring;
Olive that can only flourish
Where the fruiting sunbeams nourish;
Laurel that can never fade,
That in winter doth incline her
Lustrous branches to embraid
Chaplets for the lyric brow;
The white swan, that fair diviner,
Who in death a bliss descrying
Sings her sweetest notes a-dying:
These, all these, to thee we vow,
We thy nymphs who in a ring
Dance around thee, carolling.

THE FIRST BOOK OF SONGS

[Mortal, if thou art beloved]

Mortal, if thou art beloved,
Life's offences are removed:
All the fateful things that checkt thee,
Hearten, hallow, and protect thee.
Grow'st thou mellow? What is age?
Tinct on life's illumined page,
Where the purple letters glow
Deeper, painted long ago.
What is sorrow? Comfort's prime,
Love's choice Indian summer-clime.
Sickness? Thou wilt pray it worse
For so blessed, balmy nurse.
And for death? When thou art dying
'Twill be love beside thee lying.
Death is lonesome? Oh, how brave
Shows the foot-frequented grave!
Heaven itself is but the casket
For Love's treasure, ere he ask it,
Ere with burning heart he follow,

Piercing through corruption's hollow.
If thou art beloved, oh then
Fear no grief of mortal men!

[Death, men say, is like a sea]

Death, men say, is like a sea
That engulfs mortality,
Treacherous, dreadful, blindingly
    Full of storm and terror.

Death is like the deep, warm sand
Pleasant when we come to land,
Covering up with tender hand
    The wave's drifted error.

Life's a tortured, booming gurge
Winds of passion strike and urge,
And transmute to broken surge
    Foam-crests of ambition.

Death's a couch of golden ground,
Warm, soft, permeable mound,
Where from even memory's sound
    We shall have remission.

[Ah, Eros doth not always smite]

Ah, Eros doth not always smite
    With cruel, shining dart,
Whose bitter point with sudden might
    Rends the unhappy heart—
Not thus forever purple-stained,
    And sore with steely touch,
Else were its living fountain drained
    Too oft and overmuch.
O'er it sometimes the boy will deign
    Sweep the shaft's feathered end;
And friendship rises without pain
    Where the white plumes descend.

[Men, looking on the Wandering Jew][1]

Men, looking on the Wandering Jew,
Straightway must flee him;
My love each mortal must pursue
    Soon as they see him.
I would my love immortal grew,
Winning shy women's hearts to woo;
I from my grave would listen too,
    Would bless and free him.

[Love's wings are wondrous swift]

Love's wings are wondrous swift
When hanging feathers lift.
    Why hath Love wings,
Great pinions strong of curve?
His wild desires to serve;
    To swoop on the prey,
    And bear it away,
        Love hath wings.

Love's wings are golden soft,
When dropping from aloft.
    Why hath Love wings,
Feathers of glistening fleece?
To soothe with balmy peace,
    And warmth of his breath
    Souls he cherisheth
        Love hath wings.

Love's wings are broad of van,
Stretched for great travel's span.
    Why hath Love wings,
Mail of the sea-bird's might?
From feeble hearts and slight
    To lift him forlorn
    To a fastness of scorn,
        Love hath wings.

---

1   This refers to Bernard Berenson.

AN APPLE-FLOWER

I felt my leaves fall free,
   I felt the wind and sun,
At my heart a honey-bee:
   And life was done.

[Through hazels and apples]

Through hazels and apples
   My love I led,
Where the sunshine dapples
   The strawberry-bed:
Did we pluck and eat
   That morn, my sweet?

And back by the alley
   Our path I chose,
That we might dally
   By one rare rose:
Did we smell at the heart,
   And then depart?

A lover, who grapples
   With love, doth live
Where roses and apples
   Have naught to give:
Did I take my way
   Unfed that day?

[Say, if a gallant rose my bower doth scale]

Say, if a gallant rose my bower doth scale,
   Higher and higher,
And, tho' she twine the other side the pale,
   Toward me doth sigh her
   Perfume, her damask mouth—
   Roses will love the south—
   Can I deny her?

I have a lady loves me in despite
   Of bonds that tie her,
And bid her honest Corin's flame requite;
   When I espy her,
  Kisses are near their birth—
  Love cannot live in dearth—
   Say, shall I fly her?

[Ah me, if I grew sweet to man]

Ah me, if I grew sweet to man
It was but as a rose that can
No longer keep the breath that heaves
And swells among its folded leaves.

The pressing fragrance would unclose
The flower, and I became a rose,
That unimpeachable and fair
Planted an odour in the air.

No art I used men's love to draw;
I lived but by my being's law,
As roses are by heaven designed
To bring the honey to the wind.

I found there is scant sun in spring,
I found the blast a riving thing;
Yet even ruined roses can
No other than be sweet to man.

THE SECOND BOOK OF SONGS

[Others may drag at memory's fetter]

Others may drag at memory's fetter,
May turn for comfort to the vow
Of mortal breath; I hold it better
To learn if verily and how
Love knits me with the loved one now.

Others for solace, sleep-forsaken,
May muse upon the days of old;
To me it is delight to waken,
To find my Dead, to feel them fold
My heart, and for its dross give gold.

[Little Lettuce is dead, they say]

Little Lettuce is dead, they say,
The brown, sweet child who rolled in the hay;
    Ah, where shall we find her?
    For the neighbours pass
    To the pretty lass,
In a linen cere-cloth to wind her.

If her sister were set to search
The nettle-green nook beside the church,
    And the way were shown her
    Through the coffin-gate
    To her dead playmate,
She would fly too frighted to own her.

Should she come at a noonday call,
Ah, stealthy, stealthy, with no footfall,
    And no laughing chatter,
    To her mother 'twere worse
    Than a barren curse
That her own little wench should pat her.

Little Lettuce is dead and gone!
The stream by her garden wanders on
    Through the rushes wider;
    She fretted to know
    How its bright drops grow
On the hills, but no hand would guide her.

Little Lettuce is dead and lost!
Her willow-tree boughs by storm are tossed—
    O the swimming sallows!—
    Where she crouched to find
    The nest of the wind
Like a water-fowl's in the shallows.

Little Lettuce is out of sight!
The river-bed and the breeze are bright:
   Ay me, were it sinning
   To dream that she knows
   Where the soft wind rose
That her willow-branches is thinning?

Little Lettuce has lost her name,
Slipt away from our praise and our blame;
   Let not love pursue her,
   But conceive her free
   Where the bright drops be
On the hills, and no longer rue her!

A DEATH-BED

Her husband kept
Watch by her side; no word she spoke
Of parting; but the children crept
To bid good-night: she slept,
And, sleeping, never woke.

[A curling thread]

A curling thread
Uncoils overhead—
From the chimney-stack
A replenished track
Of vapour, in haste
To increase and waste,
Growing wings as it grows
Of amber and rose,
With an upward flight
To the frosty light.
Puff on puff
Of the soft breath-stuff,
Till the cloudy fleece
Thickens its feathers; its rounds increase,
Mingle and widen, and lose the line
Of their dull confine,

Thinning mote by mote
As they upward float,
And by-and-bye
Are effaced on the sky.

To evoke,
Like the smoke,
Dower on dower
By the power
Of our art:
To have part
In the air and the sun,
Till our course be run,
Till the sigh be breathed,
Till the wreath be wreathed,
And we disappear,
Leaving heaven clear!

[She mingled me rue and roses]

She mingled me rue and roses,
And I found my bliss complete:
  The roses are gone,
  But the rue lives on,
The bitter that lived with the sweet.

Life will mingle you rue and roses;
The roses will fall at your feet:
  But deep in the rue
  That their leaves bestrew
The bitter will smell of the sweet.

UNCONSCIOUSNESS

He with the Gentle Ones is hid from sight:
We may not follow. He hath dwelt with woes
So dread, he lays his confidence in those
Men shrink from, who remember and requite.
O comfort him, sweet daughters of the Night,
For fear of whom man's thought doth softly tread;

Within your grove let him be deeply led
To reconciliation and repose.

[When the cherries are on the bough]

When the cherries are on the bough
To my lips I raise them;
    But now, ah now
The best I can do is to praise them,
And to think all through November
Of the brightest I remember.

When the roses are opening, how
I stoop down to kiss them;
    But now, ah now
By the empty rose-bush I miss them,
And I dream all through November
Of the sweetest I remember.

The birds still sing on the bough,
They love without mating;
    But now, ah now,
No warmth of the spring they are waiting,
For they sing all through November
Of the April they remember.

[Thanatos,[1] thy praise I sing]

Thanatos, thy praise I sing,
Thou immortal, youthful king!
Glorious offerings I will bring;
For men say thou hast no shrine,
And I find thou art divine
As no other god: thy rage
Doth preserve the Golden Age,
What we blame is thy delay:
Cut the flowers ere they decay!

---

1   The Greek personification of death.

Come, we would not derogate,
Age and nipping pains we hate,
Take us at our best estate:
While the head burns with the crown,
In the battle strike us down!
At the bride-feast do not think
From thy summons we should shrink;
We would give our latest kiss
To a life still warm with bliss.

Come and take us to thy train
Of dead maidens on the plain
Where white lilies have no stain;
Take us to the youths, that thou
Lov'st to choose, of fervid brow,
Unto whom thy dreaded name
Hath been simply known as Fame:
With these unpolluted things
Be our endless revellings.

THE THIRD BOOK OF SONGS

[Already to mine eyelids' shore]

Already to mine eyelids' shore
    The gathering waters swell,
For thinking of the grief in store
    When thou wilt say "Farewell."
I dare not let thee leave me, sweet,
    Lest it should be for ever;
Tears dew my kisses ere we meet,
    Foreboding we must sever:
Since we can neither meet nor part,
Methinks the moral is, sweetheart,
    That we must dwell together.

COWSLIP-GATHERING

Twain cannot mingle: we went hand in hand,
Yearning, divided, through the fair spring land,
Nor knew, twin maiden spirits, there must be

In all true marriage perfect trinity.
But lo! dear Nature spied us, in a copse
Filling with chirps of song and hazel-drops,
And smiled: "These children I will straight espouse,
While the blue cuckoo thrills the alder-boughs."
So led us to a tender, marshy nook
Of meadow-verdure, where by twos and threes
The cowslips grew, down-nodding toward a brook;
And left us there to pluck them at our ease
In the moist quiet, till the rich content
Of the bee humming in the cherry-trees
Filled us; in one our very being blent.

[A girl]

A girl,
Her soul a deep-wave pearl
Dim, lucent of all lovely mysteries;
A face flowered for heart's ease,
A brow's grace soft as seas
Seen through faint forest-trees:
A mouth, the lips apart,
Like aspen-leaflets trembling in the breeze
From her tempestuous heart.
Such: and our souls so knit,
I leave a page half-writ—
The work begun
Will be to heaven's conception done,
If she come to it.

[Methinks my love to thee doth grow]

Methinks my love to thee doth grow
And this the sign:
I see the Spirit claim thee,
And do not blame thee,
Nor break intrusive on the Holy Ground
Where thou of God art found.

I watch the fire
Leap up, and do not bring

Fresh water from the spring
To keep it from up-flaming higher
  Than my chilled hands require
    For cherishing.

I see thy soul turn to her hidden grot,
      And follow not;
    Content thou shouldst prefer
      To be with her,
The heavenly Muse, than ever find in me
      Best company.

  So brave my love is grown,
  I joy to find thee sought
    By some great thought;
  And am content alone
  To eat life's common fare,
      While thou prepare
To be my royal moment's guest:
      Live to the Best!

      [If I but dream that thou art gone]

If I but dream that thou art gone,
My heart aches to o'ertake thee;
How shall I then forsake thee
    In clear daylight,
Who art my very joy's nativity—
Thee, whose sweet soul I con
      Secure to find
      Perfect epitome
Of nature, passion, poesy?
      From thee untwined,
I shall but wander a disbodied sprite,
      Until thou wake me
With thy kiss-warmèd breath, and take me
      Where we are one.

LOVE'S SOUR LEISURE

As a poem in my mind
Thy sweet lineaments are shrined:
From the memory, alas!
Sweetest, sweetest verse will pass;
And the fragments I must piece
Lest the fair tradition cease.
There is balmy air I trow
On the uplands of thy brow,
But the temple's veinèd mound
Is the Muses' sacred ground;
While the tresses pale are groves
That the laurelled godhead loves.
There is something in the cheek
Like a dimple still to seek,
As my poet timidly
Love's incarnate kiss would flee.
But the mouth! That land to own
Long did Aphrodite[1] moan,
Ere the virgin goddess grave
From the temptress of the wave
That most noble clime did win;
Who, retreating to the chin,
Took her boy's bow for a line,
The sweet boundary to define,
And about the beauteous bays
Still in orbèd queenship plays.
I have all the charact'ry
Of thy features, yet lack thee;
And by couplets to confess
What I wholly would possess
Doth but whet the appetite
Of my too long-famished sight:
Vainly if my eyes entreat,
Tears will be their daily meat.

---

1 Goddess of Love.

[I sing thee with the stock-dove's throat]

I sing thee with the stock-dove's throat,
Warm, crooning, superstitious note,
That on its dearie so doth dote
    It falls to sorrow,
And from the fair, white swans afloat
     A dirge must borrow.

In thee I have such deep content,
I can but murmur a lament;
It is as though my heart were rent
    By thy perfection,
And all my passion's torrent spent
    In recollection.

[A gray mob-cap and a girl's]

A gray mob-cap and a girl's
Soft circle of sprouting curls,
That proclaim she has had the fever:
How dear the days when the child was nurst!
My God, I pray she may die the first,
    That I may not leave her!

Her head on my knee laid down,
That *duvet* so warm, so brown,
I fondle, I dote on its springing.
"Thou must never grow lonesome or old,
Leave me rather to darkness and cold,
    O my Life, my Singing!"

[It was deep April, and the morn]

It was deep April, and the morn
    Shakspere was born;
The world was on us, pressing sore;
My Love and I took hands and swore,
  Against the world, to be
Poets and lovers evermore,
To laugh and dream on Lethe's shore,

To sing to Charon in his boat,[1]
Heartening the timid souls afloat;
Of judgment never to take heed,
But to those fast-locked souls to speed,
Who never from Apollo fled,
Who spent no hour among the dead;
    Continually
    With them to dwell,
Indifferent to heaven and hell.

AN INVITATION

Come and sing, my room is south;
Come, with thy sun-governed mouth,
Thou wilt never suffer drouth,
    Long as dwelling
In my chamber of the south.

On the wall there is woodbine,
With its yellow-scarlet shine;
When my lady's hopes decline,
    Honey-smelling
Trumpets will her mood divine.

There are myrtles in a row;
Lady, when the flower's in blow,
Kisses passing to and fro,
    From our smelling,
Think, what lovely dreams will grow!

There's a lavender settee,
Cushioned for my sweet and me;
Ah, what secrets there will be
    For love-telling,
When her head leans on my knee!

Books I have of long ago
And to-day; I shall not know

---

1   Charon is the boatman who ferries the souls of the dead across Lethe,
the river of the Underworld.

Some, unless thou read them, so
        Their excelling
Music needs thy voice's flow:

Campion,[1] with a noble ring
Of choice spirits; count this wing
Sacred! all the songs I sing
        Welling, welling
From Elizabethan spring:

French, that corner of primrose!
Flaubert, Verlaine, with all those
Precious, little things in prose,
        Bliss-compelling,
Howsoe'er the story goes:

All the Latins *thou* dost prize!
Cynthia's lover[2] by thee lies;
Note Catullus,[3] type and size
        Least repelling
To thy weariable eyes.

And for Greek! Too sluggishly
Thou dost toil; but Sappho, see!
And the dear Anthology
        For thy spelling.
Come, it shall be well with thee.

THE FOURTH BOOK OF SONGS

[Across a gaudy room]

Across a gaudy room
I looked and saw his face,
Beneath the sapless palm-trees, in the gloom
Of the distressing place,
Where everyone sat tired,

---

1 Thomas Campion (1567–1620), whose Elizabethan lyrics inspired
   Michael Field.
2 The Latin poet Propertius wrote lyrics to his beloved Hostia, addressing
   her as Cynthia.
3 A Roman lyric poet.

Where talk itself grew stale,
Where, as the day began to fail,
No guest had just the power required
To rise and go: I strove with my disgust;
But at the sight of him my eyes were fired
To give one glance, as though they must
Be sociable with what they found of fair
And free and simple in a chamber where
        Life was so base.

   As when a star is lit
   In the dull, evening sky,
Another soon leaps out to answer it,
    Even so the bright reply
    Came sudden from his eyes,
    By all but me unseen;
Since then the distance that between
    Our lives unalterably lies
Is but a darkness, intimate and still,
Which messages may traverse, where replies
    May sparkle from afar, until
The night becomes a mystery made clear
Between two souls forbidden to draw near:
        Creator, why?

       [As two fair vessels side by side]

As two fair vessels side by side,
    No bond had tied
    Our floating peace;
We thought that it would never cease,
But like swan-creatures we should always glide:
   And this is love
    We sighed.

As two grim vessels side by side,
    Through wind and tide
    War grappled us,
With bond as strong as death, and thus
We drove on mortally allied:
    And this is hate
    We cried.

[The lady I have vowed to paint]

The lady I have vowed to paint
    Has contour of a rose,
No rigid shadow of a saint
      Upon the wall she throws;
    Her tints so softly lie
Against the air they almost vie
With the sea's outline smooth against the sky.

To those whom damask hues beguile
    Her praise I do not speak,
I find her colour in the smile
      Warm on her warm, blond cheek:
    Then to the eyes away
It spreads, those eyes of mystic gray
That with mirage of their own vision play.

Her hair, about her brow, burns bright,
    Her tresses are the gold
That in a missal keeps the light
      Solemn and pure. Behold
      Her lashes' glimmerings
Have the dove's secret springs
Of amber sunshine when she spreads her wings.

[The iris was yellow, the moon was pale]

The iris was yellow, the moon was pale,
    In the air it was stiller than snow,
There was even light through the vale,
      But a vaporous sheet
      Clung about my feet,
    And I dared no further go.
I had passed the pond, I could see the stile,
The path was plain for more than a mile,
    Yet I dared no further go.

The iris-beds shone in my face, when, whist!
    A noiseless music began to blow,
A music that moved through the mist,
      That had not begun,

Would never be done,
    With that music I must go:
And I found myself in the heart of the tune,
Wheeling round to the whirr of the moon,
    With the sheets of mist below.

In my hands how warm were the little hands,
    Strange, little hands that I did not know:
I did not think of the elvan bands,
        Nor of anything
        In that whirling ring—
    Here a cock began to crow!
The little hands dropped that had clung so tight,
And I saw again by the pale dawnlight
    The iris-heads in a row.

[I lay sick in a foreign land]

    I lay sick in a foreign land;
        And by me, on the right,
    A little Love had taken stand,
        Who held up in my sight
    A vessel full of injured things—
    His shivered bow, his broken wings;
    And underneath the pretty strew
    Of glistening feathers, half in view,
    A broken heart: he held them up
    Within the silver-lighted cup
    That I might mark each one, then pressed
    His little cheek against my chest,
    And fell to singing in such wise
    He shook the vision from my eyes.

[The roses wither and die]

    The roses wither and die;
    Close brown is the sweet, loose red;
    Love dieth not.
    The roses wither and die,
    But their fragrance is not dead:
            Love cannot die,
            Love dieth not.

The roses are shrunk and dry;
On their dimmed rose death is fed;
Love dieth not.
The roses are shrunk and dry,
Their leaves on the earth are spread:
> *Love cannot die,*
> *Love dieth not.*

The flower on the ground must lie,
The loose, sweet leaves must be shed;
Love dieth not.
The flower on the ground must lie
To heap up a balsam-bed:
> *Love cannot die,*
> *Love dieth not.*

FROM PAUL VERLAINE

"Il pleure dans mon coeur"[1]

There are tears in my heart,
There is rain in the town;
What bodeth this smart
In my languorous heart?

O soft noise of the rain
Over earth, on the roof!
For a heart sick with pain
O the song of the rain!

Tears with no reason
In a heart out of heart.
And none has wrought treason?
This grief has no reason.

'Tis indeed the worst woe,
With no love and no hate
In one's heart, not to know
Why one's heart has such woe.

---

1   The title of a well-known poem by the French nineteenth-century poet
Paul Verlaine, which is loosely translated in the first line of the poem.

FROM POLIZIANO[1]

"Ciascum segua, o Baccho, te"[2]

On, o Bacchus, on we go:
Evoe Bacchus, Bacchus io![3]
For our heads the ivy-berry
And green ivy-leaf we get,
Serving thee we all make merry,
Nor by night nor day forget
Bacchus in our midst is set.
Drink, and I among you, so:
On, o Bacchus, on we go:
I have drained my horn, delaying
Scarce a moment: put the tun
Nearer. How this hill is swaying,
Or my brain, has that begun
Spinning circles? All should run
Up and down as I do, so:
On, o Bacchus, on we go!
Dead with sleep, I stand unsteady:
I am drunk? But am I? Nay?
All of you are drunk already,
That I see as clear as day.
Everyone should take my way:
Everyone should stagger, so:
On, o Bacchus, on we go!
Cups we empty without number,
Shouting *Bacchus, Bacchus!* then
Down our bodies drop in slumber.
Drink each one, and drink again.
I shall lead the measure—when?
For my dance is over. Io!
On, o Bacchus, on we go:
Evoe Bacchus, Bacchus io!

---

1 Angelo Poliziano, fifteenth-century Italian poet and humanist, the friend
   and protégé of Lorenzo de Medici, and one of the most notable classical
   scholars of the Renaissance.
2 Loosely translated in the first line of the poem.
3 "Evoe!" and "Io!" are calls for invoking the gods.

[I would not be a fugitive]

I would not be a fugitive
Far in the past amid the olden,
Fond times men labour to recover,
But in the age, ah, verily the golden,·
When first a girl dares to become a lover.

How sweeter far it is to give
Than just to rest in the receiving,
Sweeter to sigh than be sighed over,
Sweeter to deal the blow than bear the grieving,
That girl will learn who dares become a lover.

The songs she sings will have the glee,
The laughter of the wind that looses
Wing and breaks from a forest cover;
Freedom of stream that slips its icy nooses
Will be her freedom who becomes a lover.

What Eden unto Eve the tree
Of Life to pluck, to eat unchidden,
Then as a hostess to discover
To man the feast, himself a guest new-bidden,
Now she at last dares to become his lover!

[Sunshine is calling]

Sunshine is calling:
   River-ice grows soft,
   Trees toss the tender leaves aloft
That frost or sheath were thralling:
O Bacchus, these are drunk with that
Kindling the wine that brims thy autumn vat!

And here are dances
   Underneath the trees,
   As shadow after shadow flees
With jest and sunny glances:
O Bacchus, these are drunk with that
Kindling the wine that brims thy autumn vat!

The hills, noon-lighted,
　And the shady grove
　Become the purple satyrs love
　To quaff, by thirst incited:
O Bacchus, these are drunk with that
Kindling the wine that brims thy autumn vat!

All creatures waken;
　Warm in dappled grass
　Their gladsome wooing comes to pass;
　Wild love is sought and taken:
O Bacchus, these are drunk with that
Kindling the wine that brims thy autumn vat!

With shout and chorus
　Birds are making joy,
　Their voices have but one employ,
　To sing *The woods are for us!*
O Bacchus, these are drunk with that
Kindling the wine that brims thy autumn vat!

The happy breezes
　Sleep with humming breath,
　Then grow so still, it might be death
　Their wanton pleasure eases:
O Bacchus, these are drunk with that
Kindling the wine that brims thy autumn vat!

And flowers, sweet-hearted,
　Put away their shame;
　In openness to heaven's flame
　The honey-buds have parted:
O Bacchus, these are drunk with that
Kindling the wine that brims thy autumn vat!

Ye women, greet it!
　Light hath called you, come!
　Love, sing, no more be cold and dumb;
　Light calls you, meet it!
O women, be ye drunk with that
Kindling the wine that brims the autumn vat!

For light delivers!
  Blood as wine runs red
  When radiance is through it spread,
 When with gay spring it quivers:
O Bacchus, be it drunk with that
Kindling the wine that brims thy autumn vat!

  O Bacchus, Bacchus,
   Thou without the sun
   Couldst never do what thou hast done,
  Nor with thy fire attack us!
Nay, nay, we only can be drunk with that
Kindling the wine that brims thy autumn vat!

4. From *Wild Honey from Various Thyme* (1908)

[There was a long gap between the publication of *Underneath the Bough* and the next volume of poetry in 1908. Yet this gap does not in any way indicate a diminishing poetic output or a dissatisfaction with the genre. If anything the women's love of poetry intensified towards the end of their career and became more important to them. One must remember that the second and third editions of *Underneath the Bough*, published in late 1893 and 1898 respectively, partially filled this gap, but it is still true that *Wild Honey* gathered together a vast wealth of poetry spanning a considerable time period. *Wild Honey* represents a poetic narrative on a grand scale, charting as it does a period to which the turn of the century was central, but also a period of life-changing personal events, including the death of their most beloved pet dog, Whym Chow, in 1906 and their subsequent conversions to the Catholic faith in 1907.

The volume seems suspended around the dichotomies that structured this period of the women's lives: both pagan and Catholic and heteroerotic and homoerotic desire. The progression of the narrative from "Pan Asleep" to "Good Friday" seems to chart the biographical story of this period, as does the appearance of numerous different types of love poem, to various different recipients. "Penetration" is written from Bradley to Charles Ricketts, while "Onycha" is addressed from Bradley to Cooper (and there is that group of love poems that Cooper says were written by Bradley for her, including "Old Ivories"[1]). Yet the volume negotiates these dichotomies into a unified whole, using the motifs of the phoenix (in "Renewal") and the palimpsest (in "A Palimpsest") to insist on the intertwining of those most pressing dichotomies: old and new, life and death. Indeed, although the structure of the volume is biographical and chronological, the use of images of time and memory enables this linear temporal narrative to be questioned even as it is produced. "Embalmment" and "Balsam," particularly, suggest that past and present are wrapped into one another in a manner that suggests a much more circular and synchronic narrative to the volume. In his introduction to *The Wattlefold*, Friar Vincent McNabb wrote, "The neo-paganism which, without their knowing it, they cherished not mainly for its culture but for its cult of sacrifice, had turned their dramatic souls toward the Sacrifice of Calvary. [...] The step forward from neo-

---

1   See the diary entry reproduced in this volume, p. 294.

paganism to the Church of the Mass was but the inevitable Envoi to all they had thought and lived and sung."[1] This is certainly the narrative that Bradley and Cooper successfully cultivate from this volume onwards, and it is important to their sense of the artistic unity of their life and work that they can make it work.

The very cover of this volume places it in relation to a particularly *fin-de-siècle* imperative to produce gorgeous, highly decorated books of poetry. A gilt motif of repeated bee figures across a honeycomb design decorates the dark-green silk cover, while delicate flower bells and bees adorn the spine. This design was created by Charles Ricketts, who was not only a close friend of Bradley and Cooper by this time, but also the designer of the second edition of Oscar Wilde's *Poems* (first published in 1881, and then reissued inside Ricketts's luxurious covers in 1892)—now considered a key example of this fashion for the fine bindings. Through Ricketts this volume is connected with a rich *fin-de-siècle* culture of aestheticist production, and it should be recognised that however personal the narrative of this book is, Bradley and Cooper's work must be seen in relation to the broader concerns of their age as well as their own captivating biography.]

Source: *Wild Honey from Various Thyme*, by Michael Field (London: T. Fisher Unwin, 1908).

[EPIGRAPH]

Wild was the honey thou did'st eat;[2]
The rocks and the free bees
Entombed thy honeycomb.
Take thou our gifts, take these:
No more in thy retreat
Do we attend thine ears; no more we roam
Or taste of desert food;
We have beheld thy Vision on the road.

July 14th, 1907.

---

1 Vincent McNabb. Preface, *The Wattlefold* (Oxford: Basil Blackwell, 1930), vi.
2 This refers to St. John the Baptist's time in the wilderness during which he foretold the coming of Christ. John's visionary prophecy in the wilderness, induced by a diet of locusts and wild honey, is clearly the central allusion of the title and Michael Field's epigraph to the book.

PAN ASLEEP

He half unearthed the Titans with his voice;
The stars are leaves before his windy riot;
The spheres a little shake: but, see, of choice
How closely he wraps up in hazel quiet!
And while he sleeps the bees are numbering
The fox-glove flowers from base to sealèd tip,
Till fond they doze upon his slumbering,
And smear with honey his wide, smiling lip.
He shall not be disturbed: it is the hour
That to his deepest solitude belongs;
The unfrighted reed opens to noontide flower,
And poets hear him sing their lyric songs,
While the Arcadian hunter, baffled, hot,
Scourges his statue in the ivy-grot.

PENETRATION

I love thee; never dream that I am dumb:
By day, by night, my tongue besiegeth thee,
As a bat's voice, set in too fine a key,
Too tender in its circumstance to come
To ears beset by havoc and harsh hum
Of the arraigning world; yet secretly
I may attain: lo, even a dead bee
Dropt sudden from thy open hand by some
Too careless wind is laid among thy flowers,[1]
Dear to thee as the bees that sing and roam:
Thou watchest when the angry moon drops foam;
Thou answerest the faun's soft-footed stare;
No influence, but thou feelest it is there,
And drawest it, profound, into thy hours.

---

1   Charles Ricketts once playfully presented Bradley and Cooper with a
    bunch of flowers that deliberately contained a dead bee: this is probably
    a rather personal reference to Ricketts.

ONYCHA[1]

There is silence of deep gathered eve,
There is a quiet of young things at rest;
In summer, when the honeysuckles heave
Their censer boughs, the forest is exprest.
What singeth like an orchard cherry-tree
Of its blown blossom white from tip to root,
Or solemn ocean moving silently,
Or the great choir of stars for ever mute?
So falleth on me a great solitude;
With miser's clutch I gather in the spell
Of loving thee, unwooing and unwooed;
And, as the silence settles, by degrees
Fill with thy sweetness as a perfumed shell
Sunk inaccessible in Indian seas.

VIOLETS

These offered violets are not for regret
That thou can'st never give my bosom ease;
My fond, reservèd tears, if they should wet
Mine eyes, were of far blacker tint than these.
Nor do I give them with the idle hope
Their stealthy drops thy senses should engage;
The passion at my heart has larger scope,
A bird of sweeping pinion in a cage.
Yet shalt thou grasp the force of my intent,
Pity my doom nor do my pride despite,
Who am as one by a god's fury rent,
Cast to the dust, humbled from all men's sight:
Yea, learn how their nativity empowers—
Sprung from the blood of Ajax are these flowers.

---

1   "Onycha" was one of Bradley's many pet names for Edith, combining
    erotic signifiers of shell and finger-tips ("ony" from the Greek meaning
    nail, claw or onyx stone).

SWEET-BASIL[1]

But thou art grown a symbol unto me!
Thy speech no more hath passion to entice;
As a sad, languorous wind thou art to me,
As a wind thwarted from the beds of spice.
To look upon thee in thy varying hour,
Thy moods, no more my spirit it contents;
Rhythm I feel of a remoter power,
And sway and falling of the elements.
Thou art no more thyself; I can no more
Reply to thee; thou art a boundless shore
That I am mute beside. Away, begone!—
Some potent semblance creep into thy stead,
Like that Sweet-Basil of the buried head,
A thing that I might brood and dote upon!

[The woods are still that were so gay at primrose-springing]

I

The woods are still that were so gay at primrose-springing,
Through the dry woods the brown field-fares are winging,
   And I alone of love, of love am singing.

II

I sing of love to the haggard palmer-worm,
Of love 'mid the crumpled oak-leaves that once were firm,
   Laughing, I sing of love at the summer's term.

III

—Of love, on a path where the snake's cast skin is lying,
Blue feathers on the floor, and no cuckoo flying;
   I sing to the echo of my own voice crying.

---

1   This poem refers to the legend taken up by John Keats in his "Isabella; or, The Pot of Basil."

EMBALMMENT

Let not a star suspect the mystery!
A cave that haunts thee in the dreams of night
Keep me as treasure hidden from thy sight,
And only thine while thou dost covet me!
As the Asmonæan[1] queen perpetually
Embalmed in honey, cold to thy delight,
Cold to thy touch, a sleeping eremite,
Beside thee never sleeping I would be.

Or thou might'st lay me in a sepulchre,
And every line of life will keep its bloom,
Long as thou seal'st me from the common air.
Speak not, reveal not ... There will be
In the unchallenged dark a mystery,
And golden hair sprung rapid in a tomb.

WHAT IS THY BELOVÉD MORE THAN ANOTHER BELOVÉD?

"But what is thy Belovéd to behold
More than another?"—He is pure
As substances that grain on grain endure,
As ambergris eternal in its gold.
More wonderful and in aloofness bold
His looking forth, more sensuously sure
Than Pan's, when from great caverns that immure
He looks abroad with all his flocks to fold.

More than another he is beautiful,
Nor is there any balm that gathereth
His sweetness up, or flower that you can pull:
From his own ecstasy he incenses,
Even as a camel feeding on myrrh trees
Blows from his nostrils aromatic breath.

---

1   An ancient Jewish dynasty.

LOVE: A LOVER

To Love I fled from love
That had so madly charmed me,
    And in a summer grove
    The god enchanting calmed me.
    Warmed at his fragrant heart,
    With him I dwelt apart
    From chills of hate:
Beneath his plumes who rest
No passion doth molest,
            Nor any fate.

A VIOLET BANK

        It was as if a violet bank
Were breathing forth its purple, so profound
And brimming was the beauty, and we drank
In the discourse no meaning, though the sound
Was musical; for if a flower should speak
At its full height and richness of perfume
We could not listen, so on brow and cheek
We rested by the very senses' doom.
An instant, and the perilous charm was gone,
The charm that was even as a prophecy
Of the concentred youth, the happy years,
With all the burthen of unladen tears,
That sometimes, unaware, we find upon
A face that very soon one feels must die.

REALITY

Be but thy absence present, vigorous,
Not spectral, nor of body to appal,
As in the night I watch the genius
Of the great barges flicker on the wall:
I waken to the sputter and the noise,
I feel the speed by the race-lightning dance:
So may thy brain, if it full sense employs,
Strike on me sharper than thy countenance.
Pass: I shall feel thy stroke upon the river;

Not thou, thy voyaging is my delight,
Not thou—those gifts of thine, thou being the giver,
Not thou—the vision of thee after sight;
Yet, by Apollo, blank were my despair
If losing I should fail to find thee otherwhere.

ENCHANTMENT

He is pure symbol as the Sangraël;[1]
He lets no lure of sense the soul oppress
He gives the freedom of his loneliness
For a few footsteps, if we feel his spell.

With tufts of seedling beech leaves in his hand,
Arcadia rushes up in leafy streams:
All that Pan[2] suffers, muffled in his dreams
'Mid wanton Naiades,[3] we understand.

He leads us to the desert and its drought;
And the white sapphire at his gift becomes
Strong fountain water stinging to the mouth.

And some have watched him when, a god, he plumbs
The void, and tranquilly from troubled eyes
As from sealed vials offers sacrifice.

FROM BAUDELAIRE

There shall be beds full of light odours blent,
Divans, great couches, deep, profound as tombs,
And, grown for us, in light magnificent,
Over the flower-stand there shall droop strange blooms.

Careful of their last flame declining,
As two vast torches our two hearts shall flare,
And our two spirits in their double shining
Reflect the double lights enchanted there.

---

1 Another name for the Holy Grail.
2 Half-goat, half-man, Pan is the Greek god of shepherds and woods and
  is associated with music and sexuality.
3 Fresh-water nymphs, minor divinities.

One night—a night of mystic blue, of rose,
A look will pass supreme from me, from you,
Like a long sob, laden with long adieux.

And, later on, an angel will unclose
The door, and, entering joyously, re-light
The tarnished mirrors and the flames blown to the night.

FIFTY QUATRAINS

'Twas fifty quatrains: and from unknown strands
The Woman came who sang them on the floor.
I saw her, I was leaning by the door,
—Saw her strange raiment and her lovely hands;
And saw ... but that I think she sang—the bands
Of low-voiced women on a happy shore:
Incomparable was the haze, and bore
The many blossoms of soft orchard lands.
'Twas fifty quatrains, for I caught the measure;
And all the royal house was full of kings,
Who listened and beheld her and were dumb;
Nor dared to seize the marvellous rich pleasure,
Too fearful even to ask in whisperings,
The ramparts being closed, whence she had come.

REVEILLE

Come to us, O Dionysus,
From the Alcyonian[1] water!
By the lake the spring-tide trumpets
With their cavernous entreaty,
With their tingling, sunstruck music,
Summon thee across the ripples,
Through the depths and lowest shadows,
Till they reach the gulf of Hades,
And thine ears with slumber soulless.

---

1 In *The Golden Bough*, J.G. Frazer refers to the supposedly bottomless
  Alcyonian lake, through which Dionysus gained access to Hades in
  order to bring up his mother Semele from the Underworld (New York:
  Macmillan, 1922; p. 389).

Let the trumpets roar their sunlight
To thy sleep and draw thee sternly
From the under hollows upward!

And in tribute to the warder
Of the dead this lamb, entwisted
With the stars and clumps of blossom
From the fields in earliest flowering,
By our hand is cast a victim,
To the lake, 'mid blast of trumpets.
None of all the lambs that speckle
With bare whiteness hill and valley
Do we offer, but a black one,
Black as if by smoke commended.
Dionysus, it is drowning:
We await thee by the water!

Argives,[1] see, the waves unbroken,
And the reeds an army silent;
Not a swan with breezy plumage
On the waves that drank their victim!
Sullen water, watery meadows
Wait for raciness of purpose;
Every vale and bank deploring
That their hour is unaccomplished.
Dionysus, Dionysus!
Solidly the trumpets clamour,
With demand the gates of Pluto
Dare not frustrate in their hatred.

Fixedly the trumpets thunder
Deep-toned over the pale reaches;
And we call with mourning passion,
As they call the dead that lose them:
"Come to us, return, belovèd!"
Argives, see, within the ripple
Rhythm of a light is playing;
And the sky, behold, is lucid
As the light that chimes its current
With the current of the water,

---

1 The Greek citizens of Argos.

So that never swan more bravely
Measured out her splendid waftage.

Argives, how the spangles brighten!
Flashing trumpets, draw the presence
In the water to our vineyards,
To our farmsteads and bleak meadows!
In that light upon the water
Is our springtide, our affiance,
Buoyancy of heart and herbage,
Touch and redolence of freedom.
Veil your eyes, for none may see him
Reach the Alcyonian pastures.
Dionysus, O Belovèd!—
Blind, bright trumpets, blow him welcome!

THE POET

Within his eyes are hung lamps of the sanctuary:
A wind, from whence none knows, can set in sway
And spill their light by fits; but yet their ray
Returns, deep-boled, to its obscurity.

The world as from a dullard turns annoyed
To stir the days with show or deeds or voices;
But if one spies him justly one rejoices,
With silence that the careful lips avoid.

He is a plan, a work of some strange passion
Life has conceived apart from Time's harsh drill,
A thing it hides and cherishes to fashion

At odd bright moments to its secret will:
Holy and foolish, ever set apart,
He waits the leisure of his god's free heart.

A FOREST NIGHT

It fell to a woman, wayfaring
In a lone forest, a lion came that way,
Laying his paw upon her heart.

Soft from that heart below
She sang to him night long:
He cannot do her wrong
Such sounds to his nostrils blow.

Forever, forever I must sing,
Forever and with mortality at bay,
Must not grow weary or start—
    Things that I do not know
    Driven to me in song,
    Stories the graves among,
    Strange words in a spell that flow.

[I love you with my life—'tis so I love you]

I love you with my life—'tis so I love you;
    I give you as a ring
The cycle of my days till death:
    I worship with the breath
That keeps me in the world with you and spring:
And God may dwell behind, but not above you.

Mine, in the dark, before the world's beginning:
    The claim of every sense,
    Secret and source of every need;
    The goal to which I speed,
And at my heart a vigour more immense
Than will itself to urge me to its winning.

A VISION

Tramplings tumultuous and a charge of sound!
    Horses that paw the ground,
Mingling in a rhythm musical;
So that I hear—I hear all that I see:
    And from the blast I flee,
    Wondering what should be
The conflagration of such majesty.

And crouched down in the corner of a hall,
  Where I have fled
As from the beating pressure of a wave,
  It is spread out to me,
  That vast conclave,
Those congregated stallions rushing wide
  From north and south, outside,
And rushing up from fissures of the rocks
  As to a day of doom:
I breathe low from my room,
And in tranquillity the vision knocks.

IV[1]
THE MUMMY INVOKES HIS SOUL

Down to me quickly, down! I am such dust,
Baked, pressed together; let my flesh be fanned
With thy fresh breath; come from thy reedy land
Voiceful with birds; divert me, for I lust
To break, to crumble—prick with pores this crust!—
And fall apart, delicious, loosening sand.
Oh, joy, I feel thy breath, I feel thy hand
That searches for my heart, and trembles just
Where once it beat. How light thy touch, thy frame!
Surely thou perchest on the summer trees ...
And the garden that we loved? Soul, take thine ease,
I am content, so thou enjoy the same
Sweet terraces and founts, content, for thee,
To burn in this immense torpidity.

OCTOBER

Honey-bees by little toneless grapes,
  Bees that starve and cling,
Flowers that are distorted in their shapes,
  Bees wayfaring
  To their bowers—

---

1 This is poem 4 in a series entitled *Egyptian Sonnets*.

Bees that do not come
To the flowers a-hum,
That rove quiet, trailing up the napes
Of the sunken flowers.

EBBTIDE AT SUNDOWN

How larger is remembrance than desire!
How deeper than all longing is regret!
The tide is gone, the sands are rippled yet;
The sun is gone; the hills are lifted higher,
Crested with rose. Ah, why should we require
Sight of the sea, the sun? The sands are wet,
And in their glassy flaws huge record set
Of the ebbed stream, the little ball of fire.
Gone, they are gone! But, oh, so freshly gone,
So rich in vanishing we ask not where—
So close upon us is the bliss that shone,
And, oh, so thickly it impregns the air!
Closer in beating heart we could not be
To the sunk sun, the far, surrendered sea.

SIRENUSA[1]

Caught unawares the moments that enchant!
"Civet or bergamot, or holy basil?—
But close your eyes!" ... And while the nostrils pant,
With the kaleidoscopic sweets a-dazzle,
"Oh stay, you strive; draw in a deeper breath:
You cannot fail: do not too quick reply!"
And the great lids before me, not in death,
But vivid as one feels the sea, being by,
Are stretched unsentried. Lovely Gorgon[2] mask,
Kind betwixt me and doom! White siren coast,

---

1 Land of the Sirens—mythical creatures, who seduced sailors to their
death with their songs.
2 Powerful female figure in Greek mythology whose gaze could turn the
beholder into stone.

And all the sirens whelmèd, in their host
Trembling unseen their perilous harps! Secure,
I leave the chafing senses to their task,
And profit of those brows serene and pure.

AVOWAL

As two men smoking, though one be a youth,
And one so great he meets him as a peer
Or cannot meet at all, speak open truth,
—The God with me vouchsafing to make cheer:
"Eros, and now in disillusion, now
That thou hast purged me of thy thick blindfold,
Damon[1] is false and Glaphyrus![2] ... Avow,
Are not these creatures, I have doted on,
Thine idols, and eternal sweet to thee?
Dead loves I speak of, loves long dead and gone." ...
A noble silence settled on our glee;
And the sweet mouth grew jocund as he took
The cup to pledge, and all his glorious pinions shook.

RENEWAL

As the young phoenix, duteous to his sire,
Lifts in his beak the creature he has been,
And, lifting o'er the corse broad vans for screen,
Bears it to solitudes, erects a pyre,
And, soon as it is wasted by the fire,
Grides with disdainful claw the ashes clean;
Then spreading unencumbered wings serene
Mounts to the æther with renewed desire:
So joyously I lift myself above
The life I buried in hot flames to-day;

---

1 Just possibly a reference to "that false knave Damon" of *Damon and
   Pithias* by Richard Edwards (1571), but difficult to verify—as is the next
   reference in this line.
2 This possibly refers to Glaphyrus the flute-player (mentioned by Antipa-
   ter of Thessalonica), who is accused of stealing Athena's flutes.

The flames themselves are dead: and I can range
Alone through the untarnished sky I love,
And I trust myself, as from the grave I may,
To the enchanting miracles of change.

LIFE PLASTIC

O Life, who art thou that with scarcely scanned
Mysterious aspect breakest on my way,
And vanishest, leaving a lump of clay
As gift, as symbol, shapeless in my hand?
Kindling and mute, thou gavest no command;
Yet am I left as prompted to obey,
With a great peril at my heart. Oh, say,
Am I a creature from achievement banned?
In my despair, my idle hands are cast,
Are plunged into the clay: they grip, they hold,
I feel them chafing on a moistened line;
Unconsciously my warmth is in the cold.
O Life, I am the Potter, and at last
The secret of my loneliness is mine.

ABSENCE

Should my beloved be absent from my sight,
All work is left unfinished if begun,
Even as jealous Nature, should the sun
Withdraw himself, leaves the young shoots the height
That he had reared them to, nor takes delight
In waxy droppings of her buds undone,
Nor passion of her tendril vines to run
From pole to pole in garlands through the light.
But should the dead desert me for an hour ...
Ah me, the living may come in and out,
And the heart break not of its varying pain;
But if the dead be found wandering without,
Wandering as ghosts, scarcely the heart has power
To draw them down into its depths again!

PARTING

Lo, even memory must give up its dead!
Where he has walked we must not walk again,
Nor pause by garden borders where he led,
Nor seek his flowers; we must unknot the pain.
For, if we look not on our memory's corse,
Sweet sculpture of our memory will abide;
The eyes, the lips will take their human force,
Life's lovely images keep by our side.
Anew in the young sunshine we shall meet,
By paths, belovèd, where thou hast not been;
Thou, being by, shalt make the strangeness sweet
Of the long, silver river and the green;
And all our passion grow a child to cling
About the freshness of thy welcoming.

OLD IVORIES

A window full of ancient things, and while,
Lured by their solemn tints, I crossed the street,
A face was there that in its tranquil style,
Almost obscure, at once remote and sweet,
Moved me by pleasure of similitude—
For, flanked by golden ivories, that face,
Her face, looked forth in even and subdued
Deep power, while all the shining, all the grace
Came from the passing of Time over her,
Sorrow with Time; there was no age, no spring:
On those smooth brows no promise was astir,
No hope outlived: herself a perfect thing,
She stood by that time-burnished reliquary
Simple as Aphrodite by the sea.

BALSAM

The Past was with us and no morning rose
But we remembered something that had been,
Or thought with trembling of the summer's close,
Or clung too fast to April's tender green.

Ah, what we missed through those dull years of wrong,
Of tears, of praise, of precious laughter, how
The voice enchanting in caress and song
I heard as Orpheus' prisoned wife![1] But now,
O Loved, are we not happy? Nothing stems
The current of our freedom: all the day
We of ourselves sweet memories can make;
Nor other boon we crave than thus to stay
Watching the mists together at sunbreak,
Or gathering yellow balsams by the Thames.

CONSTANCY

I love her with the seasons, with the winds,
As the stars worship, as anemones
Shudder in secret for the sun, as bees
Buzz round an open flower: in all kinds
My love is perfect, and in each she finds
Herself the goal: then why, intent to teaze
And rob her delicate spirit of its ease,
Hastes she to range me with inconstant minds?
If she should die, if I were left at large
On earth without her—I, on earth, the same
Quick mortal with a thousand cries, her spell
She fears would break. And I confront the charge
As sorrowing, and as careless of my fame
As Christ intact before the infidel.

A PALIMPSEST

... The rest
Of our life must be a palimpsest—
The old writing written there the best.

In the parchment hoary
Lies a golden story,

---

1 Eurydice, who (with his music) Orpheus attempted, and failed, to
rescue from the Underworld.

As 'mid secret feather of a dove,
As 'mid moonbeams shifted through a cloud:

Let us write it over,
O my lover,
For the far Time to discover,
As 'mid secret feathers of a dove,
As 'mid moonbeams shifted through a cloud!

ABSENCE

Yes, but a dog's love is a true, true thing!
For, if you turn back on your doorstep, hot
In temper for a name, a word forgot,
Is there not lauguor[1] in your welcoming?
"So soon come back again and why?"—Thy spring
Whym Chow, thy raptured hurrying to the spot—
Thy face tense in the joy that thou hast got
This second, sweet return—the chance to cling
And snuff, and brood about me! Oh, renewed
As God's thy region of solicitude!
Nor could a moment of the past be dear
As this that drew me out of absence near.
Absence! And all thy glory to remit
Seven's seventy times the mortal sin of it.

WHYM CHOW

Nay, thou art my eternal attribute:
Not as Saint Agnes[2] in loose arms her lamb,—
The very essence of the thing I am:
And, as the lion, at Saint Jerome's[3] suit,
Stood ever at his right hand, scanning mute
The hollows of the fountainous earth, whence swam,
Emergent from the welter, sire and dam:

---

1 This should perhaps have been "languor."
2 Roman Catholic child martyr.
3 Translator of the Old Testament from Hebrew to Latin. This translation
is known as the Vulgate.

While Jerome with no knowledge of the brute
Beside him, wrote of later times, of curse,
Bloodshed, and bitter exile, verse on verse
Murmuring above the manuscript [in awe
The lion watched his lord, the Vulgate grew],[1]
So it was wont to be betwixt us two—
How still thou lay'st deep-nosing on thy paw!

A MINUTE-HAND

Nay, my Beloved, thou canst not keep my pace;
But, as a tiny minute-hand within
A clock's wide frame doth stand
And with the ticking of the tiny paces
    True to Time's race is,
So do thou mark my minutes—be
    My little Now perpetually—
Sense of thy sweet
Tick-tack and beat
Buzzing about the essence of the hour!
So I renounce thy pattering feet—
So, so—the heavenly din,
The rich effulgence of thy coming in,
So thou wilt mark the pressure at its source
    Of my blood's course;
And with the tiny trespass of thy being,
    In every part
Dint all my senses' seeing:
Notching—O silver chime!—
The solitariness of incurious Time.

GOOD FRIDAY

There is wild shower and winter on the main.
Foreign and hostile, as the flood of Styx,
The rumbling water: and the clouds that mix
And drop across the land, and drive again

---

1 Square brackets were used in the original publication and do not indi-
cate an intervention by the current editors.

Whelm as they pass. And yet the bitter rain,
The fierce exclusion hurt me not; I fix
My thought on the deep-blooded crucifix
My lips adore, and there is no more pain.
A Power is with me that can love, can die,
That loves, and is deserted, and abides;
A loneliness that craves me and enthrals:
And I am one with that extremity,
One with that strength. I hear the alien tides
No more, no more the universe appals.

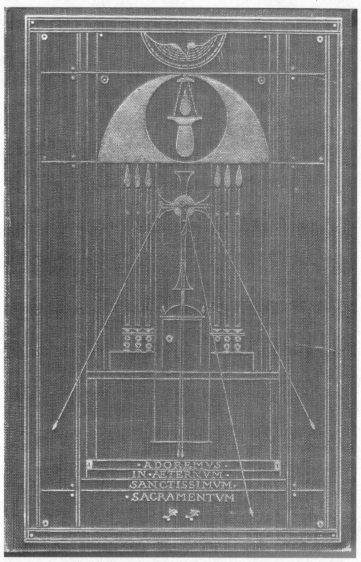

Figure 5. Book cover of *Poems of Adoration*, 1912.

5. From *Poems of Adoration* (1912)

[The next two books in the Michael Field oeuvre comprise the core of their religious writing. Although *Wild Honey* contained evidence of their recent (1907) conversion, these subsequent two books contain only poems written after the transformation and establish a new religious identity.

Although both published under the Michael Field signature, *Poems of Adoration* was written mostly by Cooper, and *Mystic Trees* by Bradley. Yet these two together form the major collaborative work of the period: they were designed as counterparts, which would form a complete whole when united with the specially made black leather strap. This new way of working still entailed close involvement with each other's work, including shared proof-reading and editing, and as such does not represent an abandoning of literary collaboration. Nonetheless, it does seem to reflect the greater distance between the two women that religion established. It is only in the posthumous collection by Emily Fortey—*The Wattlefold*—that the poems of the two women again appear thoroughly mixed within one volume.

These two major companion volumes are formed by a new awareness of how the women are seen by the Catholic community, which ensures a heavily theological text. What tends to be pushed out of these volumes is often the personal, problematic poems, expressing doubt, and desire that is less than categorically theological. The danger is that the poems become more formulaic, and the creative tension that is fundamental to the success and energy of Michael Field's poetry is resolved and defused.

Some of the successful poems in this, Cooper's, volume are, in fact, based on decadent themes or images and add on a religious framework. See for example "A Dance of Death" with its powerful turn-of-the-century meditation on the figure of the dancer, Salome, that is given a final twist in honour of Saint John the Baptist at the end. "After Anointing" and "Imple Superna Gratia" might be read in a similar way, with the former recalling the sensual delights of Symons's lyrics, while the latter is Paterian in its eulogy. Yet "Viaticum" and "Of Silence" show how religious fervour can translate wholly convincingly into poetic effusion for Cooper. The re-evaluation of Catholic doctrine and imagery in order to recognise and celebrate the role of women is another theme within the book that surfaces in poems such as "Another Leadeth Thee."[1]]

Source: *Poems of Adoration*, by Michael Field (London and Edinburgh: Sands & Co., 1912).

OF SILENCE

"Be it done unto me
According to Thy word...."
Into Mortality
Slips the Eternal Word,
When not a sound is heard.

She spake those words, and then
Was silent in her heart;
Mother of Silence, when
Her will spake from her heart
Her lips had done their part.

And only once we hear
Her words that intercede;
Her will so sweetly clear
Those lips should intercede,
And help men in their need.

Out of her silence grew
The Word, and as a man
He neither cried nor knew
The strivings of a man,
When doom for Him began.

And after He had gone
From Earth to Heaven away,
He came and lingered on;
He would not pass away,
But with His people stay.

---

1 See Frederick S. Roden, *Same-Sex Desire in Victorian Religious Culture* (Houndmills, Basingstoke: Palgrave, 2002), 211, for further analysis of this theme.

Son of the Silent Maid,
He chose her silence too.
In dumbness He hath stayed,
Dumbness unbroken too,
Past measure—as night-dew.

O quiet, holy Host,
Our pondering Joy and Light,
In Thy still power engrossed,
As a mute star pleads light,
Thou pleadest, Infinite!

REAL PRESENCE

I approach Thy Altar ... Stay!
   Let me break away!
Level stones of marble, brazen lights,
Linen spread, flowers on the shelves and heights—
    I bow down, I kneel ...
And far away, where the sun sets, would reel!

For from forth Thy altar Thou
   Strikest on me now,
Strikest on me, firm and warm to thrill,
With the charm of one whose touch could kill;
   Giving me desire
Toward substance, yet for flight the lightning's fire.

   So, if close a lover kneels,
   Praying close, one feels
All the body's flow of life reined tight,
As when waters struggle at their height;
   From Thy altar-stone,
Thou in my body bodily art known.

And I fear Thee worse than death,
   As we fear Love's breath:
Thou art as a tiger round a camp;
   And I kindle, terrified, my lamp,
    Since I cannot fly,
But to hold Thee distant, lest I die.

Thou art God, and in the mesh,
 Close to me, of flesh;
And we love and we have been in range
Of wild secrecies of interchange:
 Could I bear Thee near
I should be humble to Thee—but I *fear*!

ANOTHER LEADETH THEE

In whose hands, O Son of God,
Was Thy earthly Mission held?
Not in Thine, that made earth's sod,
And the ocean as it welled
From creation to the shore;
Not in Thine, whose fingers' lore
Checked the tide with golden bars,
Ruled the clouds and dinted stars—
Not in Thine, that made fresh leaves,
And the flourished wheat for sheaves;
Grapes that bubbled from a spring,
Where the nightingale might sing
From the blood of her wild throat;
Not in Thine that struck her note;
Maned the lion and wrought the lamb;
Breathed on clay, "Be as I am!"
And it stood before Thee fair,
Thinking, loving, furnished rare,
Like Thee, so beyond compare....

Not within Thy hands!—Behold,
By a woman's hand unrolled
All the mystery sublime
Of Thy ableness through Time!
Thou, in precious Boyhood, knew
For Thy Father what to do;
And delayed Thyself to hear
Questions and to answer clear
To the Doctors' chiming throng,
Thou, admired, wert set among.
Straight Thy Mission was begun,
As the Jewish Rabbis spun
Round Thy fetterless, sweet mind

Problems no one had divined.
But Thy Mother came that way,
Who had sought Thee day by day,
And her crystal voice reproved
Thy new way with Thy beloved.
In Thy wisdom-widened eyes
Throbbed a radiance of surprise:
But, Thy Mother having chidden,
Thou in Nazareth wert hidden;
And Thy Father's Work begun
Stayed full eighteen years undone,
Till Thou camest on Thine hour,
When Thy Mother loosed Thy power
For Thy Father's business, said,
In a murmur softly spread,
Rippling to a happy few,
"What He says unto you do!"
As the spring-time to a tree,
Sudden spring she was to Thee,
When her strange appeal began
Thy stayed Mission unto man;
Stayed but by her earlier blame,
When from three days' woe she came;
Yet renewed when she gave sign
"Son, they have not any wine!"

Holy trust and love! She gave
For Thy sake oblation brave
Of her will, her spotless name:
Thou for her didst boldly tame
God the Word to wait on her;
God's own Wisdom might not stir
Till her lovely voice decreed.
Thou wouldst have our hearts give heed,
And revere her lovely voice;
Wait upon her secret choice,
Stay her pleasure, as didst Thou,
With a marvel on Thy brow,
And a silence on Thy breath.
We must cherish what she saith;
As she pleadeth we must hope
For our deeds' accepted scope,
Humble as her Heavenly Son,
Till our liberty be won.

RELICS[1]

An alabaster box,
A tomb of precious stone—
White, with white bars, as white
    As billows on a sea:
With spaces where some flush
Of sky-like rose is conscious and afraid
    Of whiteness and white bars.
A lovely sepulchre of loveliest stone,
    This alabaster box—
Coy as a maiden's blood in flush,
White as a maiden's breast in stretch,
    Alive with fear and grace;
    Transparent rose,
    Translucent white;
A treasury of precious stone,
    A strange, long tomb ...
'Twas Maximin, who had this casket made,
The holy Maximin, who travelled once
With Mary Magdalen, and preached with her;
    Till on a wind as quiet
    As it had been a cloud,
She was removed by Christ to dwell alone.

Alone she dwelt, her peace
A thought that never fell
    From its full tide.
Ever beside her in her cave,
    A vase of golden curls,
    A clod of blooded earth.
And when she died at last, and Maximin
    Must bury her;
Being man and holy, in his love
He laid her in an alabaster box,
As she had laid her soul's deep penitence,
Her soul's deep passion, a sweet balm, within
    An alabaster box:

---

1 This poem refers in part to the story of the sinner Mary Magdelen
   taking her alabaster box of ointments to wash the feet of Jesus, drying
   them with her own long hair. It was at this point that Jesus absolved her
   of sin (Luke 7:36–50). She was buried by St. Maximin.

So Maximin gave Magdalen to God—
Shut as a spice in precious stone,
In bland and flushing box
Of alabaster stone.
And knowing all her secrets, Maximin,
Being man and holy, laid within
The priceless cave of alabaster two
Most precious, cherished things—
A vase of curly hair,
A vase of golden web;
A clod of withered soil,
A clod of blooded earth.

The curls were crushed together in gold lump,
Crushed by the hand that wiped
The Holy Feet, kept in a crush of gold,
Just as they dabbed the sweetly smelling Feet—
The curls enwoven by the balm they dried,
Knotted as rose of Sharon, when the winds
Sweep it along the desert.... Curls, of power
To float the charm of Eve in aureole
Round her they covered, till she crushed them tight
To dab the Holy Feet, and afterward
Be severed from their growth,
Stiff in their balm and gold;
A piece of honeycomb in rings and web;
Sweetness of shorn, gold, unguent-dabbled hair,
A handful in a vase.

The clod, a bit of hill-turf dry;
The turf that sheep might pull up as they graze;
Or men might throw upon the fire
At sundown when the air is loosed and cold:
A clod an eagle might
Ascend to build with, or a goat
Kick down a valley's side;
A clod dark-red
As if it mothered ruby of the mines.
The hand that gathered it one hollow night
Gathered it up red-wet from Golgotha.[1]

---

1 The place of Christ's crucifixion.

Three crosses lay about the grass—
Such arms and shafts of crosses on the grass!—
        When she, who gathered, crept
        Among the prostrate arms;
Roused a great death-bird from the ground,
            And, in its place,
Bent down and pressed her lips where it had couched,
And lifted up the ground to press her heart;
And went her way, hugging the Sacred Blood
        As in a sponge of turf,
That dried about the treasure, now grown hard,
As if it mothered ruby of the mines—
        A clod of blooded soil.

O Relics of the Holy Magdalen!
        The balmy hair her plea,
        God's Blood her grace:
Within a vase her gift,
Within a turf-clod His—
        Her relics, by her corpse;
        All she had cared to keep,
        Through hermit years of life,
        To bless her in her tomb
        Till Judgment-Day.

A DANCE OF DEATH

How lovely is a silver winter-day
        Of sturdy ice,
That clogs the hidden river's tiniest bay
        With diamond-stone of price
To make an empress cast her dazzling stones
        Upon its light as hail—
So little its effulgency condones
        Her diamonds' denser trail
        Of radiance on the air!
How strange this ice, so motionless and still,
Yet calling as with music to our feet,
        So that they chafe and dare
Their swiftest motion to repeat
These harmonies of challenge, sounds that fill
        The floor of ice, as the crystalline sphere

Around the heavens is filled with such a song
    That, when they hear,
The stars, each in their heaven, are drawn along!

Oh, see, a dancer! One whose feet
Move on unshod with steel!
She is not skating fleet
    On toe and heel,
But only tip-toe dances in a whirl,
    A lovely dancing-girl,
Upon the frozen surface of the stream.
    Without a wonder, it would seem,
    She could not keep her sway,
    The balance of her limbs
  Sure on the musical, iced river-way
    That, sparkling, dims
Her trinkets as they swing, so high its sparks
Tingle the sun and scatter song like larks.

She dances mid the sumptuous whiteness set
    Of winter's sunniest noon;
She dances as the sun-rays that forget
    In winter sunset falleth soon
      To sheer sunset:
She dances with a languor through the frost
As she had never lost,
In lands where there is snow,
The Orient's immeasurable glow.

Who is this dancer white—
    A creature slight,
Weaving the East upon a stream of ice,
    That in a trice
Might trip the dance and fling the dancer down?
Does she not know deeps under ice can drown?

This is Salome,[1] in a western land,
An exile with Herodias, her mother,
    With Herod and Herodias:

---

1 Salome danced for King Herod and was offered a reward in return. Her
   mother, Herodias, convinced her to ask for the head of St. John the
   Baptist. This poem deals with Salome's own death, also a beheading.

And she has sought the river's icy mass,
    Companioned by no other,
To dance upon the ice—each hand
    Held, as a snow-bird's wings,
       In heavy poise.
Ecstatic, with no noise,
Athwart the ice her dream, her spell she flings;
And Winter in a rapture of delight
Flings up and down the spangles of her light.

Oh, hearken, hearken! ... Ice and frost,
From these cajoling motions freed,
    Have straight given heed
To Will more firm. In their obedience
    Their masses dense
Are riven as by a sword....
Where is the Vision by the snow adored?
    The Vision is no more
    Seen from the noontide shore.
Oh, fearful crash of thunder from the stream,
As there were thunder-clouds upon its wave!
      Could nothing save
The dancer in the noontide beam?
She is engulphed and all the dance is done.
    Bright leaps the noontide sun—
But stay, what leaps beneath it? A gold head,
That twinkles with its jewels bright
      As water-drops....
O murdered Baptist of the severed head,
Her head was caught and girded tight,
And severed by the ice-brook sword, and sped
    In dance that never stops.
    It skims and hops
Across the ice that rasped it. Smooth and gay,
      And void of care,
    It takes its sunny way:
But underneath the golden hair,
And underneath those jewel-sparks,
    Keen noontide marks
A little face as grey as evening ice;
Lips, open in a scream no soul may hear
Eyes fixed as they beheld the silver plate
That they at Macherontis once beheld;

While the hair trails, although so fleet and nice
The motion of the head as subjugate
To its own law: yet in the face what fear,
    To what excess compelled!

Salome's head is dancing on the bright
And silver ice. O holy John, how still
Was laid thy head upon the salver white,
    When thou hadst done God's Will!

IMPLE SUPERNA GRATIA[1]

We may enter far into a rose,
Parting it, but the bee deeper still:
With our eyes we may even penetrate
To a ruby and our vision fill;
Though a beam of sunlight deeper knows
How the ruby's heart-rays congregate.

Give me finer potency of gift!
For Thy Holy Wounds I would attain,
As a bee the feeding loveliness
Of the sanguine roses. I would lift
Flashes of such faith that I may drain
From each Gem the wells of Blood that press!

AFTER ANOINTING

Joy of the senses, joy of all
    And each of them, as fall
The Holy Oils! ... O senses, ye would dance,
Would circle what ye cannot see,
Nor hear, nor smell, nor taste, nor touch,
Yet ye receive of your felicity,
    Till ye would reel and dance;
The joy apparent from your bliss being such
That, in a fivefold garland knit,
Softly ye would circle it.

---

1 "Fill up with divine grace." This Latin phrase is part of a medieval
Catholic hymn, "Veni Creator Spiritus," which is the Office Hymn for
Second Vespers of Pentecost.

Joy ripples through each covered lid;
    Nor are the ears forbid
Sounds as of honeycomb, so sweet is Heaven
Afar, such sweet, such haunting sound!
O nostrils, myrtle ye shall love!
The lips taste fully, as if God were found.
    Swift, under peace, toward Heaven
The hands, the feet, so still, like still lakes move.
Delighted Powers of Sense, ye dance,
Woven in such a lovely chance!

VIATICUM[1]

O Heart, that burns within,
Illuminated, hot!
O feet, that tread the road
As if they trod it not—
So lifted and so winged
By rare companionship!
No matter tho' the road
Doth unto shadow dip;
The meaning of the night
My ears, attentive, hail.
The mighty silence brings
Music no nightingale
Hath warbled from its fount;
Music of holy things
Made clear as song can make,
With marvellous utterings:
The Past become a joy
Of instant clarity,
As the deep evening fills
With converse brimmingly.
O nightingale, hold back
Your wildest song's discant;
You cannot make my heart
With such devotion pant
As He who steps along
Beside me in the shade,
Down the steep valley-road,

---

1 Holy Communion given to those in danger of death. More loosely:
  provisions for the journey from life to death.

The enveloping, dark glade!
Hush, O dim nightingale! ...
Is it my God whose Feet
Wing mine to travel on;
Whose voice in current sweet
Shows how divine the thought
And purpose is of all
That hath been and shall be,
And shall to me befall?
Stay, nightingale! Behold!
This Wayfarer, with strange,
Wild Voice that rouses gloom
Thy voice could never range,
Hath broken Bread with me!
No resinous, balmed shrine
Glows from its core as I,
When I behold His sign,
And touch His offering Hand.
O holiest journey, sped
With Him who died for me,
Who breaking with me Bread,
Is known to me as Life,
Is felt by me as Fire;
Who is my Way and all
My wayfaring's Desire!

TRANSIT

Cloud that streams its breath of unseen flowers,
Cloud with spice of bay,
Of roses, lily-breathings, and the powers
Of small violets, or, aloft, black poplars as they quiver!

Cloud that streams its song of birds—no bird
Seen to chant the song:
Yet wide and keen as sun-breath it is heard,
All the air itself a voice of voices chiming golden!

Mary hath passed by. All plants sweet-leaved,
Sweet-flowered; birds, sweet-voiced,
Round her passing have their sweetness weaved.
Let us yield our incense up, our anthems and our homage!

6. From *Mystic Trees* (1913)

[This is the second book in the pair that most centrally represents Michael Field's religious poetry. This is almost entirely Bradley's work, just as *Poems of Adoration* was chiefly Cooper's. In setting this book alongside Cooper's companion volume, we are able truly to compare the individual poetic styles of the women. Here it becomes clear that while Cooper's work is often more stylised and abstract, Bradley finds it difficult to leave behind the raw reality of the everyday, even when she most aspires to religious vision.

Ruth Vanita, in her book *Sappho and the Virgin Mary*, pays particular attention to *Mystic Trees*, in which she finds the celebration of the "power and strength" of Mary through poems charting her life story.[1] Frederick S. Roden also develops more fully this analysis, showing the various roles Mary fulfils for Bradley at this time, noting that Mary's superiority "removes her from human heteronormative desire and leaves her for God," but that this opens a space for Michael Field to present her as emblematic of a community of female same-sex desire.[2] Poems such as "Praises" show the all-encompassing nature of Mary's power.

It is not just through a co-option and development of female imagery that Bradley and Cooper inhabit the Catholic Church, however. Just as powerful in Bradley's writing is the imagery of Christ's wounds. Bradley and Cooper learned a great deal from their male mentors, such as the Decadent poet-turned-priest John Gray, about the erotic potential of the stigmata for reconciling earthly and transcendent desires. While the body of Christ is often recognised as central to the discourse of male homoerotic Catholicism, Michael Field shows that it can also play a central role in the articulation of the female Decadent-erotic. "The Five Sacred Wounds," for example, achieves this by focussing finally on Mary's intimate tending of the wounds.

Because Bradley is more troubled than Cooper by Pagan thoughts, she often writes about her new faith through the emblems of her old Pagan desire. Both "White Passion-Flower" and "Before Requiem" show how Bradley's religious verse is more rooted in nature and the secular than Cooper's often more esoteric conceits, but also how effective such a tension between

---

1 Ruth Vanita, *Sappho and the Virgin Mary* (New York: Columbia UP, 1996), 134.
2 Roden, *Same-Sex Desire in Victorian Religious Culture*, 207.

body and spirit, or natural and supernatural, can be poetically. Human frailty and inadequacy is one of the most potent themes in Western religion, and Bradley's poetry is energised rather than diminished by her struggle to find Christ's passion in the passion-flower, and by her efforts to see the church candles as emblems of a higher world rather than celebratory of the bees, spring flowers, and golden pollen stamens that occupy her mind.

Human frailty is a poignant theme of this volume in more than one way. Many of these poems were written while Bradley watched Cooper die, slowly, and painfully, of cancer. "She is Singing to Thee, *Domine!*" was written when Cooper was suffering from an unpleasant condition that produced involuntary noises from her throat. Bradley's amazing transformation of this frightening sound into a hymn to the saviour is stunning both for its courage as well as for its faith, as it does nothing to hide the pain of this "homage." Bradley's poetic achievement lies in this ability to fuse the reality of this world with hopes of another, without diminishing the former or hiding the power of its pain and pleasure.]

Source: *Mystic Trees*, by Michael Field (London: Everleigh Nash, 1913).

THE CAPTAIN JEWEL

We love Thy ruddy Wounds,
We love them pout by pout:
It is as when the stars come out,
    One after one—
We are
As watchers for the Morning Star.

The jewels of Thy Feet,
The jewels of Thy Hands! ...
Lo, a Centurion[1] stands,
Openeth Thy Side: Water and Blood there beat
    In fountain sweet:
Our Master-jewel now we dote upon!

---

1   An officer of the Roman army.

THE WINDING-SHEET

"Tuum Sindonem veneremur, Domine."[1]

I

In this is our humanity complete
That Joseph coming down the street
Bought for the Lord a winding-sheet.

II

Yours is the corse—now Pilate understands—
O women! With fair linen in your hands,
Wrap tight, enwind the Body with strict bands!

III

Dearer these grave-clothes than the seamless coat
Woven of His Mother, than the crown, reed-smote;
Yea, for He learns our little part by rote.

IV

That cry from off the Cross was wide, was loud,
As He were parted from us.... For His shroud
We famish! Women, as in fetters, shroud,

V

Bind Him our own, Jesus of Nazareth!
Sweet is your spice; but of more sumptuous breath
The redolence of that rich-blooded death.

VI

Tend Him as even now we tend the dead;
Let tears in volume on His corse be spread! ...
This Winding-sheet, the napkin at His head,

---

1 We venerate your Holy Shroud, O Lord.

Lift them, when round the open tomb we meet;
Bear them with pangs of laughter down the street;
Lay them down low, kissing His Mother's feet!

THE FIVE SACRED WOUNDS

Have compassion on me!
I thought to worship Thy Wounds in Trinity,
The Wounds of Thy Hands, Thy Side, Thy Feet;
I had no patience, no *Caritas*[1]....
Through Thy right Hand the nail doth pass!
   As a sheep standeth by
His fellow, waiting for his turn to die,
   The left hand droopeth free—
That is the Hand that *feels* the nail.
God, for my hardness pity me!

O Venerable Hands, O our delight!
We need them both: one bindeth tight
The Cup, one breaketh for all the Bread.
How pliantly they work; they wave from side to side,
As weeds that wash in a low pool-tide,
In every motion to fulfil
A motion of the Father's will!
We need them both. O lovely in our sight,
O *Amor meus*,[2] to be crucified!
O Hands, clear as a woman's in their light!

Have compassion! Side by side
They place Thy Feet, and through each they gride;
One breaketh before the other, yea,
There is a blow, and then silence, and then ...
I will have patience, wait for the blow again.
When Mary wrapt those Feet with her hair
   She was glad the two were there:
One with her hair she dried;
One she fondled up against her cheek—
God, for my lack of loving chide!

---

1 Charity.
2 My Love.

WHITE PASSION-FLOWER

I

White exceeding is the passion-flower,
When it rayeth and extendeth white.
Where is the purple thorn,
Or the robe that He hath worn?
Where are the Wounds? From the waxen flower
    The virulence is drawn, the power.

II

Dark exceeding is the passion-flower,
When it rayeth and extendeth, dark,
    The passion intricate
    Of a God in man's debate:
We beheld the Wounds, the Blood is red,
And the dark Blood gathers round His head.

III

Lovely, waxen flower, I am content
With your whiteness of the firmament:
    Even as in the Host
    The Precious Blood is lost,
On your unblooded disk I see
How the Lord is dying on Calvary.

PRAISES

O Mary, Wisdom of the early lands,
O Mary, joy of the Creative Hands!—
Behold where on the serpent's head she stands!

Child to the Heavenly Father by submission,
Spouse to the Holy Spirit in fruition,
Mother to all who seek Christ of contrition.

O Mary, lovely Bush of lightsome flame,[1]
To whom in veneration Joseph came,
And found thee tingling with the Hidden Name!

BEFORE REQUIEM

Bees from loveliest fields of light,
Make our darksome candles bright!
From the balsam beds ye come
    To build glory round the tomb.

Angels from the summer ye,
Angels to our Mystery,
That these golden rods, that stand
Sentry to our dead, have planned!

Pause upon us; stay from hell
Our poor souls with hydromel;[2]
Work us wax so fine, its flame
Be of God's the very name.

Bees, O autumn bees, that fled
Home with tribute for our dead,
Very gentle be your doom,
Dying on the ivy-bloom!

THE ROSARY OF BLOOD
Sorrowful Mysteries[3]

I

In the garden, sorrowful to death,
On Thy brow a blood that blossometh.

---

1 The biblical image of the burning bush signifies a miraculous apparition
    of the godly, often of the Virgin Mary.
2 A mixture of honey and water, which, when fermented, constitutes the
    drink, mead.
3 Incidents of great mystical significance in Christ's life.

II

By the column Thou are fiercely scourged,
And the mad, recoiling current urged.

III

Crown of thorns so planted on Thy head
We behold a crown of blood instead.

IV

Now Thy bitter Cross they lay on Thee—
With Thy blood Thou dost bedew the Tree.

V

Nails that rivet to the Cross so slow,
Force the sluices of the blood to flow;
From Thy Heart a ready cistern fills.
Blood and water the centurion spills.

DREAD ST. MICHAEL[1]

Dread St. Michael, that with God prevails—
    Priests, punctilious, insist
    That thou canst not be
    Guardian Angel unto me,
    Who am but a child.

Thou art come from Hell most wild;
Thou the awful lake dost see
Where souls wail eternally;
And dependent from thy wrist
Are the judgment scales.

    —O hist,
It is somewhere in the sacred tales
Thou wert guardian to my Jesus small.
When He cradled in a stall

---

1 The warrior Archangel.

Thou didst hold Him safe within the rails;
From the murderer beguiled,
From the adder, from the brook,
Thou didst shield Him: it may be
Thou didst guide Him to His Mother's knee,
When too far He dreamed in mountain-nook.

Egypt, with its demon-gods in bales,
And its sphinxes of the mighty fist,
Thou didst lead the little One among,
And protected Him from wrong,
     Who was but a child.

Dread St. Michael, whose I am!
Save me from the fiends that damn—
So persuasive and so meek,
I may almost touch thy cheek—
Save me, so thy power with God prevails!

SHE IS SINGING TO THEE, *DOMINE*![1]

She is singing to Thee, *Domine*!
     Dost hear her now?
She is singing to Thee from a burning throat,
And melancholy as the owl's love-note;
She is singing to Thee from the utmost bough
     Of the tree of Golgotha,[2] where it is bare,
And the fruit torn from it that fruited there;
She is singing ... Canst Thou stop the strain,
     The homage of such pain?
Domine, stoop down to her again!

---

1 O Lord.
2 The place where Christ was crucified.

CAPUT TUUM UT CARMELUS[1]

I watch the arch of her head,
As she turns away from me ...
I would I were with the dead,
Drowned with the dead at sea,
All the waves rocking over me!

As St. Peter turned and fled
From the Lord, because of sin,
I look on that lovely head;
And its majesty doth win
Grief in my heart as for sin.

Oh, what can Death have to do
With a curve that is drawn so fine,
With a curve that is drawn as true
As the mountain's crescent line? ...
Let me be hid where the dust falls fine!

---

1 Song of Solomon 7: "Thine head upon thee *is* like Carmel"—usually
translated into modern English as "Your head crowns you like Mount
Carmel." This is part of a lover's sensuous celebration of every part of
the beloved's body.

7. From *Whym Chow: Flame of Love* (1914)

[The two women owned various pet dogs over their lives, but none was as dear to them as the russet-coated Chow dog, bought by Cooper for Bradley, that they named Whym Chow (possibly after Edward Whymper, the mountaineer and artist who had recently been a huge source of support for the women after Cooper's father's death in the Alps). The dog's death, in 1906, unleashed a torrent of poems in response to the women's extreme (and some were to say, excessive) grief. *Whym Chow* is, like *Dedicated*, in large part a collection of Cooper's poems, edited after her death by Bradley. In this volume Bradley appears to be paying homage simultaneously to her partner and her pet. Indeed, the poem "Trinity" tells us that the three were united in a trinity that was both spiritual and erotic, where the dog symbolised the love the women had for one another. This is the primary sentiment of the volume, repeated in many different ways in many of the poems therein. For example, poem VI reasserts the Chow's symbolic identity as the force of love. The women had formed a tripartite configuration with the dog long before 1907, as his role as "Dionysus" in poem IV demonstrates. Yet upon the dog's death and the women's conversion this Pagan trinity morphed rapidly into a reflection of divinity, and their love became a reflection of God's love. The dog's ghost after death seems to signify a more spiritual connection between the two women than the earthly, Pagan desire he emblematised during his life.

The subtitle of this volume is a reference to a mystical poem by St. John of the Cross: *The Living Flame of Love*. Bradley and Cooper requested a loan of the poem from their friend the poet-turned-priest John Gray, a man who had an important literary and theological influence on their work. The poem is addressed to a woman, Doña Ana de Peñalosa, a rich widow, and is accompanied by a prose commentary that speaks of the Holy Spirit as a purgatory flame, and the gradual operation of fire upon the soul. St. John's poem enabled the presence of Whym Chow, in the women's holy Trinity, to be fleshed out in sacred terms with the nice conceit of the russet-coloured dog becoming a metaphor for the purgatorial "flame" that would cleanse the two women of blame for their previous blasphemy. Indeed, the first letter of each poem is in flame-coloured ink.

Yet none of this insight into the theological context for their sacred eulogy to the dog can sidestep the central impression that this volume is almost a parody of itself in its deification of the animal. The question of the book's "campness" must be addressed if we are to consider Michael Field's work seriously. Many of the poems not included here were left out because of their ludicrous sentimentality. Yet in the volume as a whole there is a hint of self-awareness that suggests Bradley and Cooper were treading a fine line between genuine sentiment and a self-conscious, quasi-postmodern parody of a long tradition of Victorian pet elegies. Why else would the book be covered in russet suede to mimic the dog's coat? There is, at some level, a certain whimsicality about this textual Whym Chow that aestheticises the loss even as it grieves for it.]

Source: *Whym Chow: Flame of Love*, by Michael Field (London: Privately Printed at The Eragny Press, 1914).

[EPIGRAPH]

"Leave the fire ashes, what survives is gold."

IV.

O Dionysus, at thy feet
The beauteous reveller, our joy, we lay—
Our Bacchic Cub, the dear tamed animal,
So often touched with ivy-coronal,
Who, breathing day
As from a mountain, found thy worship sweet.

O god, o vine, on his dead side
Stain of thy grape: above his corse we drink
In sacrament to thy divinest folly
That made all creatures of bright revel holy,
Chose them to link
With god and mænads in one rapture wide.

He loved thy torch of vivid flame,
He loved the breath of life, the rush, the glance
Of eyes from inmost happiness, and splendid
His glow as on his joyance he attended
With countenance
Of merchant over jewels of deep fame.

Receive him, tragic god of tendrilled fire—
Our sweetest, let us rove and rove with him.
We pledged him in thy grape. Leave us not lonely!
But bring him and thy wine-cup with thee only—
Our Chow, our Whym,
And thirst should end, and passion bind desire.

V. TRINITY

I did not love him for myself alone:
I loved him that he loved my dearest love.
O God, no blasphemy
It is to feel we loved in trinity,
To tell Thee that I loved him as Thy Dove
Is loved, and is Thy own,
That comforted the moan
Of Thy Beloved, when earth could give no balm
And in Thy Presence makes His tenderest calm.

So I possess this creature of Love's flame,
So loving what I love he lives from me;
Not white, a thing of fire,
Of seraph-plumèd limbs and one desire,
That is my heart's own, and shall ever be:
An animal—with aim
Thy Dove avers the same....
O symbol of our perfect union, strange
Unconscious Bearer of Love's interchange.

VI.

What is the other name of Love?
Has Love another name?
Yea, one that, when he came
To his Creator's feet above,
Met his lone ear and thrilled
His grievous want, and filled
The chamber of his birth with new live fire.

"Response, my Answer" was God's cry.
O gift of joy to hear

The Godhead's welcome clear.
As heart to heart the vast
Desires were gathered fast—
Love as the source of Love, Love the Reply.

Response! O little Love, O little Chow!
O Answer! What is Love's most answering bliss?
What is Love's happiness alert but this
To welcome? And thy rage of welcome how
Should words tell dim—the bound,
The dances round and round,
As if the sun had come down carrying love
Instead of light, with all his rays and power,
With the wild spinning of his heat above,
And in thy body had his hour
Of cabriole and circle on the ground!
What beating of fine, little feet!
What slouch of ears like banners drooped
To the great Victor all the soul would greet!
Thy tail—the thyrse of flame that Delphi[1] knew,
Thy dance—such dance as on Cithæron[2] tossed!
Thy cries as circling sea-birds mew;
Thy stretched paws the defiance of all fear,
With the adored in sight and near
To touch and smell—the fine nose stooped
In midst of ecstacy to prove it sure,
Not a vain presence in its visit lost:
Athwart thine eyes the fierceness of a gem,
That drowns its flashes and then rescues them,
Casting on lucent gold about them set
Magnificence still with doom's flooding wet—
Eyes that no separation could enure[3]
To loss of their one love, their utter fate.
O Chow, the glory and the gold-furred state
That smote beyond the strength of any verse,
And all its pride in gold, even to rehearse—
The state that surged around a daily chance,
If thy Beloved should enter: in thy Dance
A worship; in thy light, a universe.

1   In Greek mythology, the site of the legendary oracle.
2   Mount Cithaeron: a range of mountains between Attica and Boeotia,
    which was the setting for many legendary events of classical mythology.
3   Perhaps this should have read "endure."

VIII. OUT OF THE EAST

Jasper and jacinth, amber and fine gold,
The topaz, ruby, the fire-opal, grey
And lucent agate covered thee with glory,
O Eastern Prince from fuming China hoary,
That on thy orient rug celestial lay,
Thy coat a web of treasure manifold!

And from thy glinted eye what lust of eye,
What joy in having joy to thy desire,
What potency out of thy gold to fashion
Thy slaves to aptness for each regal passion,
What ambush and what ease of rampant fire!
What somnolence of ancient cruelty!

And what endowment of what frenzied joy,
That our cold flesh of the Hesperides[1]
Can reach not, ... eyes and teeth and feet all blended
In pomp of dithyramb[2] that only ended
By sleep, through which the god remitting frees
His votary from fire-flames that destroy.

Yet in thee such a bowing-down to doom:
Docile and proud with humbleness a spell,
Thy talisman of universal splendour—
That with necessity by still surrender
Thou wouldst be level whatsoe'er befell,
Nor by defeated light establish gloom.

And mysteries, old mysteries like stars
Rose in thy spread gaze, and thy thought was filled
With worship, with perpetual adoration;

---

1 Daughters of the evening star (Hesper): singers of sweet song, and the
   guardians of the golden apples that were given to Hera on her marriage
   to Zeus. These nymphs were described as living in the extreme West,
   and this reference seems primarily to refer to the West in opposition to
   the mystical, colourful East.
2 In ancient Greece this was a hymn to Dionysus. It came to signify more
   generally a choral lyric with vocal exchanges between the leader and the
   chorus.

Thy very breath of being an oblation;
Infinitude a faith life never stilled,
The lustier for its chains, its wrongs and jars.

O Orient Prince, thou Asian Bacchant, dear
To Eleutherius,[1] how thou knewest love!—
Thy Mistress thy hot self thou couldst not render;
Yea, with indifference, a strain untender,
She being thy very self, thou would'st not move
Even to caress her, for caress too near.

Thou would'st not break thy trance save at the hour
Of welcome: then the glories of thy race,
Then dance and sovereign courtesy, elation
As thou would'st heap the substance of a nation
At feet that had the ritual of thy face,
And all thy gems in flash, thy gold in shower.

IX.

My loved One is away from me
Whom thou dost love. O Chow,
That with my outward eyes I may not see
Thy gaze that fathomed how
Intent were thy furred ears with such emotion,
As in a shell is straining for the ocean!

My loved One is away from me;
I may not turn to find,
Chow, in thy senses the infinity
That in my senses pined
For her we loved in absence and together,
My feet, thine eager paws, questioning whether

The loved One would come back to us
Or now, or soon, or late.
Oh, in our vigil to be solaced thus,
By the unbounded pressure of one yearning
Vaster than we, no pause in it, no turning!

---

1   "Eleutherius" means "deliverer," and sometimes represents Dionysus or
Zeus.

Our loved One was away from each:
Your eyes burnt signals, mine
Sprang the same flambeaux the same aid to reach
Of Guardian Love divine—
That it would give us back our sole possession,
For whom our thoughts, breath, hearts kept holy cession.

Our loved One was away from you—
O Chow, the sighs, our sighs!
And what I murmured you would listen to
With your far-open eyes,
Raised in the anguish of a want immortal ...
Lo, than didst sweep as hawk against the portal!

For, lo, our loved One surely came,
Lo, she was at the door!
Your eyes demanded Yes, in running flame;
Mine gave them Yes—no more:
And we had reached our vigil's end in gladness
Of so great ease from terror it seemed madness.

My loved One is away from me.
O Chow, no more, we twain
My lovely fellow-lover, hear and see
And breathe for her again!
You ever have your Love ... yet do not leave me,
Nor in my mortal wake of love bereave me!

My loved One is away—my cry!
Be at my side, unseen,
Alert, like strange Anubis,[1] toward the sky,
As you so oft have been.
O Chow, my little Love, you watch above her;
Watch still beside me, be with me her lover!

---

1 One of the Egyptian gods of the Underworld, who guided the souls of
   the dead. He is represented in the form of the dog (or a human with a
   dog's head)—an animal greatly revered by the Egyptians. Anubis was
   often represented as the guard of other gods and was associated with a
   dog's ability to keep watch by night as well as by day.

XXII.

Sleeping together: Sleep,
The lull of thy breath on the air
That held the lull of our breath there;
Or movements in that former deep
Of night that was before the world—
Movements of thy form re-curled,
On a sigh, a pearl in seas
Shut down dark in mysteries;
Or a snuffling by the bed
Of thy fair-created head;
All of Genesis from dense
Covert gloom, till, issuing thence,
Motion, sigh of heart, caress
Came through sable void to bless.

Eating together: food,
Rest of continuance! Like a Song
To feel it made us blithe and strong!
To see thee greet with us the good
Of such nurture as could hold
Thee so eager, bright and bold,
We with all our deeds and dreams
Re-illumed, as were the gleams
Of thy savouring body, till
Complement of power did fill
Thee and us, that side by side
We in newness might abide.

Breathing together: breath,
The friendship of all things with us,
The means by which just then and thus
What word the sun in sunshine saith
We could hear and welcome it,
By our mingled eyes sunlit.
And of breath we shared the breeze,
Listened to the mammering trees,
Elf-possessed to make such sound;
Or against the river's bound
With thrilled trepidation ran.
Yea, of breath, the breath of man
And of beast we knew the spell

Of our bodies, relished well.

Loving together, love,
The flame that even in locked-up sleep
Had place, as in the rock, closed deep,
Is set the spark with rock above;
That in our morning-open eyes
Took on flash of full replies—
From the couch, where thou had'st slept,
To our bed unwavering leapt,
And from us in thee would light
All the sanctuaries of sight:
Flame that, did we only eat,
Made a sacrifice of meat,
Something eaten from the fire
That had brought a god down nigher:
Flame that while we breathed made air
As itself a warmth and fair
Shining through us of content—
Life with sacred passion blent.

Joying together: joy,
The call to us of ivy, pine
And a Voice of One divine
Who kindled the wild creatures coy
Even as he kindled women, men
Into choruses and then
Set them to life's dance of praise,
Rhythmic over devious ways;
Who with flambeaux hung bright spears,
Lifted panthers' tingling ears,
Taught the bliss that must express
Unity of blessedness
When a god to mortal things
Their delight for worship brings.

Grieving together—No!
Scarce any sorrow save the dull
Shades that will mar things beautiful,
The cloud upon day's promised glow,
The walk along the hills denied ...
We no longer at thy side!—
That was absence, deathly space,

Holding not the Loved One's face,
Sorrow at Creation's blank
While drear distance slowly sank
Coffin-timbers in each heart:

Absence; oh, we grieved apart.
Now that thou art dead we meet
Still together in the sweet
Company of close-drawn breath,
If we banish grief from death.

XXIX.

O Chow, the Peace of her I love above
All else, O feeder of her heart forlorn,
Sustainer of her torn,
Conflicted Nature with a seamless love!

Her Silence!—Light her, as with torch of fir,
O little flambeau, that hath never smoked,
Never grown dim, but ever leapt for her
Forth of its Bacchic resin; and evoked
By breath of her alone, would blaze and stir
Through desolation mountain-mists that choked
Dead hollows, till its presence came
Through them triumphant, with unbated flame.

Still love her, little Chow, still love thy Own,
For solely by thy leaping love she keeps
Live now on earth; and, of thy light alone,
By surety of thy brand that never sleeps,
Will she tread out her wandering with no moan,
Nor die! Unless thy ruddy flambeau leaps,
Naught can assuage her grief,
No mortal nor immortal give relief.

8. From *Dedicated: an Early Work by Michael Field* (1914)

[Two days after Cooper's funeral in December 1913, Bradley suf-
fered a haemorrhage. Severely ill, she could do no more than "rail
angrily against" Cooper's obituary notices. "Nothing in the least
adequate has yet been done—nothing of her work given," she
wrote.[1] In March 1914 she began to collect Cooper's early work
to be published under the title *Dedicated*.

Most of the poems date from 1900. In July of that year, after
a long illness, the women went on holiday to the New Forest and
stayed there for seven weeks. In direct contact with the wood ("I
am the Forest's and the Forest is mine," she wrote in *Works and
Days*), Cooper found again her poetic voice and began to com-
pose a series of poems based on Bacchic themes. In her last
evening in the Forest, and feeling "a Poet again," she decided to
put the poems together under the title *Dedicated* and give them to
Michael as a gift. Back in London, Cooper asked Charles Rick-
etts to design the volume. Thus, though the posthumous publi-
cation suggests a dedication to "Field," the volume was in fact
"naturally & inevitably Dedicated to Michael": Cooper gave it to
her on Michael's birthday, 27 October 1900 (see "Diaries"
Section, p. 269).

In this powerful selection of poems, we find Michael Field
again reverting to the pagan, to Dionysian themes. "Dionysus
Zagreus" represents the wine God eluding his hunters, the
Titians (who will eventually tear him to pieces). "Genethliacs of
Wine," a birthday poem, describes Messalina's excessive passion
for, and Bacchanalian marriage with, Silius. "Sylvanus Cupres-
sifer" sings the divinity of fields and forests. Many of the poems
explore transgressive, often even aggressive, sexuality. They sing
of myths associated with heteroeroticism, homosexuality, trans-
vestism, and transsexuality, as in "Caenis, Caeneus." The poem is
based on the story of the daughter of Atrax, Caenis, who, by the
will of Poseidon, was changed into a man and renamed Caeneus.

The final poem, "Fellowship" is a touching conclusion to both
the collection and to the work of Michael Field, and can be read
as Bradley's obituary of her beloved Henry, "Her Glory, Her
Delight!"]

Source: *Dedicated: an Early Work of Michael Field* (London: G.
Bell, 1914).

---

1   Sturgeon, 56.

DIONYSUS ZAGREUS

Ai, ai! The pursuit of my hunters illuded,
I pant, I stretch on the spines of this desolate forest.
Rock on rock, as bone on bone in a body
Sucked of its flesh by the wind and sunshine and days,
Rock is loose-piled on rock; and below, a continuous whiteness
Roars in my ears and swirls through my sight. O torrent,
Beguiler of those who would murder me, savage to keep
My anguish in prison to hear and to watch thy flood
Crave, as no multitude craves for its prey,
      For my loneliness, sorrow,
All pain I can know 'mid the pulses of breath,
All fears with their smarting languor, all wrongs I suffer
That heave the sources of grief and yet, as an earthquake
    swallows
A fountain, banish my tears down their blinded gulfs,
O torrent, you need my godhead in manhood to stay you
From hunger so infinite ... those whom thy fury baffled
Had need but of flesh, my flesh and the jets of my blood.
I lie on the spines that prick me, on moss-chilled soil,
No longer pursued.... Ai, ai! but above me, around,
Beneath me pursuit, as a Power of the earth and air,
Rules in the silence, the silence no Men approach.
The rocks evoke a terror, like lions that c[r]ouch;
The stream gives the terror of appetite fierce to spring
On my passions in lust, and the wind moves around my form
As it wandered in stealth to capture: the mountain eagle
Watches grey on the roofless walls of rock.
I, who love the shooting and summer of trees,
See the pale firs above, the constant-hued,
The mad-rent boughs of mourning that has no end,
Cybele's tortured grief for the love-lost Atys.
Grieving trees of the dark shade, how I dread you!
I, the son of a god, in the form of man,
Lie on the troublous spines with a mighty burthen
Thrust on my human weakness, the burthen of craft,
Of Nature's patience and craft that pursue a mortal
Steadily, open-eyed, with terrible gold in the gaze,
Sunshine's pitiless blank. I ran from men, the cruel,
That sought my life; but here I lie down, I slumber
Struck with the charm of the elements, held submissive
To vast inflictions, to impious, secret Death.

O trees, pale firs of the dark, dark shade,
O scenting wind, O rock-edged quietude,
O voice that slides like thunder through the gorge,
O eagle-wings at poise, I yield, I sleep,
   Laid on the moss-chilled ground
   With rhododendron's hard tufts
A ridge about my body as a tomb's,
I yield to die. I who have fled from men
In gnashing hate, with speed as swift as hate,
   I yield undone
To you, the great, obliterating airs,
To you, the world's rapacious substances
Grown still to feed—earth, sunlight, and yon bird
That watches grey above the roofless rocks.
   My father's bird,
   His witness looking on—
Not sent to feed on me, his child, but sent
To bear the record of this great temptation,
And how it fails or triumphs, to the sky,
Where in unthwarted power the gods abide.
   O kingly feathers sweep the stone!
   It may be I mistake
The meaning of these watchers at my side,
As I mistook, O bird, thy hoary guard.
   Zeus, can it be,
My father, that this dreadful peace is made
About me for my glory, not defeat?
I must lie quiet and humble on the ground,
As if in very deed obdurate Death
   Were on me parched and cold....
Thus I must lie until the silence break
Again into disclosure: yet no more
The wilderness repels, where all things wait.

  .   .   .   .

   The preying, slant-head bird,
   With eye and beak intent upon my sloth,
   Wheels, now I raise my limbs,
   Reveals himself august,
God's messenger, my father's twin-throned joy.
   I rise, I bend the pale firs to my grasp,
I break the whitened whorls, the honied cones;
I of such sorrows, greater than a man's,
I, the rejected, hunted, mad, unwelcome,

I weave these tragic bunches in a wreath,
Fit crown for ever, of my misery;
Yea, I am crowned with the dark-shading boughs
I dreaded and I choose them as my own;
Heart's anguish in a garland, in a knot
Of cones and shadow-spines upon my wand,
My wand cast down beside me when the force,
Next to a god's, of Nature laid me low.
                    Evoe! Ye rocks,
A King leaps over you with crown of fir,
With sceptre of the hard fruit of the fir,
Choosing to turn all sorrow into life,
All darkness into motion, all mad pain
And burthen into realms beneath his sway.
O torrent, from thy writhing voice I learn
The rhythm of this my empire, dithyrambs
That rush and break and rage ineffably,
Songs of the Clamour-King. O rocks, O rocks,
One day my ritual shall beat your floors
With dance and feet that scorn you, scoop your sides
To show amid you to the world my grief,
My conquest—you subservient. And, O breeze,
That coveted my breath, to you I give
My victor-cries, the waving of my garlands,
The carriage of my music through the air.
            Evoe! Hence, hence, O Eagle! Fly, yea, fly!
            The wings stretch.... He is gone.
Zeus welcome him! O terrible, strange Powers,
That plotted for your prey, receive your lord.
O solitude of rock and stream and fir,
I stand erect amid my enemies,
And draw them into sanctitude and faith,
                    Making the woe-struck fir
My chaplet, and the hungry rocks my haunt,
The stream, the stream my anthem turbulent.
I climb! The eagle in Olympus lights
Beside my father's knee: the heaven receives
My father's smile. The terrible still forest
Breathes conquered.... If I climb into the snows,
And through them where the unseen slopes descend,
It may be there are vineyards, it may be
Some streak of gay, gold leafage for my hair,
Some grass, some noiseless waters: but I climb.

THE GENETHLIACS OF WINE[1]

Rome and the Palace-gardens and October,
And vintage on the trellises, great weight
Of stony-massive clusters, drab and sober,
Their purple screened in umbrage against Fate:

Their leaves with hint of blood-stain on the tarnished
Warm green of autumn and their tendrils dry.
'Tis vintage, and the trellises are garnished
With wreathing limbs of vintagers, sky-high.

Who catch and rend away and then drop under
The mass of turbid grapes that on the ground
Shoot out in light confession they are plunder
Worth laughing to receive: a jewel-mound.

And laughter breaks from boys and girls, commingled
With children, baskets, tuns and stammel juice;
A seething troop where nothing can be singled
As coy to let the mirth-distraction loose.

With hats of sunlit straw and garlands heavy
Of branching vine-leaves and of clumps of fruit,
The youths and maidens in an amorous bevy
Their pile of grapes down in the presses shoot:

Where crimson feet receive the rush, and splashes
Of grape-must give to clowns the stain of war,
As bunch on top of bunch, with melting flashes,
The harvest runs to wine, the presses pour.

While jests and toyings and wild untuned noises
Love feasts on pertly nor will be appeased;
The lads are satyrs and each girl that poises
Her pannier on her head is rash and pleased.

The Palace-gardens echo, for the revel
Around the running vats and web of vines
Is taken up with rapture from the level
Of the great platform where the Palace shines.

---

1 "Genethliacs" means predicting the future events of life from the stars
that preside at birth.

The sobbing cry that cleaves the grapes when trodden
Dies round still feet; the vintagers are dumb:
And from a bosomed heap of fruit half-sodden
An infant cries . . . The mother does not come.

She listens, as a chorus, mid its thunder,
Star-spotted faun skins and slant ivy-staves,
Its ribbon-fluttered drums, the hands that sunder
On cymbal-clashes, down the garden raves.

With hair afloat and wanton silks wide-flowing
The Empress-harlot Messalina[1] speeds
The rout of Bacchanals, her forehead glowing
Toward Silius, the enchanted youth she leads.

There is unknown profaneness in her carriage:
For mid soul-stricken witnesses—her lord
Away at Ostia—she in open marriage
Has knit to her the lover last adored.

Her passion cried for vintage; she was weary
Of lust unpunished, unwithstood excess.
What was her love but dereliction dreary
Without an end or pleasure's painfulness.

She would be mad and smart with joy and tingle
With ache of panic; she would clasp despair
And win it death by dying; she would mingle
A candour with a courage past compare.

So she has claimed defiant by the altar
To sanctify her paramour her own;
To publish such desire as will not falter,
Co-equal with her life-blood, with her throne.

And now she feasts intractable, the sunny,
Loud revel in her wake, her lover gripped
Beside her, on his brow the sun like honey
Spread flat, his mouth impassionate, red-lipped;

---

1 Third wife of Roman Emperor Claudius. In his absence, she married
   Caius Silius. Her promiscuity was notorious. She came to be synony-
   mous with all the faults and vices of the Roman world.

His eyes a glory as when steel is flooded
At battle-heat with noon; to right and left
His golden-tressèd neck, dark ivy-hooded,
Beats with the music as if sense-bereft.

The husbandmen are scattered and their labour
Is turned to sport by noble vintagers:
Some dance upon the press with hoisted tabor,
A dozen heap the ground with cumbering furs.

The tumult of bare limbs and veils together
Is like a whirl of doves above new seed:
And one might doubt, who stood to listen, whether
A cry could pierce the storm from brass and reed.

But no one drains the vessels overrunning;
The vat stands flooded and the soil drinks deep
As old Silenus, while these Bacchants, shunning
The ladders, pluck from lower vines that creep.

The Empress dances: she has lost the measure
Of mortal empire, and the heaven and earth
Have added wings to freedom, wings to pleasure;
A calm is made for dizziness of mirth.

Young Silius, frantic, rocks his head, surrounded
By arms that shake the castanets amain;
While boyhood and his early youth confounded,
As he were drowning, glide before his brain.

The orgies at their height—as fire is riven
By wind in devious streams, so restlessly,
With sudden panic from the concourse driven,
One, Vettius, starts aside and climbs a tree.

Then terror circles through the dance, an anguish
Of limitless constraint; the pipes break off
Upon a shriek, the whirr and triumph languish;
Some dancers, struck with guilt, their badges doff—

Their panther-skin and garland: all would follow
The climber's eyes; they shout, they wait, they yell;
And he sees nothing save a distance hollow
Of any sign that might disclose their spell.

The tragic moments pause, as dead for token;
Till to unblenching life each ear awakes,
For Vettius from the turret-tree has spoken,
And made the silence valid that he breaks.

"Io, Io! I see a cloud." The Empress ceases
Her dance to laugh an echoing laugh and cry
"What further portent?" "The small cloud increases,
It moves above the plain, benights the sky;

"A cloud of dust." Impatient of the story
Their satyr-watchman tells, the maddest climb.
"It moves from Ostia"—Every face turns hoary.
"It will sweep on us in a little time.

"The Emperor leaves his sacrifice impassioned
To strike our treason, aweless of his pride.
That cloud is by his furious coming fashioned;
His armed centurions through the country ride."

The Empress throbs, yet turns her eyes elated
With desperation, a sweet rage, a charm
Devoted on the eyes of him new-mated,
Yet binds his neck with her remorseless arm.

He wakes as children into youth must waken;
Response is gold in eyes and smile; he finds
Profusion where was nothing, and, unshaken
By fear, his arm about her body winds.

And now the turning spheres, the endless quiver
Of tides and light are rivalled by these two
That dance on threatened and sublime deliver
Their perfect life to motion as a clue.

All may behold their mystery; a stranger
Would see that death alone could break their dance,
An end engulf it; there could be no danger
From interception nor discountenance:

None, for the God of Vintage loves such lovers,
The god whose sap is wine, who ripes for doom,
Who in the transport of the year discovers
Divinest mettle that exacts a tomb.

They breathe to end their joy, they dance as fellows
Of Spring, the ocean-waves, the stars, the rain,
And of the movement of that zest that mellows
The grape for autumn, cornlands for the wain.

A blow! The Emperor's tribune strikes abhorrent
The impious boy to earth, the Empress down
On bursting grapes, that in her life-blood's torrent
Lose all their started rivulets and drown.

She sinks into the spume and plants a whiteness
Deep in the ruddied clusters of her bed:
And thus she sleeps a Bacchanal the brightness
Of noon's impartial flame avouches dead.

Then round her crowd the vintagers, returning
A chorus to the field her passion trod:
And over her magnificent, unspurning,
Rests as her meed the harvest of their god.

DE PROFUNDIS[1]

The grey world of the dead is conquered—all
Its coolness, unconcern; its misty pall
Of cavern-air, its sacred tripod-fumes
Prophetic, all its sunken gems and metals,
Its germs of plant and fruit and summer petals,
Its laws that breed the world, its roots and tombs;

Conquered! The shadows know it by their breath
Warm on lip-ridges of the ice of death;
They know it by the comfort in their eyes,
And by the flute-like sympathies that waken
Each pulse and vein, of music long-forsaken;
They know it by a passion to arise:

They lift themselves and move. They cannot see
The spring-tide changing Dis[2]—that cannot be,

---

1 The title of Oscar Wilde's famous love letter to his lover, Lord Alfred
Douglas, which was written from his prison cell at Reading Gaol in 1897.
2 Another name for Hades (also known as Pluto), King of the Under-
world and god of the dead.

Where all is solemnness of blindfold glades;
They cannot see the spring, but in the hollow
Unmirroring, vast, their feet are blessed and follow
Some bent of beauty twilight overshades.

And then the dusk grows blue across its web;
The sable in the blue begins to ebb
To pure sky-azure, and the ghosts sweep white
As clouds of April: in the mighty clearness
The gems and metals shake themselves and drearness
Reels with their chequer. Pluto, there is light;

And in the light thy Conqueror! He lies
All love across a shadow's knee, his eyes
Beneath her gaze as if he were a child;
The budded vine-stems of his hair declining
Down to her feet, his level body shining
Under her bosom with the grave-clothes piled,

His bloom of life surrendered to her arms:
His mouth, soft, open for her kiss, embalms,
Like crevice honey-filled, the air she draws.
This youth that is her babe she looks on powerless
To fondle him, for she has tasted hourless
Duration of despair that slowly thaws.

Then first across her brain the image dawns
Of Thebes, her city, and those genial morns
She parted from a god unseen as sleep;
Till, by sore lust for seeing him o'ertaken,
Fire swept her blind. And can her eyes awaken
To look on joy and yet their vision keep?

Can she at last behold her very son,
Who might not see her god, or must she shun
His grace divine of smile and laughing touch,
That claim her from her cinder-desolation,
That are her mighty lover's own creation
Soliciting her eyes to feed, to clutch.

Again flames spring in rage; they swell and smite
Her orbs; there is jagged frenzy in her sight,
That fails resplendent with its quick desire;

But from the lightning-stroke her son has wielded
Tears rain: the Mother, from her passion shielded,
Weeps silently above the lightning's pyre.

And thus she bows herself and seeks the mouth
That never sought her breast: she stills her drowth
With kisses ... and the Dead refresh their love
Beholding; all the coverts pulse and listen;
The roots, a fringe round yellow corms that glisten,
Drink rain in Hades for the spring above.

Rose-tender mid the phantom's direful clothes,
The child of Zeus and Semele[1] still glows
As sun throughout its morning to a height
Of triumph—for the phantom glows with rapture,
And is the woman he has lived to capture
For Heaven and Zeus and unforbidden sight.

"Mother, I knew thee when the nymphs bent down
On Nysa's[2] sward to touch me, and my frown
Met their smooth finger-prints; at shadow-fall
I sorrowed for thee, till I sought thee, lonely,
Round olive-boles, believing thou wert only
Warm-screened among them, hiding for my cry.

"I knew thee when the lambs lay still and slept,
A single tree above them: and I wept
On summer banks to feel how firm it were
To own thy comfort; I have never striven
For joy but I was seeking thee, nor thriven
Save for such hopes the want of thee would stir.

"Mother, when Ariadne[3] smiled her smile
Brought me this sun-glow on thy face. Awhile
I triumphed over earth, the kings, the laws;
Then old Silenus[4] told me of thy story,

---

1 Dionysus.
2 The place where Dionysus was raised by Nymphs.
3 Dionysus married Ariadne, who was known for helping Theseus kill the
   Minotaur.
4 Satyr associated with Dionysus.

Told me of Pluto's kingdom, deep and hoary,
The thwarting rivers, the hound-guarded doors.

"Through coils of rock I reached the Stygian flood,[1]
That came as sodden snow upon my blood;
But the black oarsman, dazzled, took his seat,
Rowed and forgot he cleaves the flood for money;
The hell-hound licked my hand as if for honey,
The groves became aware and voiced my feet.

"I broke a spell, and yet with no surprise
The shadows raised their heads and gave me eyes
Full of the earth and lenient. Hades' tomb
With all it held took heed I sought my mother,
Not spouse nor bond-maid, nay, nor any other
Than she who bore me darkling in her womb.

One tall grey form among the thousands more
Drew me and owned me by the look it wore;
Those veils would cling to me, the unseen face
Be as my birth-star, holy, sure, and fateful.
The shadow's solitude was cursed and hateful ...
A son was in thy arms' abiding-place."

"My child, my love ... My child! But thou canst speak;
I cannot: my unfathomed want grows weak
Before its bliss; and thou canst never hear
What pain has called for thee, what sunk thanks-giving
My dearth of thee yet made shouldst thou be living,
The light upon thee, while my breast lay drear.

"You raise me from my ashes to the throne
Of Zeus within the heavens: and not alone
You take me past the star-sparks to my youth,
But to my future also, to the lover
No fearful vow, no fear, nor shame shall cover
Away from worship eagle-eyed as truth.

"Let us go hence, above; for at thy side
There is no fire I may not now abide,

---

1 The River Styx, river of the Underworld.

No lightning and no deity." The souls
Pant with the sweeping motion through their valleys
Of son and mother as they pass, like galleys
Tide-borne, while severed Dis together rolls.

The visit of the Conqueror fades away
From each convinced recess: yet day by day
The Dead are cheered of those who carry grapes,
And smeared bold masks and flutes across the river,
Who tell that Eleutherios[1] is the giver
Of these new pledges to the Stygian shapes.

SYLVANUS CUPRESSIFER[2]

Et teneram a radice ferens, Sylvane, cupressum.[3]
Georg. I.

A forest glade: a muffling sound of boughs,
One ominous, sweet coo, small breaths about;
   And then a scowl, a doubt
If sun will fall through to the moss again;
Then floating on the floor a tide of wind.
One fir-tree joint creaks, with a twang of pain,
That lifts the feathers of the startled dove;
While the green pathway has a sense that comes
   Not from rude shades above,
Nor breezes with the pattering leaves behind,
But from one coming as the robber comes.

His little body, that can hardly serve
To keep itself on goat-haired, swagging legs,
Trembles and pauses, still and terrified
From creeping on; the little hairy side

---

1 The Liberator. This refers to Dionysus.
2 "Cupressifer" means "wood-bearing." The poem is about the love
  between Sylvanus (God of the forest) and the young boy Cyparissus,
  who was one of Apollo's lovers. Michael Field presents an idiosyncratic
  version of the myth in which Appollo turns Cyparissus into a cypress
  tree.
3 Virgil, *The Georgics*, Book I, line 20 (Latin): "And, Wood-king, thou,
  with a slim young cypress uptorn in thine hand."

Lifts with its terror: one hand stretched in span
For solitude most desolately begs,
The other hand lets drop with timorous swerve
A plant so black it seems beneath day's ban.

And straight I feel the wood-depths apprehend
That I, of mortal race, shall hold him bond;
Reluctantly they fear
As when the thunder-rain is gathered near
I see the flowers of wood-sage that before
The light had hidden, plainly see one frond
Of fern above all others twirl elate....
O panic! I could run; but hold the tighter
This half-god creature, while the nutted floor
Cracks with his strife against me, as I wait
His peace, yea, wait till the dulled woods flash brighter
        From threatening end to end.

A sunbeam grows: the butterflies are tilted
Each toward the other through the amorous air;
Wings speak of joy; wings, wings through every alley
Unstartled now are up and down, or dally
Or dance or pasture, but are everywhere.
Gone is the panic as of daylight thunder,
For he and I are reconciled, are still.
Beneath the growing beam of sun his wonder
Grew gentle: then a bird, whose every motion
Had been a start while terror lay around,
Rose from a holly-branch that trailed the ground,
And from a topmost branch of holly lilted,
        With open dew-drenched bill.

And we are friends, and I have led the creature
I know divine to roots where we may sit,
Have lifted from the track his sable plant,
Have shaken it from fly and ant,
And placed it in his hand that folds on it.
Now first I see his eyes and then his face ...
The eyes where confidence itself is hidden,
And all the other gentlenesses bidden
To lurk before they spring in one dark blaze,
Jump from their refuge to a stranger's heart:
And in the sheltered countenance I trace

No boorish sullenness, no churl disfeature,
But through the shyness woe
Of long ago.

Crowsfeet and little wrinkles weave their maze
Under the squills and birch-twigs of his crown,
And yet his front is simple with no frown;
And the lips, soft as women's, fall apart.
I woo his voice: words tread upon its tone
As feet on spines and moss of fragrant pile;
And on his mouth the fir-seed as he chews
Moves glidingly or drops or clings awhile:
He snaps a fly and now and then will muse
Till all the wood deep through is quiet as stone.

Yet hour by hour I learn from him his story,
For I have loved the woods and I may hear;
And I can listen till the pines are hoary
With eve and surgent moonlight and the dew.
He tells me he is Sylvan—and a fear
Booms from the doves' nest—how he once loved dearly
Young Cyparissus of the lovely locks;
How sweet the boy was in his eyes, how clearly
He was more godlike than the starry flocks,
Though bred on Earth and they withheld above.

He tells of the boy's love
For one red fawn, of how that shaggy head
Lay on the brilliant side, a spot of shade,
And his white arms clung tight,
Strained to the beast at noontide and at night;
Of how he watched it feed and as it fed
Enjoyed it and its appetite. Ah, never
Could Sylvan win the fair boy's fellowship
Unless that ruddy fawn were close or lying
At rest or softly sighing
Where scarce a breadth of shaded turf might sever;
And all the while from Cyparissus' lip
Bubbled a language chosen for his pet,
More tender than the tenderest human phrase
He used to Sylvan in the dear sunset
When they were close at heart in the last rays.

He tells of how, one August afternoon,
Wandering apart from the fantastic lad,
      He shot the forest deer,
And ate the ivory filberts as a boon,
And drank the stream from its brown shelves,
And lay, as hunters loose on leaves and glad
      To cool themselves;
And how, while lying thus, he chanced to hear
A movement through the deeps of fern, and shot.
      Ah, had he not!
He would have died to gather back that dart:
A cry went through the tree-tops, through his heart:
And in a dimple of the level fern
A well of darkness had been sunk and there
He found the boy he loved who would not turn
His face away from what was stretched below;
And Sylvan saw a rim of ruddy glow,
And knew what he had done and shuddered with despair.

And well he might despair: for on the sun
Cool evening breathed, yet Cyparissus lay;
And night entrenched itself among the pines,
Then waited, then made sortie and then won
The dales and chases from the green of day,
      Yet still he gave no signs,
No comfort, no forgiveness to the grief
That moaned beside his form, with no relief
Of tears, though dew was on the cloakless cheek.
Space filled with doom; leaves turned and slept once more;
A fruit fell ... and Sylvanus strove to speak,
But something smothered every sound before
He spoke: and then the strong adjacent wild
Was blown across ... and loneliness was made
For Sylvan evermore through bourn and glade.

At dawn he saw the stately firs were fresh
With shower, he heard them sigh.
The fir-pricks fell, the fir-boughs spread their mesh
Of foliage for laments from age to age;
While voiceless sorrow that could only die
Was huddled at his feet. He would assuage
At least the cold restriction of that wrong:

And at his word a funeral tree arose
Where Cyparissus lay, and there was song
Full through the tree and freedom of its woes.
Poor Sylvan heard; he saw the mourning fir
Rise up instead of that soft-greeting boy
   He loved so well;
He heard its music swell
With piteous plaint, and then he heard the joy
He had in love been powerful to confer.
He wept, he cried aloud, he bathed his hands
With weeping, and he came and broke some strands
Of foliage, that his sorrow might be able
To touch with lover's touch its misery.
Then the sun smote him; day received the tree,
And Sylvan wandered with his branches sable.

I listened to this story hours by hours,
While butterflies approached their fans to flowers;
While the green woodpecker was gliding hither
And thither 'mid the crannies of his bark;
While jays shook sky-ribbed feathers with a jeer,
And seeds or leaves or insects in the dark
Of silent shadows crackled far or near.
At last we parted; and I knelt to win
The drear serenity his blessing shed.
I saw his swagging goat-hoofs pass within
A bowery path that slanted round his head,
   And covered him away.
O Sylvan, I have known your lore, your sway,
O mourner of obscure and unhoused death,
   That reeks up from the balm
Of fallen leaves, of falling autumn fern,
At instants, through the fresh woods, on their breath,
I too have known, O little, gentle King,
   Your comforting—
To hear a sorrow of all sorrows sing:
   And I as you can turn
With measured feet afar where boughs are calm.

CAENIS CAENEUS

Yea, from the sea she won her will,
From Neptune of the restless waves,
The changeful channels and unfathomed caves:
By Neptune she had stood and prayed
He would her fickle need fulfil,
Give her a solace unessayed,
And let her life be altered to the core,
Dissevering it from what had been before.

He heard across his billows' fret
Her dear petition haunt his foam,
And echo down the waters of his home.
He climbed his car—it spouted brine;
And bannered with sea-ribbons wet,
His dolphins 'mid their issuing shine,
Paw in the daylight, and disclose their King,
Propitious to the maid's petitioning.

He heard her discontent make moan
Even as the ocean round his wheels
Itself will voice impatience when it feels
To yearn for alteration, yearn
For other being than its own,
And other tides to flow and turn,
And other shores and streams, and gulfs and bays,
For any end at last to weary days.

He loves to see her urgent face,
'Mid banners and 'mid ribbons wet
Of floating tresses the foam-bubbles set;
So covetous to have its prayer:
He loves to find it in that place,
To meet such lips and eyes as dare
Press for a mercy that the sea in vain
Cries after in fatigue nor may attain.

His realm for ever he would lose
If he could give dejected waves
The new existence that his ocean craves:
But he will grant this maiden's hope,
And let her reach, as she would choose,

Her goal of wellnigh impious scope,
She shall be changed—a very change be wrought,
And she become a man in form and thought.

For so she prayed, and so he heard,
And looked on her—with billow-crest
Bowed on her little foot and splashed her breast;
While from his head of mounded snow
His azure-netted veil he stirred,
That his compliance he might show
To the fair woman the last time she prayed:
Then toward her with magnificence he swayed.

Close in a mist he shut her round,
And with a voice that drew its tone
From welling deeps of prevalence unknown
He rent her soul away, he breathed
A valiant breath ... The mist unwound;
And, turning, with his veil he wreathed
His hoary mound of hair and waved adieu
Light-fingered to the youth that stood in view.

The shore was desolate, the boy
Saw the curled dolphin-tails divide
A coming wave and in blue fathoms hide:
Then turned to scan the cliff that rose
Up to the land. A curious joy
Hath made him to himself propose
The conquest of that overhanging height,
That faces him with challenge of its light.

He climbed, he feasted on the air
Drawn up from seaward by the rock;
He circled many a precipice and block,
Discovered, rifled in their holes
The sea-birds' nests, while everywhere
He started birds to veer in shoals,
And reached the grasses, shivering with nods,
High on the summit's scarcely-woven clods.

Affrighting was the silence high;
He felt no fright, he knew no pain
In treading over the unpeopled plain;

Sureness was on his nerve, his heart;
The tang of fern as he passed by,
The herd of deer, their eager start,
Their bound and their alluring eyes on him
Roused up the hunter's lust in every limb.

He wanted but the dart to slay:
So chased the fleeting creatures wide,
And breathless came where countryfolk abide.
A stranger, on the grass he laughed
And ate with them at close of day,
And of their liberal vintage quaffed.
He had no tales to tell, but they were bred
To chat in legend while they drank and fed.

It came to pass that Caeneus won
Men's praises when along the street
Or market-place he trod with buskin'd feet;
Though oft he strove with them in fight
And would no chance of quarrel shun,
Yet never was his piercing might
Struck down nor staggered by the rival's blow,
Nor any wound delivered by a foe.

Fame gave him of her noblest sport—
He hunted the Arcadian boar,
Across the forest heard its whining roar,
And stood beside its spiny heap;
He sailed on Argo[1] from the port
Of fell Iolchus[2] to the deep
Sicilian seas, and many wonders met,
And loved the sea he never might forget.

For when upon the sea, he felt,
As he beheld it fall and climb,
Misgivings, intimation of a time
Before he lived a man as now:
Against the vessel's side he knelt,
Or stood apart upon the prow,
And thought, till ever-baffled in his quest,
He put the strange, unguarded thought to rest.

---

1 The ship on which Jason sailed in quest of the Golden Fleece.
2 Jason's home.

Though when it came to him it charmed,
It harrowed him and made him reel
With sense of things too far away to feel:
And then he joined the sailor-throng,
For from that trance he woke alarmed;
Yea, ample-throated sang their song,
But with his eyes still on the fluent bars
Of sunny foam or grey beneath the stars.

And when on shore he passed a maid
Who tangled flowers about her hair,
She caught stray smiles, a question in the stare
That Caeneus fastened on her coil;
And by the bridges he delayed
To see the washers at their toil;
And when he wooed the girl whom he would kiss
Oft deemed he shared her shrinking from her bliss.

And so he loved and sailed and sang,
And fought in battle with his peers,
And laboured for his joy through glorious years;
Till at Pirithous'[1] marriage-feast
The fair Thessalian meadows rang
With fratricidal war, increased
By fumes of wine, as flashing Centaurs strove
To rape the women whom the Lapiths love.

There Caeneus roused him 'gainst the crew
Of ravishers, a mortal fight.
The cunning Centaurs weighed his wound-proof
  might,
And came on him with forest trees,
Rent and uprooted, that they threw
In masses, with gigantic ease,
Against the hapless warrior buried deep
By firs and oak-trees in a funeral heap.

Crushed down, he fainted in the sod,
Immovable, but living long

---

1 Pirithous was the King of the Lapiths, a tribe of Thessaly. At his
wedding, a battle broke out between the Lapiths and the Centaurs (who
were half-horse, half-man).

Without a sigh through the hot summer day:
His victors, who had wrought such doom,
Far over other valleys trod,
And left him proudly in his tomb;
Nor did they watch how through the trees amassed
Above their foe a bird, the Caenis, passed.

Then a fresh life began in air
And on the wing and in the tree:
Song, when the Spring was striking sunnily
Deep to the greenwood's heart-felt green;
Rest, when the night was everywhere,
And leaves for warmth and not for screen
Were blindly sought; and feasting, when the day
Touched into laughter dews that crept away.

The little space of wingèd time
Soon ended, and a nipping frost,
That over the black woodland crossed,
Laid low the Caenis-bird in death;
Still were the feet that loved to climb
The topmost bough, and cold the breath
That made aloud their music for the flowers,
And note on note more sweet o'erbrimmed the hours.

Thus earth is left behind at last,
And Hades covers in a soul
That nevermore will follow any goal;
The world of judgment is her home,
And here the lives that she has passed
Under the sky's tremendous dome
The maiden Caenis in her narrow days
Must ponder on, dividing blame or praise.

"And I am Caenis: once again
Her life of shadow I resume,
Closed in by walls and by prevailing doom,
Unable with my hand or will
The dreaming in me to attain,
Or any impulse to fulfil.
O ghost, thou art the Caenis thou wert born,
And Hades is thy fitting house forlorn.

"Well that I once could breast the sea
And lure from it the gift of change!
My maiden life could win no valid range,
Aye waiting impotent to win;
But with my manhood's sovereignty
I struck where woman's hopes begin:
The world was in each plan, in every deed;
Mine was the doing: for the rest no heed.

"God of the sea, I loved my life
Should leaven earth; I loved the heat,
The calm events, the merrymaking meet
For triumph and the ease of choice:
Then all was possible to strife,
And every moment might rejoice
In what it bred of its affiance high;
While every moment pushed the zest to die."

So she bemoans herself and weeps
Her spectral days and bends her sight
On heroes as they strive in spectral fight.
The vanity of all she sees
Or faintness on her sorrow sweeps,
For with a sudden run she flees
To a dark wood no tremble ever stirred,
And there she sobs "Ah, would I were a bird!"

EROS

"I have no Temple!"—"O young god,
Give me that wide, protecting hand ...
        No Temple in the land!"
He gave the hand, and foot by foot we trod.

Supine before us lay the Earth,
Held of impregning light and half-enskied,
        Yet adverse—woe betide!—
Uneasy, as the starving in their dearth.

A restless bull clanged on the air;
Bitten young buds, once red, were pressing red
        Up to frost-edges dead:
And on young things fell an unwearied care.

Birds were dark-cradled lutes, and men
And women listened, tho' they knew it not,
          But in a trance forgot,
Till from their flesh lutes echoed back again.

And secret in a green-leaved place,
The Beautiful, the Idalian goddess lay
          Watching a spring-flower's way
Up from the dark, with tremulous breast and face.

THE MASK

How bold the country where we danced ...
Great uplands, headed dark
With trees, as if night's sombre mark
Had sealed the vivid pasture hers,
With seal of convocated firs—
A noble country by her sign enhanced.

How wide the air and silence too,
A single bird's wing heard,
Save for the voices 'neath the bird
Of masqueraders on bright grass.
"Whose is this form I cannot pass?
Who is she?" And they breathed a name I knew.

She passed me in black velvet mask,
Black as the fir-knolls, black
As they upon the fields. Alack!
Why must I see her as once seen,
With tender pearl of face, a sheen
Of childhood in her face? What would I ask?

She came as comes a wind that treads
Round hill-brows in the night;
We stood together: "Oh, for sight
Of thee, my lost of many years!
I have forgotten, in my fears,
The way the hair about thy forehead spreads."

Powerless the Masker stood: I laid
The velvet softness by.
The curving mask ... Oh, I should die

To speak the bare face underneath;
It were the last moan of my death ...
In cottage-smoke of age it will not fade.

I shrieked and fled—how slow my feet,
And wild as they were chained!
She fled ... but where she stood remained
The empty sable mask. Alas,
That I had cast it on the grass—
O silent pastures and the bird's wing-beat!

FELLOWSHIP

I

In the old accents I will sing, my Glory, my Delight,
In the old accents, tipped with flame, before we knew the right,
True way of singing with reserve. O Love, with pagan might,

II

White in our steeds, and white too in our armour let us ride,
Immortal, white, triumphing, flashing downward side by side
To where our friends, the Argonauts, are fighting with the tide.

III

Let us draw calm to them, Beloved, the souls on heavenly voyage
    bound,
Saluting as one presence. Great disaster were it found,
If one with half-fed lambency should halt and flicker round.

IV

O friends so fondly loving, so beloved, look up to us,
In constellation breaking on your errand, prosperous,
O Argonauts!

.   .   .   .

Now, faded from their sight,
We cling and joy. It was thy intercession gave me right
My Fellow, to this fellowship. My Glory, my Delight!
    March 1914

9. From *The Wattlefold: Unpublished Poems by Michael Field* (1930)

[This volume consists almost entirely of poems written in the final part of Michael Field's career, after both women had converted to Catholicism. These poems remained unpublished (except for the few that had appeared in Catholic magazines while the women were alive) until Emily C. Fortey published them in this format in 1930. In her brief note at the start of the edition, Fortey writes that she had simply gathered together all the religious poems Bradley and Cooper left behind on their deaths (vii). What makes this collection interesting is that we are, by and large, seeing what the women decided not to include in *Poems of Adoration* and *Mystic Trees*. This makes *The Wattlefold* an apocryphal text, and one that is all the more interesting because of this. While *Poems of Adoration* and *Mystic Trees* tend to contain poems that shore up the women's new religious identity and vocation, the rejects in *The Wattlefold* often express the creative tensions involved in formulating that new identity. As such, this volume is uneven in quality, but at its best it offers successful and insightful expressions of the problems of reconciling their old pagan desire with their new Catholic fervour. "Blessed Hands" is a key poem in this respect, fusing the erotic touch of hands with an act of religious benediction. The confusion, in these later poems, between the women's love for each other and their love for Christ seems a deliberate poetic strategy. "Lovers" in particular uses this technique to assert the naturalness and propriety of their love. It is not just their love that has to be reconciled with the new faith, however. "How Letters Became Prayers" and "How Prayers Became Letters Again" also depict that struggle to retain aspects of the women's old identity in the face of a new and all-encompassing religious calling, but this time it is writing itself that must find a way of co-existing with the demands of their new faith.

As well as displaying a concern to reconcile their desire for each other with that for Christ, this volume still includes the poems written by the women towards the end of their lives, poems that convey the deepest and most passionate of love between the two women. Sometimes these poems make the reader feel voyeuristic for breaking in upon such tender sentiment, but always these poems are carefully crafted poetic works, as well as personal documents. For example, "I am thy charge, thy care!" was written by Bradley after Cooper's death and seems to be an attempt to commune with her ghost: to bring her back in whatever form is possible. And that form seems to have been a poetic one: it is as if by writing imaginatively with Cooper, and re-inscribing once again their joint authorship, Bradley can summon her presence to her again. "Fading" as a counterpart to this poem expresses much more directly and starkly her fear that she is losing the memory of her mate. Vincent McNabb writes in his introduction to the volume that it was "[t]he full self-efface-ment of each in the life and life's work of the other" that provided the dramatic spark for their writing, and this seems to have been true right to the very end of their lives (v).]

Source: *The Wattlefold: Unpublished Poems by Michael Field*, Col-lected by Emily C. Fortey; The Preface by Fr. Vincent McNabb (Oxford: Basil Blackwell, 1930).

BLESSED HANDS

I

Virginial young finger-tips
Offered eager to my lips
To confer more blessing of the Chrism
Filtered down from God's abysm!

What of dew, kissed as it shone,
Wild rose I have fed upon—
Flesh that fortifies and wins,
Finger-tips forgiving sins!

Flesh that bears of sin no trace
Flesh that is of Mary's grace,
Bough from Heaven let down that we
Kiss of Paradise the tree.

Lovely and incarnate things,
Clean as violets at their springs—
Let us touch them, kiss them, pray
For our Resurrection-day!

II

Hands just blessed and consecrate
Blessing my low head—
Then each one outspread

With joined tips as on a bed
Of sea-sand the sea-shells mate
Shining valve with valve rose-red.
From God's sea, O priestly hands
Ye are shining and so sweet,
Held to me, my homage is complete
And the kiss I fall on you
Is softer than a Bridegroom ever knew.
Soft as that brine that swathed you in its bands,
That moves your young and shell-like finger-tips
Up to the softest motion of my lips.

1909

MY BIRTHDAY

Sixty years! But I would say
A requiem on my birthday
For the soul that sixty years
Of contrition knew not the deep tears.

For the soul that walked in sight
Of its disesteemed birthright,
Withered fig-trees overhead
Of the summer disinherited.

Of those years that knew Thee not
Christ, let Thy compassion blot
The iniquities; erase
Their dull, arid plateaux from Thy face!

Doggedly that soul outcast
Through Emmaus'[1] village passed
With no knowledge of the road
Where the Lord through all His Scriptures glowed.

But one circuit round the sun,
All Thy will in me being done,

---

1 A reference to Luke 24:13–35, the story of Christ's appearance on the
road to Emmaus, after he had risen from the dead.

Counteth more than all the rest—
Of its importunity is blest.

For a twelve month that with Thee
In the deep security
Of Thy Sacraments I spend
Is of substance that can have no end.

Aug. 28th, 1908

POETS

Consider them thy poets, how they grow,
    Thy lilies of the field![1]
Brown and gold and tiger-brown,
Wreathing many a spotted crown,
    Or looking up
As a child from their cup;
Or as kings bowed lowly on their stem,
    Consider them!

Consider them, as Solomon they glow,
    Incense they yield.
Burnished, tumultuous, immense,
Where are they in Thy Providence?
    They do not spin
And yet such fabulous beauty win—
Surely, King, Thou dost delight in these,
    Thy field-lilies?

Oct. 5th 1908

---

1 A reference to the words of Jesus in the Sermon on the Mount when he
   asked his followers to consider the lilies of the field—whose beauty was
   separate from material toil and advancement—in an effort to take their
   minds from their worldly needs.

HOW LETTERS BECAME PRAYERS

Nothing in Nature can exceed the change,
　　Hawthorn nor roses that must berries be
　　Like this that falls on the simplicity
And loveliness of our thoughts' interchange.
Letters we wrote; letters we did exchange,
　　Laughter and woe there was to you and me,
　　As lovely coral waving in the sea,
　The words now grown so rigid in their range.

For now in my obedience I pray
　　And every virtue of dear silence boast
　　　　Giving thee lordships, kingdoms, as I kneel
Behind my quiet, crowding an array,
　　　　A pressure of petitions in appeal
As golden as the silence of the Host.

Dec., 1910

HOW PRAYERS BECAME LETTERS AGAIN

Nay but my prayers—I pray them back again,
　　For life is so miraculous inside
　　My beating brain, it were a suicide
To give no record of it to the pen
Gossip! Sweet wings are given to her when
　　As an annunciation, glorified
　　And full of dream, experience that had sighed
A mortal sigh, comes laughing into ken.

All of my senses to your ear belong
　　By swift transition: this is art's own way,
Her privilege. Oh yet I fear me wrong!
　　Who lived in Nazareth so many a day
And with the Word Incarnate, for all that
Kept in her heart-sob her Magnificat.

Jan., 1911

POMEGRANATES

Proserpine, Proserpine,[1]
Give us of lovely stems,
Give us your fruit—
We with pomegranates will crown our bowers,
So feel the flowers,
So fails desire—
So your fruit is ruddy as a fire.

Winter again, how quick,
Comes! and my loved is sick:
'Proserpine'.
Shuddering she pleads 'I do not want
The pomegranate'—
Desire in tears
Claims an eternity of love and years.

O Love, thy voice! ... My breath
Warm on thee startles Death.
Mythology
Shrivels as a ghost, beholding me
My lips, O Sweet,
To thine the heat,
Stir of coals, immortal cherishing!

Nov. 8th, 1911

LOVERS

Lovers, fresh plighting lovers in our age
Lovers in Christ—so tender at the heart
The pull about the strings as they engage—
One thing is plain:—that we can never part.
O Child, thou hauntest me in every room;
Not for an instant can we separate;
And thou or I, if absent in a tomb
Must keep unqualified our soul's debate.

---

1 Another name for Persephone, who was taken and kept prisoner in the
   Underworld by Pluto (otherwise known as Hades). He tricked her into
   eating pomegranate seeds as a way of preventing her leaving his realm.

Death came to me but just twelve months ago
Threatening thy life; I counted thee as dead—
Christ by thy bier took pity of my woe
And lifted thee and on my bosom spread;
And did not then retire and leave us twain:
Together for a little while we stood
And looked on Him, and chronicled His pain,
The wounds for us that started in their blood—
We, with one care, our common days shall spend,
As on that noble sorrow we attend.

1912

['Lo, my loved is dying']

Lo, my loved is dying, and the call
Is come that I must die,
All the leaves are dying, all
Dying, drifting by.
Every leaf is lonely in its fall,
Every flower has its speck and stain;
The birds from hedge and tree
Lisp mournfully,
And the great reconciliation of this pain
Lies in the full, soft rain.

Oct., 1913

RESPITE

They have told me presently that I shall die,
   Earth, I kiss thee,
Mother, Mother, I shall miss thee,
   Yet another spring—
Pray for me, O Mother, Mother!
   Yet another!
For the sake of the swallow on the wing,
Days of orchard and the hedgerow-briar,
   My desire,
Yet, yet another year,

Till the change to the Autumn breviary,[1]
  That the saffron-crocus may appear,
The saffron-crocus of which I am so fond,
  And the myrtles, smelling sweet
   In their trickles of close, warm peat,
In their trickles of close, warm peat by the forest-pond—
I would smell them again, for their smell I cry,
I would smell them again, when I come to die—
       By and bye—
          Mother!

Aug., 1913

THEY SHALL LOOK ON HIM[2]

Jesus, my Light,
How, when it comes through darkness I love light,
Mysterious air's adornment, white
Chrysolite[3] of the water, striking free,
  And beamingly
Through the dull currents of the stream at dawn
    Beam after beam
From the suspended jewel drawn;
   While swans go by,
Swans through the jewel pass, go by,
  Ponder and go along
Through gem-strokes strong,
    O perfect sight
    Of entire chrysolite!

November, 1913

['I am thy charge, thy care!']

I am thy charge, thy care!
Thou art praying for me, and about my bed,
About my ways; but there are things one misses—

---

1 The book containing the daily services of the Roman Catholic Church.
2 Edith Cooper's last poem.
3 A gem of a green colour.

It is the little cup
That I drink up,
The cup full of thee, offered every day—
I come for it, as birds draw to a brook—
It is the reflex of thee, in thy nook,
Caught sideways in a mirror as I pray—
    My precious Heap,
My jewel, in the casket of thy sleep.
Beloved, it is the little wreath of kisses,
I wove about thy head, thy withering hair.

January 28th, 1914

A CRADLE SONG

Yea, thou restest—dost thou rest?
    Yea, thou sighest, as one opprest:
    In the shadows blue and gray
    Sad thou liest, far away—
Far from thy hearth, in a wood alone,
And no path that windeth along—
    Art thou remembering?
I must sing to thee,
Sing thee asleep with a cradle-song.

    A song of one string,
    Our sharp, keen love!
I remember so many a little thing
Too slight for remembering,
    And sing and sing,
    As a wave from its crest
Drops over, bows down to its rest.

    I found thee asleep
    In a wood alone;
—A wonder over thy face was spread;
Thou smiledst, as thou wert smiling dead;
Then I sang thee the days, the winter days
When we crooned by the fire and stirred the flame—
    The days self-same
When we laughed and fondled and read.

Almost it was as a flicker came,
　Almost doth a flicker creep—
My Love, I have sung thee asleepen, the praise,
The breath of the years, the breath of the days,
　I have sung thee fast asleep.

1914

FADING

Nay, I have lost thee and I cannot find!
No image of thee wavers in my mind,
—My memory is growing blind.

I utter my past knowledge of thee—fond
I leave thee as a book that I have conned.
Thine eyes were dusk as alder-shadowed pond,

Thy face how full of augur, hidden will,
When thou wert silent, dreaming, very still,
Some of thy whitest mischief to fulfil.

The little happenings to thy voice, the drop,
As when the warblings of the linnets stop,
While tiny sounds from twig to twig still hop.

How thou didst covenant thyself to please,
From lifted eye-brow uttering prophecies,
Till thy will's treasure tangled all the seas.

Dead is thy mirror, dead as of desire,
The alter dumb, uncommuned with the fire,
Lacking of life the little curling spire

In pliancy. Stiffly the rustus bowers,
Blank is thy sun-room of thee; purple flowers
Rise, wither, fall, uncrossed by dial hours.

1914

['What shall I do for Thee to-day?'][1]

What shall I do for Thee to-day?
        What service, pray?
I will carry a basket all the way
        And strew and strew
    Flowers of forgiving
    On each mortal living.
And I will sing as I hold the flowers
    Of the hours and hours
            Of Thy loving me
            On Calvary
I will extol Thy Powers
Then scatter the herbs and the heartsease free.

        May, 1914

---

1 Katharine Bradley's last poem.

Life-Writing

NOTE ON TRANSCRIPTION POLICY

Anything in square brackets is an editorial intervention. For this reason, on the very rare occasion where square brackets are used by the author of the manuscript, we represent them with curved brackets.

The following symbols are used:

[<] [>] surrounds text inserted by the author later into a line.

[?] when directly preceding a word, shows we are not certain of the transcription.

[illegible] denotes an illegible word.

[illegible, deleted] denotes an illegible word that has been deleted by the author.

[...] indicates where the editors have cut passages from the middle of a section of text.

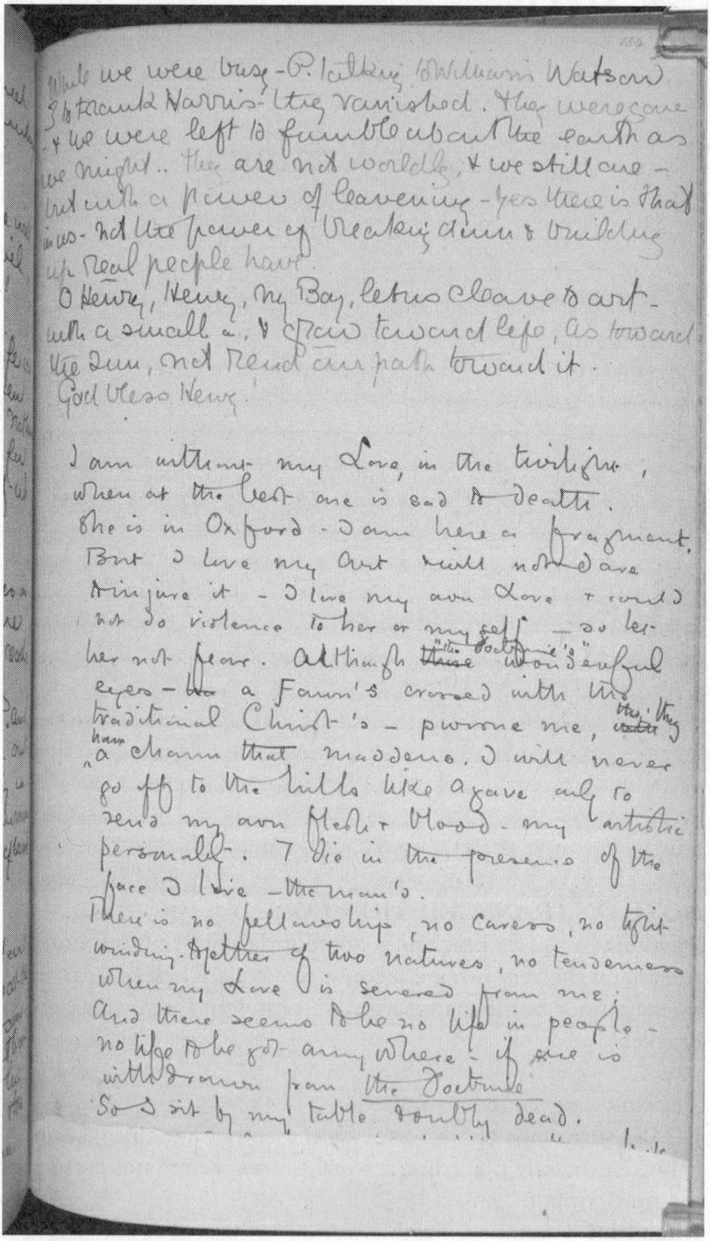

Figure 6. Michael Field's Diaries, *Works and Days*, 1892.
© British Library Board. All Rights Reserved (Add. 46780, f.134r).

1. Diaries

From *Works and Days*: The Diaries of Michael Field, 1888–1914

[Katharine Bradley and Edith Emma Cooper's joint 28-volume journal, *Works and Days*, dates from Saturday 14 April 1888, when the poets started their journal, to 18 September 1914 (Bradley's last entry four days before her death). Left to T. Sturge Moore with "instructions to open, at the end of 1929" and to "publish" it, this journal is an extraordinary text. It is a public account of their life as "Michael Field." But the journal is more than an autobiographical narrative. It is a riveting dialogue between "Michael" and "Field" as well as a captivating palimpsest of letters to and from Robert Browning, George Meredith, Walter Pater, Oscar Wilde, John M. Gray, and W.B. Yeats, amongst many others; it includes reviews of their work, drafts of their poetry, and travel writing narratives (the volume for the year 1890, for instance, is devoted to their journey to Dresden via Paris). Thoughts on the aesthetic are articulated side by side with large extracts from Friedrich Nietzsche's writings (copied by hand by Edith Cooper). The journal is a montage of descriptions of their journeys across London in omnibuses and underground trains; critical discussions of lectures by Verlaine and Pater; narratives of their talks with Charles Ricketts and Charles Shannon; detailed critical studies of works of art, including Whistler's *Nocturnes*; press cuttings; and notes on thoughts for drafts of poems and new plays. We hear from "Michael Field" first-hand accounts of the art world of the turn of the century, as the journal discloses the world of male and female aesthetes (including Vernon Lee, Dollie Radford, Oscar Wilde, Arthur Symons, Amy Levy, A. Mary F. Robinson, Louise Chandler Moulton, Algernon Swinburne, Ernest Radford, and Andre Raffalovich), whilst still offering Michael Field's own assessment of British aestheticism, nineteenth-century gender ideology, and their position within the different aesthetic and intellectual bohemian circles of *fin-de-siècle* London.

When reading *Works and Days*, it is important to appreciate that the writer of the entry might not actually be writing her own words. For example, Cooper often copied Bradley's extracts into *Works and Days*, and vice versa. For clarity, we have included in square brackets the initials of the woman in whose hand the entry appears. Whilst written by both women, Bradley and Cooper, the diary also contains a few annotations by Edith's sister, Amy (some of whose letters are attached or glued to the pages of the diary). However, none of Amy's extracts are transcribed here.]

1888
[K.B., May]
The time drew toward [Robert] Browning's birthday & I wrote to him:

"How absolutely the simple greeting—many happy returns of your birthday, expresses my wish for you it is difficult to say. Yet to the Poet of Prospice[1] I cannot give words that ignore death, & what parting—parting that I often feel one of us will be the first to begin—maybe. It is an undeveloped creed of mine that the dead live on—in & with us—influencing us as they never have before, if we will let them; & if in this life only, dear Mr. Browning, we had hope in you, we should be of all poets most miserable. But we will never lose you. We are confident you will be bounteous & friendly to us always. Still it is getting lonely singing in England now that the voices of [Dante Gabriel] Rossetti & Matthew Arnold are hushed. & we beg that you will stay with us & help us through the harsh, draughty bit of century remaining to us. We send you 18 more fragments, 8 of which are the work of Erinna.[2] I am sorry they are not so good as the others. It will be time, I think, to put in the sickle, & bind them in the sheaves for the printer, after they shall have received your corrections, &, I trust, additions. We love to have in & out among our verses a golden line from you. Please give my dear love to Miss Browning,[3] & tell her how we esteem "blessedest Wednesday"—not "Thursday"—"the fat of the week."
    Affectionately yours.
    K. H. Bradley.

---

1 Browning's poem "Prospice" (1861) was written shortly after the death of his wife, the poet Elizabeth Barrett Browning. It begins "Fear death?"
2 The Greek poetess, and another nickname for Cooper. These poems were part of *Long Ago* (1889).
3 Sarianna Browning, Browning's sister.

[K.B.]

On Wednesday May 9th we were asked to visit Mr. Browning. [...] We found the drawing-room at Palace Gate[1] full of flowers. Under one of Pen's statues,[2] in a pale blue roc's egg were our carnations. Mr. Browning came in greeting us as his "two dear, Greek women." He opened ὦ τέκνον[3] a feint of kisses. Ardently then & afterwards he spoke of the Sapphics, expressing especial interest in <u>Tiresias</u>[4] wh. he had once himself thought of treating. When I remarked I wished he had treated it—he said "No: it ought to be treated by a woman.["] He said to Edith he liked the 2nd series of poems even better than the first, & prophesied they would make their mark. But he refuses to write a preface. We must remember we are Michael Field. Again he said:—<u>Wait fifty years.</u>

1889

[K.B.]

On Tuesday Feb. 12th. We went to lunch at De Vere Gardens. The poet was restless, dissatisfied with his own moods, & the psychic entertainment he could give us. But he was infinitely sympathetic over <u>Long Ago</u>. He spoke to me of "the tragic largeness" of the lyrics. As he tore us down to lunch he stopped before Penn's Dryope & said it had been worthily sung, referring to Edith's "There was laughter soft & free."[5] He seemed to regret that ~~Edith~~ [<] Pen [>] could not embody the 2 moments—the tortoise—& the serpent. We showed him the archaic head of Sappho.[6] Miss Browning could not forgive the smirk; but the Old Gentleman looked at it with thoughtful consideration—"If I were an artist I should like to paint what the artist strove to express—

---

1 The poet's house at De Vere Gardens, Kensington (London).

2 A pupil of Rodin, Pen Browning was Robert and Elizabeth Barrett Browning's son.

3 "O child!" It could also be translated as "Oh dear!"

4 See Poetry Section, *Long Ago*, poem LII, p. 72.

5 Pen's 1883 sculpture "Dryope Fascinated by Apollo in the Form of a Serpent" shows a nude woman wresting with a serpent. Browning is linking the statue's subject matter (Dryope's seduction by Apollo, disguised as a serpent) to poem LXI from *Long Ago*, "There is laughter soft and free," which shows Apollo's cunning transformation from tortoise to serpent. The entry identifies Cooper as the sole author of the poem.

6 The cover illustration for *Long Ago*.

but could not—for instance the firm round chin shows that this is a young face, & the smile is an attempt to express a sweet smile—& the great eyes show that he was struck by the beauty & size of Sappho's eyes—that he felt them beautiful ...["] He also said of this third batch of Sapphics that they seemed to him so much better that the others—there was certainl[y] no falling off.

[K.B.]
Sunday even May 19th—& yet Zaehnsdorf's Long Ago (10 copies) not yet come.[1] On Wednesday I read at the British Museum—learning much of Carloman,[2] especially from a dictionary of the popes, & Italian life of Zacharias. [O]n Thursday Mr. Bell[3] sent a specimen copy of Long Ago—a red marker raw against the lovely orange-Greek. I arose—& at Marshall & Suelgrave's matched the very tint. Yesterday I joined the Fellowship of the New Life[4] at Mersthen. Lord Eltham threw open his grounds to us—& after listening to a paper at the end of wh. allusion to the robberies of the lords of the soil was made, he courteously asked us to come into his hall, & look at his pictures. The scene was significant—the best of the old time benign towards the new. And the moment was apple-flower time in May. Men gave up their doubts & faiths to the women of the company; it was good to feel that every one of that motley group was, in his or her fashion, seeking "a better country". And the fair land, full of buttercups & deep grass, yielded her beauty. A way to more genuine companionship in verity the fellowship has found. In June Percival Chubb[5] goes to America "to hear & ask questions," I surmise.

[K.B., 12 July]
Mr. Walter Pater hopes we shall be able to call on him about teatime at 5 oclock [sic] on Monday.

---

1 Joseph William Zaehnsdorf (1853–1930) was the son of one of the most influential bookbinders of his time, Joseph Zaehnsdorf. He took over the bookbinding company at his father's death.
2 The main character of a new play, *In the Name of Time*, published posthumously by The Poetry Bookshop in 1919.
3 Publisher of *Long Ago*.
4 An advanced, proto-socialist society dedicated to developing models of alternative societies.
5 Founding member of the Fellowship of the New Life and of the Fabian Society, a socialist society whose members included William Morris.

[E.C.]

Jan. 2 Thursday

We got into the train for London at Redhill,[1] as a gentleman was taking possession of a discarded foot-warmer. When he sat down, he addressed me "I can easily push it further that you may share the warmth." I bowed with thanks. Then ~~we~~ [<] he [>] became absorbed in a paper. The scales fell from my vision almost instantaneously—it was <u>George Meredith</u>: Sim had a suspicion, which she put by as nonsense. Perhaps he became aware of an interest in our looks (I had whispered to Sim <u>G</u>.) for every now & then the fulgent eyes swept us in survey. We were reading the <u>Contemporary Review</u> (containing the "Lumber Room," just received by post from Percy Bunting) together.[2] Sim says my eyes grew sharp as crystal points in their brief search for the traits of ~~Hollyer's likeness of the novelist~~ person fixed in ~~Hol~~ his portrait by Hollyer.[3] He drew out letters from Turkey & dropped an envelope under the seat. At Cannon St. he got out—our eyes flashed into one another as he passed—easily raising the window at the very moment of descent from the train. He made a step or two on the pavement, & then doubled back a minute's space to throw an uncertain glance into our carriage. I was sure of our man— <u>Why</u>? I recognised him on the instant—the iron-grey hair & beard, the forward sweep of the moustache, the large beautifully modelled eyelids, the unusual shape of the ear's "porch." Only the eyes were new, for in the portrait they are covered—quick, much the colour of nuts at Christmastide; yet, with all their rapidity, a certain profound languor emerges & show recluse smiles, that send their ripple no further than the orbs themselves. Must I confess! I took the envelope—(all is fair in war) but it gave no clue, having been evidently enclosed: on it was a list—"a few packets of envelopes—a banjo-case—a stick of sealing-wax" (not in his writing)[.] We still thought that imagination might be fooling us with a mere London man.

---

1 Suburban village close to London where the writer George Meredith lived.

2 A short piece of prose written by Bradley. Bunting was the editor of the journal the *Contemporary Review*.

3 The photographer Frederick Hollyer (1837–1933) was known for his excellent photographic reproductions of works of art and his artistic photographs of artists and writers.

On our return, at Cannon St., the same figure paused by our carriage, went to the next, & finally returned to ours. His appearance, thus sudden, was so like the portrait I was certain, but the name on a document in his hand made assurance sure. At first this document absorbed all his attention, & I could watch the grave profile. [<]~~Then~~[>] Finally I took out my pocket Shakspere [sic] & read <u>Othello.</u> He put up his document, took a paper out of his bag, & then seemed to wake to the fact that his travelling companions of the morning were again in the same carriage. He laid the paper on his knees, & his hands on it, & turned full round to watch & receive. I was obliged to read closely for his eyes were well-prepared for my least look in his direction. Sim, who could only see his hands, says they were folded, determinedly observant. Soon after, she came to sit by me, & we talked vividly each to each. Sometimes his lids covered his eyes as in the portrait; but if we took the ~~opportunity~~ [<] moment [>] for a study of his features, the brave lights were upon us, like a tiger's through the jungle. We actually went on to Reigate[1] to give him a clue to what he ~~had~~, I am sure, more than guessed: it had a strong effect on him.

[E.C., 3 March]
We went to meet <u>Herbert Spencer</u>[2] at lunch, invited by our sweet Miss Bakers. [...] He speaks like a man whose every sentence is connected with a general principle—yet there is humour & interest in his talk. It is delicious to hear him making disarmed fun at [?]Mary's perfect frankness of most sweet folly in conversation. He laughs till the tears flow. I am certain our friends are reforming him, for there is the possibility of disagreeable things in his features. He is very faddy about the small[<]nesses[>] ~~things~~ of eating & drinking & comfort. It was sad to find the great Altruist so self-concerned. For all his giant powers of thought, Robert Browning far surpassed him in moral dignity. At the end of lunch, he said childishly—"My feet are cold, I must warm them"[.] "We will all turn to the fire & warm our feet" suggested gracious Miss Rosa; but no!—off he went to his own room, &, unless reminded, would have left us without salute in the oblivion his creature need occasioned. I was shy, for he put on his spectacles to examine a creature so strangely & hopelessly poetic—Sim was mightily

---

1 The women lived in Durdans, Reigate, a suburban village in London.
2 Victorian philosopher famous for coining the term "the survival of the fittest."

audacious. We were talking of picturesque old houses & how beauty endeared a home for us. He said he was devoted to the useful & what tended to life. "We live by admiration, hope, & love" rang out Sim's voice. "But if you get a fever & die?" "Then I shall go on admiring, hoping, & loving more & more" was the intrepid answer. "You comfort yourself like that" he said, but his glance appreciated the independence of the stranger.

[E.C., Wednesday, 5 March]
By underground we reached Portland Rd. & soon found Fitz-Roy Street,[1] & a white door with dull brass ornaments [&] fittings— no number on its [illegible, deleted] lintel. Here lives Herbert Horne, editor of the <u>Century Guild Hobby Horse</u>,[2] here Selwyn Image[3] has his studio, & other artists & art-men dwell in unity. The various storeys represent the arts from architecture to design—hence Selwyn Image has his place at the top of all the stairs, & his walls are inhabited by the great figure-designs he makes for stained-glass windows—spaced into ~~thinck~~ thick irregular lines for the inevitable leading. One of these designs (for the Church at Morthoe) has great force & originality—Raphael as the Guardian-Saint of travellers, with heaped cloak on his shoulders, lantern in his hand, staff along his arm, & a baffled, searching look in his eyes. In another the hair of the women's heads floats up into the traceries of the window & fills them decoratively. Another large design of the Angel of Life has a strikingly fine background of blossoming roses, thickety leaves & briar-stems with their grand, injurious thorns—In looking at this rose-tree one was reminded of Blake's—"her thorns were her only delight"—In another design of the Bridegroom, the background was pomegranites [sic] with their split discs so perfect a fruit for artistic treatment. Selwyn Image himself is very "likeable," with firm lips, indicative of that self-control essential for the art of design,—yellow eyes illumined with genius—giving the element

---

1 Station on the Metropolitan Railway Underground Line. Fitzroy Street was famous in the 1880s and 1890s for its colony of artists and writers.
2 The talented typographer and book designer, author of the book of verse *Diversi Colores* (1891). He was also the editor of two beautifully produced art magazines *The Century Guild Hobby Horse* and the *Hobby Horse*.
3 The famous illustrator, founder of the Century Guild, an arts and crafts organisation.

of brightness & freedom, without which no combination of lines will live & combine into symbolism or beauty. His complexion is parchment, his hair cropped, his grasp of hand assured & frank— his age above 38—I should fancy. As we gave him clue to our conception of Queen Mary, the flame in his eyes grew intent.[1] He ~~was~~ set down every suggestive point—& made a special note as to the Carnation as the Stuart Flower. His business will be difficult—to draw a design imaginatively symbolic of our conception—yet without trite Scottish Emblems.

[E.C., 14 May]
Miss Heaton also knew & knows the Rossettis. To Dante Gabriel she gave five or six commissions. The first picture he painted for her was <u>Paolo & Francesca</u>. Ruskin said "it was not suitable for a lady," & Miss Heaton weakly made an exchange with him. There is to me a speckled silliness in Ruskin's dealings with women— spite of his chivalry & exaggerated estimate of our sex as Queens.[2] Rossetti had a constraining fascination. His sister[3] is striving to work out his redemption by prayer & denial. She is bent on being Love's martyr for his sake. There is a small chance we may be able to call on her. I should like to see her once.

[E.C. Account of their trip to Paris]

<u>Pictures in the Louvre</u>[4]

[...] <u>Leonardo da Vinci</u>
<u>Mona Lisa</u>—Treachery in its utmost loveliness. Sea, Rocks, Atmosphere—Sidelong, historical, implicating eyes, smile that

---

1   Their 1890 play *The Tragic Mary*. Image's stunning cover and book design for the play is a masterpiece in bookbinding. He also designed the book cover of their 1892 play *Stephania*.
2   Ruskin's 1865 essay "Of Queen's Gardens" offered a conservative view of Victorian womanhood: "Her intellect is not for invention or creation, but for sweet ordering," he wrote. Ellen Heaton was one of Rossetti's early patrons. Ruskin offered in exchange for *Paolo and Francesca* 35 guineas and Rossetti's 1855 watercolour *Dante's Vision of Rachel and Leah*.
3   Poet Christina Rossetti.
4   On 5 June 1890 they travelled to France and Italy, visiting Paris, Verona, Florence, Bologna, Pisa, and Genoa among other cities. The women left space within the diary to be filled in afterwards. A diary of their trip, reproduced here, appears on pages 243–44.

makes velvet cushions of the cheeks, & leads the calm lips upward, skin of ripe tone with shadows dusky as a bat's dusk, soft, glowing hands with the patience of cruelty in their rest— all are infamously, perfectly treacherous to the point of infatua- tion—& with to the extent [<] measure [>] of universality. It is no portrait, it is a dream of power and occult influence. Rocks & Seas in nature are the powers types of the inconstant & perilous—they are the chosen background with Da Vinci of his concave smiles on the lips of woman, & the full space be- tween their lids & eyebrows which is bewitched by subtlety of Expression.

[E.C., entry in red ink]
<u>Wednesday, 23 of July</u>
Father came back from London this evening with the news that Durdans was bought for us. That we had a home on the earth— a sacred acre our very own.

[K.B.]
English souvenirs
Yesterday, Monday July 21, we were suddenly summoned to Mrs Chandler Moulton's[1] last "at home" in Weymouth Street. The first moments were misery and humiliation. Mrs. Moulton intro- duced us as a poet, as Michael Field, & we stood, our wings vibrating in revolt, while hollow, fashionable women lisped their enchantment at meeting with us. A moment came when this could be borne no longer, I laid a master-hand on the hostess, & told her to introduce us by our Christian names. After that George Moore[2] was brought to us. He had heard our names across the room; but he is a brother-one of the guild of letters. His admiration for <u>William Rufus</u>[3] is unbounded.... By Jove it's fine ... ma foi it's good. That old fellow with one eye & the passion of the hunting. The scenes in the forest—I have only read the play 5 or 6 years ago—the moment it came out—& <u>once</u>—I never read a book twice—yet I see it before me now. (?) He has even

1 The American poet (1835–1908).
2 George Moore (1852–1933), influential Anglo-Irish writer. He was a friend of Manet and Zola.
3 Michael Field's 1885 play.

proposed it to the theatre libre[1] as one of the English plays to be acted./ Long Ago had disappointed him. We were engaged on an impossible task. It had not the versification of Keats, still there were some fine things in it.

Edith continued the conversation for I from far recognised Oscar Wilde, &, desiring to make his better acquaintance, found him by my side talking easily.

He has a brown skin & coarse texture, insensitive surface, & no volcanic blood fructifying it from within—powerful features, a firm jaw, & fine head—with hair that one feels was much more beautiful some years ago. It is pathetic when bright hair simply glows dull, instead of turning grey. The whole face wears an aspect of stubborn sense, & the aesthete is discovered simply by the look of well-being in the body (soul take thine ease!) the soft comfort of the mouth, & a lurking kindly laziness in the eyes. But the dominant trait of that face is humour, humour that ridicules & gently restrains the wilfulness, the hobby-horse passion, the tendency to individualism of the rest of the man. There is an Oscar Wilde smiling ironically at his namesake the aesthete, smiling with almost Socratic doubt.

"There is only [<] one [>] man in this century who can write prose." "You mean Mr. Pater." Yes—take Marius the Epicurean[,] any page.[2] We spoke of the difficulties of writing prose, no good tradition—he had almost quarrelled with Watts[3] because he wanted to write the language of the gods—& Watts sought to win him to prose....

"French is wonderfully rich in colour words."

We agreed English was poor in such—I instanced bluish-grey as a miserable effort, & he dwelt on the full pleasantness & charm of the French [<] colour [>] words ending in âtre bleuâtre &c. But we should grapple with this colour difficulty. It should bear faith that everything in the world could be expressed in words. I spoke of L'embarquement pour Cythère[4]—of the impossibility of expressing what was happening at that fairy-water. [...]

---

1 Parisian theatre company founded by André Antoine in 1885. An international playhouse, it was a showcase for experimental naturalist theatre.

2 Pater's novel Marius the Epicurean (1885) was the "Bible" for aesthetes and decadents. It is the story of a young man's spiritual and aesthetic awakening in ancient Rome from paganism and stoicism to Christianity.

3 Theodore Watts (1832–1914), poet and principal reviewer of poetry for the journal The Athenaeum.

4 Watteau's painting, poeticised in their 1892 volume of verse Sight and Song. See poem "L' Embarquement pour Cythère" in Sight and Song, p. 107.

We agreed—the whole problem of life turns on pleasure. Pater shows that the hedonist—the perfected hedonist is the saint. *
<u>"One is not always happy when one is good; but one is always good when one is happy[.]"</u> [...]

[H]e is determined to write in a language that will only be understood by minds artistically-trained. The writing shall not be obscure—quite clear, but its meaning will be seized only by artists. He once wrote a story of Spain—a story in black & silver—in wh. he had endeavoured to give something of the dignity & gloom of Spanish life—like heavy, black velvet cushions—& this story when translated into French came out [<] ~~blue~~ [>] pink & blue. It taught him that after all there were certain colour forces in English—a power of rendering gloom not in French.

He has a theory[,] it is often genius that spoils a work of art—a work of art that should be so intensely self-conscious. He classed the Brontes, Jane Austen[,] George Sand,[1] under the head genius. This was when I said to him there was one sentence of Mr. Pater's wh: I would not say I could never forgive, because I recognised its justice; but from wh. I suffered—a[nd] wh. was hard to bear—that in wh. he speaks of the scholarly conscience as male—adding I did not remember where the passage occurred. "Yes" he said "it is in Appreciations, in the essay on Style, page 7—left-hand side—at the bottom—& in all this memory the one tiny error was that the page is page 8 ... Genius, he continued, killed the Brontes. Consider the difference between Jane Eyre & Esmond.[2] Owing to their imperfect education the ~~only~~ only works we have had from women are works of genius.

[E.C.]
Monday—24th [November].
In heavy mist Sim & I stepped into a cab & reached the station, two bundles of shawls—but a great pleasure drew us on through the weather to town—Pater's lecture at the London Institution on Prosper Mérimée.[3] Till the appointed hour we took refuge in the National Gallery, simply guessing at the outlines of the new pictures, & divining the new ones by memory.

---

1 Pseudonym of the French novelist Amadine-Lucile-Aurore Dupin (1804–76).
2 Thackeray's eponymous novel *The History of Henry Esmond* (1852).
3 French writer (1803–70), famous for his 1845 novel *Carmen*.

Yet so perversely human were we that we started to Finsbury Circus a little after four, though we had come to town early ~~only to be in time~~ & knew that the doors opened at 4.30. To gain time we drove for some distance by the Embankment—the merest block of building, the commonest trailing barge were ~~a~~ soft wonders in the mist. After all we had good seats—at first beside Mrs. Barrington. Selwyn Image came up & told us there was a great opportunity we must not miss—<u>Orfeo</u> at the Italian Opera—he had spent all his money on it—Horne sat by Lionel Johnson[1]—a learned snow-drop, (his friends say he is so old he has become a child again)[.] He is quite young, quite pale, drooping under book-love, with curved ~~lips~~ lids, nearly as fine as Keats' Hyperion's.[2] Oscar Wilde ~~to~~ on our left gave to the tiers of faces ~~the~~ [<] his [>] lambent eyes. A. S[ymons]. was the last to enter. He was charming to watch, with the crossness of isolation on his brows & mouth. His colour dazzles, even from a far distance......"but I love his beauty passing well"!![3]

Pater ~~entered~~ [<] came forward [>] without looking anywhere, & immediately read his "slips" with no preface & into the midst of movements & coughs ~~that had not settled~~. He never gave his pleasant blue eyes to his audience—there was a weight of shyness athwart them—Above his eye-brows the light so fell as to throw up two ridges ~~above~~ [<] over [>] them, with strange effect. What determination—almost brutality (in French sense) there is about the lower part of his face; yet it is under complete, urbane control. His voice is low, & has a singular sensitive resonance in it—an audible capacity for suffering. I always feel that, like every Epicurean, his courteous exterior hides a strong nature, not innocent of barbarism. There is something of Prosper in him—a strain of "Denys l'Auxerrois"[4] wh: he has expressed in the creation of that northern Zagreus.[5] Would'nt [sic] one give much to surprise The Bacchant in Walter Pater! The even flow of his reading went

---

1 1867–1902, decadent poet and a member, with W.B. Yeats, of the Rhymer's Club. He introduced Lord Alfred Douglas to Oscar Wilde.

2 "Hyperion arose, and on the stars / Lifted his curved lids, and kept them wide." John Keats's "Hyperion. A Fragment. Book I" (1820).

3 Cooper is quoting from Alfred Tennyson's poem "Sisters" (*The Lady of Shalott, and Other Poems*, 1833). The poem speaks of a sister's revenge against the lover who caused her sister's death.

4 The title of Pater's 1886 essay, which recreated a medieval myth of the return of Dionysus (Denys). It was first published in *Macmillan's Magazine* and reprinted as the second portrait in his *Imaginary Portraits* (1887).

5 Dionysus Zagreus. See poem "Dionysus Zagreus" in *Dedicated*, p. 194.

on—save for a break when the same voice asked if all could hear. Oscar was "visibly delighted" ~~when~~ [<] to find [>] that Mérimée regretted the decay of assassination. ~~in~~ The lecture ended, as it began, abruptly through disregard for any popular ~~customage~~ customariness.

[E.C.]
Paris

June 5. Arrived at Hôtel St. Peterbourg.
June 6. Friday. First glimpse at Notre [sic] Dame. Breakfasted with Symons at Céline's. Visited Miss Gérente.[1] Afternoon with the Pictures at the Louvre. Settle comfortably at 20, Avenue Victoria. An evening visit from M[r]. Symons.
June 7. Sculptures of the Louvre. Visit to Hôtel Corneille & the Book-stalls of the Odéon. Abortive call on Rodin.[2] [...]
June 8. [...] Visit to Mrs. Chandeler [sic] Moulton. Miss Gérente to afternoon-tea—delicious on ~~Bernard~~ [<] Bonnard [>] & Impressionism.[3] [...]
June 9. Bought Verlaine & some nos. of "Les Hommes d'Aujour-dui [sic]"[4] at Vanier's; went to Symons's Hotel Corneille & saw his collection of photographs from the works of Gustave Moreau:[5] then to the Odéon bookstalls & bought Rabelais, Flaubert—indeed a dozen books. [...]
June 10 The Louvre (Venus, Bacchus, the head of Theseus & the Antique Sculptures—then the Room VII of Early Italian pictures, where we met Mr. Berenson, a young Russian, qualifying to become an Art-historian, introduced to us by Mrs. Moulton[6]—the Drawings)—then a visit to ~~of~~ Marie Bashkirtseff's pictures,[7] shown to us by Rosalie [...] with A. Symons to see Redon's wonderful, almost unknown drawings.[8] In the Evening a visit to Mrs. Moulton with exciting intimate conversation.

1 Bradley's companion during her first trip to Paris in 1868–69. Sister of Bradley's first platonic love, Alfred Gérente.
2 The French sculptor (1840–1917).
3 French impressionist painter Pierre Bonnard (1867–1947).
4 Verlaine's literary magazine, *Les Hommes d'Aujourd'hui*.
5 French symbolist painter (1826–98).
6 The women first met Berenson at a Mrs. Chandler Moulton's "at home" in Paris.
7 The Russian painter and diarist (1858–84).
8 Odilon Redon (1840–1916), French symbolist painter.

June 11. A long morning with the Italian Pictures in the Louvre, instructed by Mr Berenson. [...]

June 13 A long morning at the Louvre with Berenson. The Visitation of Piombo & the works of Ribera & Zurbaran. After breakfast with him, we returned to receive Mrs. Moulton & A. Symons. We met the latter at Céline's for dinner & returned to his hotel to hear & discuss his article on Rodin for the last no. of the Art Magazine.[1]

[...]

June 15 Sunday. [<] A walk down to Tuilleries' Gardens— [>] A short visit to our beloved Sculpture & pictures at the Louvre, where we met Berenson & Mrs. Moulton. The mid day all spent with A. Symons at the river up & down—breeze & grey light. A long talk on the drama, its forms & future at a Café near the Palais Royal—a visit by ourselves to Mrs. Moulton: she read some lines on Amy Levy, & some of Marston's poems with a deliberation of voice that gives strange emphasis to passion.[2] We dined with A.[rthur] S.[ymons] for the last time at Céline's.

June 16 [...] Lunch with Madame Darmesteter[3]—full of tidal interests: she was genuinely friendly & most anxious we should meet her in Savoy. Prof. Darmesteter proffered us his book on Shakspere [sic]. In the Luxembourg Gardens we met A.[rthur] who looked literally like the angel of that garden with bright bluets in his button-hole & beaming a feast of "grosses fraises," an offering, a fête Champêtre for Michael ere the moment of departure.

1891

[K.B., Cambridge]
A sudden invitation from Miss Clough;[4]—on Friday Feb. 13th I start.

---

1 Edited by poet W.E. Henley (1849–1903).
2 Aestheticist poets Amy Levy (1861–89), who committed suicide in 1889, and Philip Bourke Marston (1850–87), admired by D.G. Rossetti and Swinburne.
3 Married name of poet A. Mary F. Robinson (1857–1944). Her first husband, James Darmesteter, was an influential Oriental scholar.
4 Anne Jemmina Clough (1820–92), first principal of Newnham College and sister of poet A.H. Clough.

The green scum of the ditches affects me as I drive to Newnham. Beholding it, I feel how vain it is to try to belong to Oxford. The stones of my heart grow moist with tears. And yonder is the Cam:—& King's; but it is not these great things that draw me;—it is the dear green scum.

I pass a long range of rosy buildings—I pass & am almost thankful. It would be too formidable to go under that gate of honour. But lo! the cabman in his stupidity has passed. He turns the horse's head. We are in Newnham.

And that night I lie in my strait college bed &, watching the firelight flicker on the walls, muse on many things. Sixteen years ago I came to Newnham empty-headed, with vague ambition, vague sentiment—the pulpy lyrics of the N.M. in my brain.[1] I return a poet & possessing a Poet. I look forth on the stars, kneel down, & give God thanks.

[E.C.]
April 8. Wednesday. Arthur's [Symons] first Tea-Party in his [?]attic. Daffodils crossed in the mantel-shelf, and embossing two pots on the book-case. Tea poured out in face of the old roofs by May Morris (she will never be called by her spousal name!)[2] Her features are harsh, demure—her complexion old parchment, her eyes cold blue—her hair suggests the hereditary power that in the mother's held Rossetti. The child-wife, Mrs. Radford,[3] looked up to the guests, like a dove with its soft little head aside. Her husband held me long in talk—he has a slow voice, aquiline features, & fixed eyes, curiously pied. He converses in the "middle Voice"—hearing himself all the time; but he says individual things, ~~that~~ it is worth one's while to wait for. [...] I ~~went~~ was aware while talking that some-one passed into the tea-room—I did not see, but I had instant knowledge, who it was. As I was handling some of our host's books, Sim stood by me & George [Moore] smiled with a smile of milk & honey. I found myself seated & talking to him.

---

1   *The New Minnesinger*, Katharine Bradley's first book of poems.
2   1862–1920. Daughter of pre-Raphaelite poet William Morris and Jane Burden Morris, lover of D.G. Rossetti. She was married to Harry Sparling, secretary of the Socialist League.
3   Socialist poet and aesthete Dollie Radford (1858–1920), wife of poet Ernest Radford (1857–1919).

[E.C.]

Tuesday—June 17

We visit Oscar Wilde—being received by Mrs. Oscar in turquoise blue, white frills & amber stockings. The afternoon goes on in a dull fashion till Oscar enters. He wears a lilac shirt, a heliotrope tie, a great primrose pink—very Celtic combination, ma foi!

His large presence beams, with the heiterkeit[1] of a Greek God [<] that has [>] descended on a fat man of literary habits.

He sat down & told us that in his belief our Tragic Mary (Zaensdorf [sic] vol.) & Rossetti's Poems were the two beautiful books (in appearance) of the century[2]—but he was going to surpass us, & wd. send us an early copy of his Tales to make us "very unhappy"[.] He was delicious on the illustrations, that are not taken from anything in the book, only suggested by it—for he holds that literature is more graphic than art & should therefore never be illustrated in itself, only by what it evokes.

[K.B.]

Yesterday (July 21st) Amy & I went to Mrs Chandler Moulton's. I saw [Thomas] Hardy, kind & austere[.] Near him was Theodore Watts. At the name of Michael he leapt into the air & glittered[.] Both these men found it inscrutable, incomprehensible that 2 people could write poetry together. Hardy seemed apprehensive & said the Eckman-Chartrions had remained united too long.

The Miss Hepworth Dixons[3] give me the delicious flow of their free, ~~rippling~~ [<] bubbling [>] nonsense. One of them is in the very hey-day of pessimism[.]—"So delightful to be free—to have no fear of shocking any one—to enter into the joy of the moment. To have broken with convention, to live."

---

1 German for "mirth," "jocularity."

2 Zaehnsdorf produced sixty exquisite copies of *The Tragic Mary*. Wilde is presumably referring to Rossetti's 1870 collection of poems. Wilde's book of fairy tales *A House of Pomegranates* (London: McIlvaine & Co., 1891) was designed by Ricketts and Shannon.

3 Ella (1857–1932) and Marion, daughters of William Hepworth Dixon, a former editor of the journal the *Athenaeum*. Ella distinguished herself as a journalist and novelist. She is best known for her celebrated 1894 New Woman novel *The Story of a Modern Woman*.

[E.C. August–October. In Dresden, Germany, visiting galleries. Edith is unwell.]

Monday. August 10

In feebleness of body and pallor of soul we take a cab for the Gallery.

A poor Zurbaran, a passage of Dutch pictures—little things that the eye cannot sift, a turn into a square room, and there she is—Giorgione's Venus!)[1] This is perfect womanhood; the Earth is holy ground about her, it has itself the round, unconscious curves of her sex. There is in the picture that ideal sympathy between woman and the land, which the nations have divined when they made their countries feminine.

She lies asleep: her chestnut, braided hair only a little brighter than the bank above, which is shaggy as a wolf-skin; from the outer edge of this bank a brown, light spray throws its leaves against the sky. Her pillow is a heap of pomegranate-red—that fertile red that is the right bond of colour, between the solemn flesh and the grave slopes. She lies on white linen, somewhat black in the shadows. Her right arm is bent back over her head, & the curve from the elbows to the knee has the extensive soft-ness of undulating land............

[E.C.]

Of the Venus she writes:[2]

She lies pure, bare, in deep unconsciousness; and this unguarded beauty is without spot. She rests against a deep red cushion, under a russet bank; she lies on soft undulating Earth. To the right there are houses and sheds—for she is Goddess of the Earth—the Earth is her temple, she is no foreigner, no visi-tant—but of long, quiet summer afternoons and restful skies, of swelling lands and sacred country-life. There is nothing rustic in this picture. It is only Italian landscape that could thus take flesh in a Venus. There is about her nothing bitter or barren—every-thing is of harvest—silent ripening, fulfilment.

---

1 Giorgione's Venus is underlined twice, in red and black ink. The red symbolises Greek eroticism.

2 Venus is underlined in red and black ink. The excerpt is by Katharine Bradley, but Edith Cooper copied it into the diary.

[E.C.]

I continue my impressions of the <u>Venus—Giorgione</u>.

Her face is oval, the tint olive, with the scarce rose that stays on olive cheeks; the brows restfully crescent-shaped; the lids in their profound slumberousness wrinkle a little where they begin to orb over the eyes. The nose is long & Grecian; the lips have a steady red, the upper one so short that the shadow of the nose meets its lovely curves. The mouth expresses unconscious, dreamless rest: all is asleep in this face—the brain, the sweet blood as well as the features. Other painters give us a mask of sleep. The breasts are almost invisibly veined, firm, unseductive in their holy loveliness; the left arm follows the lower heaves of the body & the hand lies over the thigh, the fingers bent inward with unashamed simpleness—that profound universal pleasure of sex that sleep itself will not, dare not[,] invalidate. The right leg after forming a divine little bay above the knee, bends under the left which is [<] lo [>] stretched in one downward line to the foot. The ~~foot~~ instep makes another divine little bay. The Earth is shadowed under & round her, then it passes into olive-green light on the near slope—beyond this is a brown hillside on which is a castle, very severe & simple roofs & sheds. A round olive-green tree on the steepest descent toward the uneven plain of hedge-banded fields—grassy, with the after-harvest breadth. In their midst is a single slight tree of olive-yellow, & intensely blue & definite mountains close the horizon, against a basking stretch of almost level cloud, that at the right side foams up into white <u>cumuli</u>. The sky itself is of intact blue. There is a small nick of hay on the nearer slope. A few violets and yellow flowers bloom in the long grass by her side. Here we have beauty with us, by our home-steads—no stranger from the sea, no apparition, no enchantress, but simple as our fields, as nobly-lighted as are our harvests, pure as the things man needs for his life that use cannot violate. No-one watches her; there is no figure to be seen: she is closed from the sense of her perfection.....

Here Sim becomes too ill to stay longer in the Gallery. It is painful with noise & figures, & straining faces. We find the fountain playing outside & the sky quite grey. I have a ~~burn~~ hot sense of regret in leaving the Zwinger,[1] a kind of <u>malaise</u> & disappointment. My throat is fearfully swollen & gives me continu-~~ous~~[<]al[>] pangs.

---

1 The Dresden museum was housed at the Zwinger Palace.

Afternoon

I lie on my bed, I gargle with Eau de Cologne that increases the atrocious pain in my throat, we have an early tea & start for Tannhaüer [sic][1] at the Opera House.

[E.C.]
Wednesday—Aug. 19th

Again a long waiting for the Doctor. I lie almost voiceless. At last he comes, looks at my feet, & says that I have got scarlet fever.... There is a pause & I feel that a sentence is gathering against me— I know what it is—You must go to the Hospital[.] Dismay scatters our fortitude. [...] We make a vow, we neither speak, that nothing but death shall sever us.

[E.C.]
Saturday, Aug. 30th.[2]

At last this morning even the Herr Geheimrath says there is no danger from the fever—only she must lie in bed. She looks very pretty in her short boy's hair & fresh cotton jacket.

(On Friday I must have had the locks cut off. Sim asked the H.G. if nurse should do it or should I have "un Barbier"[3]—Little Waggie & his companion Dr. Millar, broke out into laughter they could not hide. I was very grave & depressed at the thought of being clipped. While Sim was in the Garden, I got sister to do it, while I held a glass & directed her scissors from tuft to tuft.—The little white cotton jacket with black & red spots was chosen by Bernie [Berenson], bought by Mrs. C[ostelloe]. & brought on Thursday)

This morning I brought in for P. from the garden 2 dove-feathers, some wild-strawberry leaves, a fresh spring of delicate mountain-ash & plane-leaves (with the strong drawing of Botticelli, she says)[.] Again & again her soul is swept with agony that she has missed so much that would have the very highest experience.

---

1 Wagner's opera.

2 The author of the entry is Bradley ("Sim"), who presumably wrote this episode in a notebook in Dresden. On their return to London, Cooper ("P." or "Puss") copied it into their *Works and Days* diary. Note in particular how she responds and adds to Bradley's account of these events in the brackets.

3 "A barber" (French).

[E.C., 18 September]

Whilst I am away P. drink [sic] "Kaffee" with sister for an hour. Sister kisses her with a kiss that plunges down among the wraps ... (yes, as the wolf did when he sought the child—O Eros!—in Browning's "Ivan Ivanovitch"—a fatal kiss!)

This evening we (officially) part with Hemmer.

* My Love & I have our first springtide kisses—shy & brief & full of the future. Pussie feels his cheeks reclaimed by life. Oh, how Love is better than & as <u>Bad</u>!

("My Love was a little jealous, stormily tearful that nurse should have forestalled her on my lips ... but I know whose kisses were vernal—not received for what had been, but for what should be. Still the motherliness in the wonderful passion of nurse's gave me delight[.]")

[E.C., 22 September]
<u>Tuesday afternoon</u>

I go into the garden & watch the fish, leaving P. with Schwester, who encloses her with passionate arms & plunges down on her cheeks with kisses. "Ich bin so hungrig"[1] she said on a stifled sob that came out as a smile of anxious love. P. told her when two nestled together, we called it in English "ein Love." "Meine Edith giebt nich Kein Love"[2]—she said with jealousy that is jealous of the loved one's receptiveness. P. kissed her cheeks, & then giving a little clap to the round, honest cheek, & kissed her lips. "Danke, danke" she said, & it was her heart that spoke. Then she kissed P. again & again on her lips—great, spreading kisses.

[E.C., 26 September]
Afternoon

[...] I must fight nurse's unreasonableness. She comes while I am resting, throws herself about me & kisses with the persistency of madness: I manage to make her understand she grieves & fatigues me—instantly with repentance she retires to the arm-chair, & I pretend deep sleep with anxious ears. She is called away & I slumber. She strives with herself & scarcely ever breaks out after——but the strain makes me dull by the time my Love returns.

---

1 "I am so hungry" (German).
2 "My Edith don't give no Love" (incorrect [dialect] double negation).

P. is with me—she has spent her holiday in the age of gold. Illness has made her sweeter, younger, more a Child. Heinrich has been born.

1892

[E.C.]
<u>Sunday</u> Feb. 14

My ~~own~~ Love is away with Amy Bell—I am away from my own identity. I want & want.... My own Love, & nothing else. Last night I wrote the wee Preface for <u>Sight & Song</u>.

[E.C., 30 March]

A trying half-hour with the Elk & the Roadman.[1] Something has worried them—they have an anxious East-windy manner. <u>Sight & Song</u> is found to be too bulky to be held by the parchment (unmounted) cover of <u>Fêtes Galantes</u>.[2] Suddenly our little book is disappointed of its clothes & we do not know how to cover its nakedness. Olive-Cloth is suggested.

Lane brings out a Privately Printed vol—1838—without a cover, called <u>Graphidae</u> or Characteristics of Painters.——not of Paintings. Truly, Solomon, there is nothing <u>quite</u> new under the sun ... & yet, forgive me, great Pessimist, there is—a room of Whistler's Nocturnes.

[E.C., Saturday 23 April]

A lovely morning—the leaves more like dewdrops than leaves in their lucid joyousness, the sky pale & happy. My love & I go to the Station that I may see her off to Dover. We swear ~~in the~~, with the bright world round us, that we will remain Poets & Lovers whatever may happen ~~that~~ [<] to [>] hinder~~s~~ or deflect~~s~~ our lives.

Sim wrote in the train:

---

1 The women's nicknames for publishers Elkin Mathews and John Lane, founders of the Bodley Head.
2 Paul Verlaine's 1869 influential volume of poems, many of which focused on Watteau's paintings.

It was deep April & the morn
Shakespeare was born;
The world was on us, pressing sore:
My Love & I took hands & swore
        Against the world to be
        Poets & lovers evermore;
To laugh & dream on Lethe's shore,
To sing to Charon in his boat,
Heartening the timid souls afloat;
Of Judgment never to take heed,
But to those fast-locked souls to speed
        Who never from Apollo fled,
        Who spent no hour among the dead:—
            Continually
            With them to dwell,
            Indifferent to heaven or hell.

[E.C., 2 May. Invited for the first time to Lunch at George
Meredith's, with decadent poet Richard Le Gallienne and his
wife.]
He [Meredith] asks wh: of us "does the <u>Males</u>"? (The highest
compliment implied in any question asked of Michael.)

[E.C. Between 20 June and 13 July the women stay in Paris at
Mary Costelloe's. The account of the trip is all in the hand of
E.C.]
[Monday 20 June] We go into our bedroom, wh: leads from the
salon—It looks impossible at first sight—so small a bed, such
dingy wash-stand, few chairs, & Mary's boxes. We have a sense we
are beginning a life in which the impossible easily becomes pos-
sible. As I pass through the door Bernard says "How charming
you are looking!" and I feel an angry self-depreciation [sic] at the
remark. [...] [After a walk with Bernard] We light our own lamp
in the dark little Salon. A young Americaine comes in—a little,
shapely dusk thing, with fire-flies in her pupils—A despair lies
over me—I cannot play with life as she can. Bernard plays too, &
I feel heavy.
    In course of conversation he says that a place becomes provin-
cial by believing it is not so. No place is so provincial as London.
    He talk[s] with a dazzling assurance that produces torpor &
irritation in the listener. The Americaine goes—will Bernard go is

a question that almost stops up our hearts. Yes—he gives his hand to all, and goes at midnight.

Tuesday—June 21st
We wake to a vine at our window (Evoe, Evoe!) & Mary, in a tawny dressing-gown, with streaming hair above it & naked feet below, comes to prepare our cold bath. We open our bedroom-door: Bernard twists round to us—he is there—& bids us good morning. Mary is in a white gown—she looks very positive, clear, & lovely. Seeing her & seeing him, I have a speechless weight on my whole nature—the beginning of "peine forte et dure."[1] I scarcely say a word at breakfast, except with my eyes, that can always talk, when my voice is [?]clownishly awkward.

Bernard drinks his coffee, eats his roll, eggs, while he talks as naturally as he breathes—of God, fate, art, & man.

"My God is a great machine, going along, digesting every-thing. What is bad & stupid is difficult to digest: when we are happy and joyous, we are aiding the digestion of God. ([H]ow inevitably this Lithuanian Jew, for all his American training, drifts to Spinozism!)

The talk began through Mrs. Costelloe saying that she spoke of the English devotion to gloomy sorts of work & duty to reli-gion as devil-worship.

Yes, truly,—answers the little Blasphemer—long ago the god of the Christians is dead and his rival is in his place. I believe in a God who suffers when we suffer, who rejoices when we are happy. His one command is: Be contemporaneous! The people who are so make tomorrow. To be contemporaneous is to digest today's meat. The great people of all ages are those who have been contemporaneous.

There is no beauty like the beauty of freedom; no grace that must not be foregone for freedom. Even male costume now is beautiful & graceful.

He goes—we unpack. Mary shows me the studio under our vine-tree where a painter lives with his mistress—a grisette.[2] We seem to live in the air of a French novel; there is a great strange-ness in us—an awe that is not sacred. Then she speaks to us of life, of the dissolution of family-bonds, of the divorce she hopes

---

1 Literally, strong and hard pain.
2 Literally, cheap dress made out of grey material. In the nineteenth century, the term meant a young working-class woman with a modern and urban lifestyle.

to get, by residence in America. With her soft voice ... Oh, it is like the delicious sweep of the scythe, mowing down what is ripe for destruction!

[E.C., 22 June. After a visit to the New Salon.]
By ourselves we go out into the Luxembourg Gardens—it is green & very peaceful; we sit beside a bed of white & crimson foxgloves that are almost as full as they can hold of bees.

There we face our situation.

When we joined Mary, at her proposal, in her brother's flat, we had no idea that her life & our lives would be spent [<] entirely [>] with Bernard—we had no idea that he & she were inseparable companions—we had no idea that we cared so much for him—that I should sicken of very passion for him. We did not know he had lost the £400 a year, granted to him by an American millionaire for 4 years, & that therefore he was needy & beset with a grasping hunger for cash. We are in a tragic coil, as it is— We cannot go, without breaking all friendship with the only friends who attract us—Mary is perfectly sweet & full of confidence: also an explanation would be required in England. Probably knowing that as Michael & Field we are insepa[<]ra[>]ble they have counted on long absences from our company & refreshing <u>recontres</u> at breakfast, afternoon-tea & at night. Yet such a hope on their part is unfair; for we were induced to visit Paris on the ~~understanding~~ [<] condition that [>] we should receive guidance to an understanding of recent art & Morellian help in the Louvre. However, independent action is our only shield; we agree that we will walk together, plan our separate plans, have no expectancy in our manner—but this wisdom comes from the bitterness of our hearts, is sour & unripened. We feel there is much that we cannot grasp in the circumstances we encounter: the magnetic trouble Bernard & I awake ~~in~~ each ~~other~~ in each is an incalculable element: & we cannot trust the Sapphic frenzy that ~~drags~~ [<] forces [>] us, in spite of ourselves, to follow him.

[E.C., 26 June]
We meet Mary & Bernhard outside Duval's.[1] The crowd is dense inside. Sim nearly faints, is tetchy over her food, and makes us all

---

1 One of several Parisian bohemian restaurants established by a butcher called Duval. It was immortalised by Pierre Auguste Renoir in *A Waitress at Duval's Restaurant*, painted ca. 1875.

cross & anxious. At night, in the little Salon, Bernhard criticises
several poems in <u>Sight and Song</u>. We challenge him to show how
impersonal he can be as a critic, face to face: at last he begins—
not without fear and some unwillingness.

We have confused the material of poetry, which is <u>feeling</u> with
colour & outline the materials of painting. If we looked on a
picture till we were on fire with it, the language we used would be
poetic. In <u>St. Jerome</u> we have <u>felt</u> the picture so intensely that
unconsciously we have evoked the feeling of a St. Jerome like the
St. Jerome painted or rather moulded by Tura. Wherever this
burning sensation is maintained there is life in the words we use.

Then he gives a verbal criticism of <u>The Magdalen</u>, <u>The Pietà</u>,
<u>St. Jerome</u>, <u>Bacchus & Ariadne.</u>

At afternoon tea B. had said that someday we shall give the
very picture itself, drag the animal from its shell: then we shall
write a <u>great</u> poem, as Rossetti did on the <u>Vierge au Rochers</u>.

[Thursday, 30 June. Still E.C.]
At Duval's we choose a table—They come in—the tall figure with
the gracious face, the small one, with a look ~~in~~ [<] about [>] the
face of restive unworldliness. We watch them—they come up to
us. I forget what we are talking about—he says—"Miss Cooper &
I should marry—& be miserable ever after." I am powerless to
shake off such remarks with irony or wit. I suffer & hate. But it is
true—we give one another no pleasure; the fascination we have
for each other makes us wretched.

[E.C.]
<u>Thursday</u>—July 7th

I am very poorly still & obliged to take a day in bed. The Doc-
trine asks if he may come & see me. I send word I will receive him
& should be very glad to have a lecture on the Lombard School,
as time is so short.

The Concièrge makes my room & by 11 I am ready for my
lecture, in my jasper-red dressing-gown. He greets me "O Field,
how picturesque you look."

Then he begins, sitting by my bedside. But Mary will not let
us have him to ourselves & she totters in to lie ~~again~~ by me, like
a drift of snow. I stoop to kiss her—half to teaze [sic] him! With
a flash of envy that ends ~~with~~ in a smile he says "For once in his
life he would like to be a girl."

[K.B.]
Monday even. July 18th.
*We came home on Wednesday July 13th.

Dionysos [sic] is not young; he is quite old, care-worn with crossing the mountains between Persia & India! I leave P. to tell the Paris story: we are back in Durdans, with every feather plucked from our wings, convinced of folly in dress, of poverty & affectation in English, of false method in art (see S. & S) of "taking things personally, of being Anglo Saxon, of living away from Life.["] We have heard of a new god whose sole command is—<u>Be Contemporaneous.</u>

[K.B., 29 July]
O Henry, Henry, My Boy, let us cleave to art—with a small a, & <u>grow</u> toward life, as toward the sun, not rend our path toward it.
God bless Henry!

[E.C.]
I am without my Love, in the twilight, when at the best one is sad to death. She is in Oxford. I am here a fragment. But I love my art & will not dare to injure it—I love my own Love & could not do violence to her or myself—so let her not fear. Although ~~those~~ [<] "the Doctrine's" [>] wonderful eyes— ~~ha~~ a Faun's crossed with the traditional Christ's—pursue me, ~~with~~ [<] tho' they have [>] a charm that maddens, I will never go off to the hills like Agave¹ only to rend my own flesh & blood—my artistic personality. I die in the presence of the face I love—the man's.

There is no fellowship, no caress, no tight winding-together of two natures, no tenderness when my Love is severed from me; And there seems to be no life in people—no life to be got any where—if one is withdrawn from <u>the Doctrine.</u>

So I sit by my table doubly dead. [The end of this entry was cut out by the writer.]

[K.B., 12 October]
It is lovely autumn, when we come out [of Tennyson's funeral]. And so closes the Victorian epoch.— ~~It is~~ an epoch already yesterday: it is for us, England's living, & yet unspent poets to make

---

1 The maenad Agave, in her frenzy, believing her son was a wild beast, tore him apart.

all things new. We are for the morning—the nineteenth century thinks it has no poets—nothing to lose—verily it has nothing: for we are not of it—we shake the dust of our feet from it, & pass on into the 20th. century.

[K.B.]
New Year's Eve

[...] There is much to make this year close in cynicism. We have published two books that have been received with silence or with hate. Most of our friends are further from us than last year—at least none of our bonds have been deepened, with the exception that I have grown to love Mary more.—The Man we love has been stamped & sealed another's, & the time we spent with him was one of trouble & unrest. Still I feel that much of our misery springs from the fact that we have not drawn on the infinite, we have asked for a happiness that could not have been given us without being taken from others.

We need to come under the blessing of peace to the men of good-will.

[E.C.]
Yes: the year 1892 has been almost the bitterest I ever spent—We have given our work to a silent world—twice have we given to the silence.

We have no friends who believe in our work—they are all in the grave—Encouragement is a sound that would make me start.

I love in a deathly way—the torment spends me—mind & nerves—as a prodigal devours his capital. In Love's domain I walk with Keats & Sappho.

"The modern" claims me—I am bound to live among old-fashioned conditions; I long for all things to be made new, & have to remain [<] keep [>] old myself. I long for freedom. England's a prison! I scarcely care to learn. I do not care for my work as I used to do—It does not grow up in me like a quickened seed—it grows from node to node like a yew. Now & then the spring [<] it [>] stirs it verdantly & I am happy.

[E.C.]

<u>Thursday Jan. 26th</u>

Elkin Mathews has offered for our Song-book[1] ~~at~~ only the terms offered for <u>Sight & Song</u>. Sim has consulted Ernest [Bell] & stirred him up to make an offer—half-profits on a good sale & for the rest Elkin's conditions.

So Sim goes to settle the matter at York St. Ernest is flattered we want to go back to our old publisher.[2] Certainly we have lost prestige greatly by giving to Elkins—we have had scarcely any reviews. There has not been a notice of <u>Stephania</u>[3] in one of the leading journals, that used to give us articles directly after publication.

The book might be a <u>deader</u>. We have not got on friendly terms with any of the Bodley Head set, & younger authors than we are have been pushed before us. No, we want a grave publisher & a little good company—Bridges, Patmore.[4] We are not made to go with those to whom literature is a scramble as heady [?]as that of the stock-exchange. The Artist must have a quiet hand & live in quiet ways.

I go to Paddington Green to arrange for an Empire Evening dress. I hear that A.[my] B.[ell] wears a magic ring wh: has brought her "old ladies—lots of money, & joy in the affairs of her heart"—O superstition!—I wish <u>we</u> could have such a ring.

My Love & I meet over Tomatoes & our Club chops, & then drive to the Athenaeum, 73, Tottenham Court Rd.[5] It is crowding—we get places that front the press of people ~~that~~ who [<] enter [>]—Among them Arthur [Symons], much the same in looks. He shakes hands & passes on. So does Selwyn Image. George Moore avoids us. He shines like the inside of an oyster-shell on the pretty woman who is with him. We are desperately alone in this world that shuns us. What can it be! <u>Stephania</u> cannot be responsible for it all. We are boycotted in the papers, by the men (Pater, Meredith, Hutton) to whom we have sent our book, & by even literary society. It is mysterious.

---

1   *Underneath the Bough.*
2   George Bell and Sons.
3   Their 1892 play.
4   Poets Robert Bridges (1844–1939) and Coventry Patmore (1823–96).
5   Athenaeum Hall (not the Club) was located at Tottenham Court Road. Socialists such as Eleanor Marx, for example, lectured here.

[K.B.]
Wednesday, July 12[th.]
Wet, wet, thunder-storms in the air.

The dear study is one the eve of spring-cleaning. This morning the battle of the ~~past~~ [<] modern [>] raged. The past was repulsed with great slaughter. Every Millet, every Turner has been banished from study & blue-room. Italian art alone remains. This new god's single command—<u>Be Contemporaneous</u> is harder to keep than all the ten old commandments. Our eyes no longer desire the Turners, our heads testify against them, yet the pain of parting from them is keen. Memory is a harpy—pluck her roots & she bleeds.

To-day's dreams & desires—the tongs with wh. the angel makes living corals of our lips to-day—these are the things to be expressed on our walls, in our furniture in our dress.

[K.B.]
Sunday Sept 10th
A day of perfect autumn. The Athenaeum Review of <u>Underneath the Bough</u>[1] is taken up to a high knoll top, encircled with bushes of oak. We read, rejoice dance madly, pluck the oak-apples.

[E.C. They moved to III Verulam Buildings, Gray's Inn, London, on 13 October 1893 to be close to the Opera Comique Theatre (Strand), where <u>A Question of Memory</u> will be performed.]
This afternoon I dare not go to the theatre—I have such a chill. It is difficult for me to stay away, I so love Rehearsal. It is ~~so~~ wonderful to see one's words growing pictures, movements, persons—to watch a play being secretly fashioned down in the Earth. I descend the ~~black~~ stairs & triumph in the bald dirt, the hangman-ropes, the gape of the stage. I triumph; & in the dim-obscure is a small table, ~~a few~~ [<] some [>] chairs, the extinct footlights, & a few puppets—men & women in whom I take an interest second only to that I take in the creation of my brain.

---

1 See "Reviews" Section, p. 367.

[E.C. 27 October, Bradley's birthday, first and last performance of <u>A Question of Memory</u>.[1]]

<u>5 o'clock</u>. The gas-lamps are lighted—the sun is setting.....

<u>Oct. 28.</u> It seems more natural to be dead than alive. We wake to the surprise of finding every morning paper against us; little Fleming falls before the crisis—he is too small a soul—but my love ~~was~~ [<] is [>] strong, pour~~ed~~[<]s[>] him out his tea, crack~~ed~~[<]s[>] jokes with him, and ~~was~~ [<] is [>] able to convey our gratitude for this Gray's Inn Refuge. I ~~was~~ [<] am [>] in helpless pain like a dumb animal at first. The <u>Times</u> & the <u>Telegraph</u> are worthy of respect in their blame; they have some good words for us & for our actors; the rest howl!
[...] Not a flower had any one sent us yesterday, not a flower was given to us. No word, no letter, no visit, only the execrations of the Press!
[...] The Evening papers are worse than the morning—they are like a lot of unchained tigers. We are hated as Shelley was hated by our countrymen blindly, ravenously.

[E.C]
<u>Tuesday November 22.</u>
Verlaine reads his own poems at Barnard's Inn—a most "seizing" occasion (in the French sense). The picturesque ~~apartment~~ hall—so to 100 intellectual listeners, many of them women—the personality of the reader, that can be summarised by Strafford's <u>Thorough</u>[2] (for Verlaine is as extreme a devotee as he is extreme a sinner), the ~~midsummer~~ [<]June[>]-rose beauty of his young neophyte, Symons, the low melodies of that cracked instrument, ~~Verlaine's~~ [<] his [>] voice, and the congruity between the poems & the poet—all these things made the time from a quarter to nine until ten most singularly new.

---

1 Directed by H. de Lange. Cast: Ferencz—Mr. Acton Bond; Stanislaus—Mr. A. Hamilton-Reveille; Haynau—Mr. John Beauchamp; Austrian officers—Mr. Neville Doone and Mr. Charles Rutland; Ferencz's mother—Mrs. Theodore Wright; Fina—Miss Mary Keegan; Thekla—Miss Hall Caine; Elizabeth—Mrs. Charles Creswick.
2 This seems to be a reference to a policy set up by the Earl of Stafford (1593–1641) to manage Church and State affairs, but the relevance is not clear.

1894

[K.B.]

.........I go on to the Bodley Head, & learn that Henry Harland is to be the editor of a new quarterly magazine, to be called <u>The Yellow Book</u>.

I return with Louie Ellis[1] who spends with us Sunday Feb. 4th.

Tonight, (Feb 4th), I have sent ~~Edith~~ Henry's <u>Garden</u>, & my few little typed things to Henry Harland, in proposal, for his <u>Yellow Book</u>. Louie has been very caressing, but she & all our friends avoid allusion to our art as if it were a dead husband. After all, Mary & the Doctrine are the only people who at any points touch our lives vitally.

[E.C]

Wednesday—April 17   The Yellow Book[2]

We have been almost blinded by the glare of hell.

When we started to town we were feeling depressed; it was one of those morose & leafy days wh: are the curse of summer in England—& it is almost summer after the heat of the last three weeks—days when the young green is viciously out of tone with the muddied stretch of rain-sky. We went to the Bodley Head to ~~buy~~ [<] purchase [>] our copy of <u>The Yellow Book</u>.

As we came up to the shop we found the whole frontage a hot background of orange-colour to [<] sly [>], roistering heads, silhouetted against it & [<]half-[>] hiding behind masks. The window seemed to be gibbering, our eyes to be filled with incurable jaundice. <u>La Réclame</u>, hideous beyond Duessa or any Witch ever seen by the mind's eye, stood up before us as a shop where contemporary literature ~~was~~ [<] is [>] sold. One felt as one does when now & then a wholly lost woman stands flaming on the pavement with the ghastly laugh of the ribald crowd in the air round her. One hates one's eyes for seeing! But the infamous window mocked & mowed, & fizgiged, saffron & pitchy, till one's eyes were arrested like Virgil's before the wind of flame.

And the inside of the book! It is full of cleverness such as one expects to find in those who dwell below light & hope & love & aspiration. The best one can say, of any tale or any illustration is

---

1 Sister of Havelock Ellis. She designed clothes for the women.
2 This entry is by Edith, but the title of the entry, "The Yellow Book," is in Katharine's hand. See letter 23 (K.B. to Mary Costelloe: 1894).

that it is clever—the worst one can say is that it is damnable.

But George Egerton does not even deserve damnation, but something weightier—crushing-out silence.

Education Sentimentale by Beardsley & his Bookplate are night-mares from some exotic house of ill-fame. Faugh! One most go to one's Wordsworth & Shelley to be fumigated.

We think of changing our name to Messalina Garden[1] to escape from the company of George Egerton!

[... K.B. continues] These George Egertons, George Flemings &c &c. We are threatened with a fresh Hanoverian curse!

[E.C.]
Thursday—July 17
Got off heaps of letters.

A few days ago Michael, in full disgust at the Yellow Book, wrote as follows to the Editor Harland—à propos of our little prose-poem Rhythm he had accepted for the 2nd vol.

Dear Sir,
I must request you to return my typed copy of Rhythm. I dislike the Yellow Book both in its first and second number & greatly regret that in a sudden rashness of sympathy I proposed to contribute to it—It has been all my fault, & I should not ask you to return an accepted paper if your delay in printing had not convinced me that you feel M. F. is not an ingredient in the Yellow Book —broth ... as for metaphor's sake I must name it. Trusting you will see that I do not write in a spirit of contention, I am
                Sincerely yrs &c

In response we have the following on an open p.card—
"The Editor of the Yellow Book can in no case return rejected MSS. unless stamped addressed envelopes for that purpose are provided by the sender."

————————

We reply to the Cad—"Durdans
                Reigate—July 17

Dear Sir,
I extremely regret the unbusinesslike omission of stamps. I punish myself for the informality by enclosing a half-penny stamp

---

1 See the poem "The Genethliacs of Wine" in *Dedicated*, p. 197.

for the card on which you explained ~~by~~ my mistake. And I enclose fully addressed stamped envelope as the return fare of the M.S. I have asked you not to insert. Sincerely yours &c.["]

This means a break forever with the hated Bodley Head—it is like a noisome dragon dropping from one dead—so utterly the pollution drops form our lives—as far as our wills go in the matter.

1895

[E.C.]
March 21st
An offer from The Atlantic Monthly for two of our Wild Honey Poems—if we will set our price on them: we have bated them with £10 each—will the American mouse bite?

[E.C. April. The women go to Italy. There they meet Bernard Berenson and Mary Costelloe, and Vernon Lee and her partner Clementina Anstruther-Thomson.]
Sunday [21 April]   Alice Pearsall Smith [and] her husband Bertrand Russell come for the day, & we have a merry peep at them before we start for Vernon Lee's. The walk is white-hot—we creep under walls, at the top of which the olives scintillate.

Lunch is as tactless a meal as one would expect in so un-homely a home. Vernon's brother Eugene,[1] who was twenty years on his back as an invalid, in wh: time he became a poet with ~~some~~ ghoulish ~~power of suggesting~~ diseased colour in his sonnets [<] & good form [>], has risen from his bed & walks—but has completely lost poetic power & general brain power. He sits by one, a flabby man, with great peevish blue eyes—wearied with the life given back to him in ~~old~~ [<] middle [>] age, restless for change of scene. He wants to see the real ocean again—the Atlantic, "with its tides and jelly-fish"—what keen longing in that last item ... one minute desire that has ~~has~~ grown a hunger, after twenty years! The pathetic bore grates his sister's nerves, till the ~~air~~ [<] atmosphere [>] all round her becomes uncomfortable. She left us much to him—poor intellectual Vampire disappointed of her discussion. There is something uncommonly kind about her ... &

---

1 Poet Eugene Lee-Hamilton (1845–1907).

she is well-instructed with a gigantic memory; but the instruction does not serve an able mind.

She is like a museum, rather untidily arranged.

[E.C., April]
On Sunday night after talk about Carducci's <u>Satana</u>[1] & about Oscar, I dream that we stop at a restaurant half way up a mountain & a woman far down the table begs to speak with us when the table d'hôte is over, for she has heard things against us. "Oh," says a woman on Michael's left "what an interesting talk that will be—I ~~know~~ [<] suspect [>] it will be about your works." Michael replies "I have no fear at all about my works—I know quite well they all came from Satan"[.] At her right hand I whisper "For goodness' sake, don't say these things—remember the Oscar Scandal!"—How characteristic both remarks!

[E.C., October]
But I have read more Nitzsche [sic] ... & what I have discovered! That <u>every thought</u>, almost, that Bernard presented this spring with the marvellous personality of voice & language that is his, came straight from Nitzsche <u>without acknowledgement</u>. When I think that B. stood in the way of our reading Nitzsche, & and presented him as a German Whitman, lacking the American <u>quality</u>.—I recoil against the doer of the infamy. The man is in an asylum ... & another man simply day by day charms people with the madman's originality, & never even says "all this was suggested by Nitzsche."

1898

[K.B.]
Whym Chow[2]
Friday evening, January 28th Whym-Chow arrived—a dusky sable—a wolf with civilization's softness, an oriental with husky passion—white-rolling eyeballs, & the power of inward frenzy—velvet manners & the savagery of eastern armies behind.

---

1 "Hymn to Satan" (1865), by Italian Nobel Prize-winning poet Giosuè Carducci (1835–1907).
2 The dog was Cooper and Amy's joint present for Bradley.

I suppose our new love of animals is a desire to get into another kingdom—we reach after the kingdom of the dead—we can penetrate into the kingdom of animals. Mortals all round us defeat or mislead for the more part, we seek a companionship we can determine.

[K.B., 3 February]
I will never make him [Whym Chow] a Christian dog. I will civil-ise the seven devils.
—Oh, I love him!
Hennie loves him.
He is Michael's own little brimstone soul.
    Hennie loves him!
            Amen.

[E.C. 31 December]
[W]e have been detaching from Durdans—our adored little home, with its garden & the twining about it of <u>his</u> memory who gave [<] it [>] to us. I trust this year looks on the death-bed of our home—for I feel we need a new life, a resurrection; & a great Chance has been offered to us at last—the Chance of founding a home, where my Love & I can live a married life & make our own associations & weave our modes of enjoyment, & be our Best Each to Each in newness as of green spring.

The courage we shall need will be gigantic—it will grow in might if we seek sincere quality in it.

We have made no new friends—but the Artists are more & more our male-doubles in what they enjoy, live for & assimilate.

1899

[E.C., 9 February]
It was exhilerating [sic] to gather my Love out of the very wet rain & tell the news through a kiss that 1, Paragon[1] is ours—I feel <u>renewing</u> as a process that is as yet a wild confusion in me—but the certain movements of the confusion tell me it will become a dance.
"Sweet Thames, flow softly till I end my song."

---

1 In the suburb of Richmond, London.

Indeed the Song in my heart is an Epithalamium—a marriage-song of absolutely joined lives: a dream that Eros returns to us after the years of a lifetime as a gift.

[K.B., 11 October. In their new house in Richmond.]
Love & I sit on the yellow sofa, curled up.—A boat is moored in mid-stream, its keel reflected clear in the water. Henry says— "How that boat measures the silence."

"I like the air when the stars come out" Love says, & then our spirits close up together.

We sit together in the dusk now[.] The timber-barges with their lights, one orange & two clear gold, add [<] in their swift passing through the mist [>] to the strong excitements of sunset.
　　And with the eyes with which we shall see god—vision puri-fied by the beauty on which it rests—we gaze & wonder.
　　Just that we want to watch, as the light alters, just that, nothing else, & no more.
　　Two in accord, four panes of glass, a stream, a misty meadow, & the sun falling through the rounded elms.

1900

[K.B., 21 January]
—It is very much to me, the news of his [John Ruskin's] death[1]—touching me not with grief at all—with music—with music one has not heard for years,—& an indescribeable [sic] sense of pre-cious relics that one has not seen [<]—for a moment exposed [>]—of the past that is with one for ever, & has been neglected—of the past that is only attaching—when it is fugitive, & lost, & re-appears.
　　How I loved him!
—For years, best of all creatures on the earth.
Good is it that he is away from the misery of this sinful world ... but as I sit, & watch the dick-birds hopping about, & the sky already a little restless with the spring—I don't like to think his eyes will enjoy these things no more. For the earth was his & the fulness [sic] thereof.

1　John Ruskin died on Saturday 20 January 1900.

And he has left us for creed so much—labour, & peace, in worship—the joy of the servant of God—that recognizes the smallest little chickweed His, & loves His work—all the six days through.

—And this joy is simply unknown to the moderns, who love their [?]cribbled, idol-orchids, the work of men's devil-hands,—love the spotted, tainted flower, in its mimicry, its self-absorption, its grotesqueness, & care nothing for the creatures that bear us the honey, the light, the dew.

[E.C., c. 27 January]
After wandering the Tower we return to the Sun Room: Michael, Mary [Berenson], Logan,[1] & Roger Fry[2] sit close on the settee, black figures resolved, it seems, to break down the old[,] came by mass. So strange to see four faces together against the all-judging white wall—but the judment [sic] must be unrecorded.

[E.C.]
Tuesday April 9th.
Nutt sends statement of Anna Ruina[3] a good name Ruina—Queen of Ruin. Only 19 copies have been sold! We have to pay £15, as by agreement, & the excellent David is then still a loser.

No wonder I regard publication as merely Fire Insurance.

We have no readers; before our work a beautiful desert swims golden ... who shall say what is on the other side—But I am soothed by the solitude—Michael is wearied by it, alas! [...]

A. Symons has written well & Pateresquely on Symbolism—a book that has West-Wind influence, searching out life in our quiescence & prophesying over it. [4]

---

1 Logan Pearsall Smith (1865–1946), Mary Berenson's brother. Their sister Alys Whitall was the first wife of Bertrand Russell.
2 The famous post-Impressionist painter and a member of the Blooms-bury Group.
3 Their 1899 play.
4 Arthur Symons's influential *The Symbolist Movement in Literature* (London: Heinemann, 1899).

<u>Good Friday</u> April 13th—

A wild wholesome West Wind—its noise & sun are about us.

At breakfast Michael & I were talking of our different attitudes toward the Spiritual World. Michael sees it ~~like~~ [<] as [>] an Umbrian Painter[1] sees the sky, trees, with adoration in her eyes … I see it as Whistler sees this world through an atmosphere, & as long as I can keep within that atmosphere I have found the condition by wh: I can live in it. This atmosphere is what light is to our world—no more mystical—the dead are in it, as flowers & beasts & men are in the sunshine.

[E.C. Still Good Friday, Ricketts is visiting.]
Then talk ~~turns of~~ [<] begins [>] on Arthur Symons' <u>Symbolists</u>—R.[icketts] finds Symbolist a meaningless word—Evocation has always been the poet's aim. Mysticism is equally meaningless as a word of praise, of quality. It describes a state of obtuseness to impression or an attitude of Dandyism toward Language. The mystic is in a state of diseased fear before his impressions[.] Maeterlincks'[2] persons will not put out a hand to open a door they curdle at. Maeterlinck is consumptive, & unintelligent—for intelligence is the death-knell of mysticism: Mallarmé is not a mystic, he is wholly a learned experimentalist in words, a man with an <u>idée fixe</u>, a passionate ~~technilia~~ "technician." All the men Arthur considers are men of 2nd-class importance (men of diseased temperament) with a "precious" way of looking at life. Verlaine alone counts—he is a simple force, extremely human & wonderful.

Ricketts understands why Huysmans has become a Catholic. He has shared the restless, intoxicating life of the Cafés till the necessity of finding a quiet, unchangeable basis has become essential to him. Think what it wd. be to an <u>habitué</u> of the Cafés to meet a Catholic priest with his quietude, his sense of manners, his ordered hours—what a relief. In France if you hate a rival artist, instead of backbiting him as you wd. in England, you draw him to the Cafés & urge him to write there—put the pen in his hand as Catulle Mendes did with Verlaine.[3] You have done all an enemy can do. The Fairyman speaks touchingly of our frailty—of

---

1 Fifteenth- and sixteenth-century Italian school of painting represented by Perugino and Raphael.
2 Belgian symbolist poet Maurice Maeterlinck (1862–1949).
3 Parnassian poet Catulle Mendès (1841–1909) was the founder of *La Revue Fantaisiste* (1861). He published the work of Gautier and Baudelaire.

how even Peter denied Christ—It is so hard to keep up any of that strength that forms life into beauty.

The moderns bring disintegration with them. One is coming to dine at Spring Terrace[1] next week; & Ricketts cannot tell what a bad taste his visit will leave. The few chosen friends lose their places—life becomes a railway-station, all jostle, disorder; one's relation with existance [sic] is falsified, one's personal dignity suffers [?]cloud.

[K.B. July]

It is very sweet! It is the Sunday of convalescence. Henry is sitting up in my gay, west bedroom, in lovely ivories, & lace, & turquoise & diamonds—my Bride, my Shining One. And we have been reading all the Marriage-songs in <u>Long Ago</u>. "Oh Hymen, Hymenaeus!"[2]

[E.C., 21 October]

While Michael was away in town last Thursday I grew bold enough for a magnificent audacity. My chief birthday gift is a vellum copy of all my poems (written by myself) that are naturally & inevitably <u>Dedicated</u> to Michael.[3] I felt they would begin with a spell if Ricketts designed the page of dedication. So I send a page round by our Cherub-Boy Herbert to 8, Spring Terrace.

My note began—

Dear Painter, Be reassured! This is only a page of my Book of Poems I am going to give as a gift to Michael on the 27th. Could you letter for me the title <u>Dedicated</u> & [<] if [>] it might be[,] you could surround the title with a swirl of altar-flame, of vowed garland & or insence[sic]-cloud, my gift wd. come to Michael with a spell.

[E.C.]

<u>October 27th</u>—The great Birthday & Wedding Day.

As soon as I wake I bring <u>Dedicated</u> to Michael. Her joy is a shock to her—she can hardly receive my supreme gift, made

---

1 Ricketts and Shannon's house in Richmond.
2 God of marriage.
3 Cooper wrote most of the poems later published in *Dedicated* (1914) during their holiday in the New Forest.

beautiful by the Fairyman's creative tact. I tell her all the story of my audacity for her sake.

1901

[E.C.]
Jan. 6th
At last nearly a week after I record the New Century Dinner on New Year's Day in which [<] when [>] the Poets & Painters[1] pledged each other.
I must give the <u>menu</u>
~~Tomato~~ Tommato Soup
      Cod à la Crème
      Poularde rôti
      Plum Pudding
      Cherry Pudding
      Stone Cream
      Croûte au Caviar

      English Pine, Almonds & Raisins
      Newtown Pippins

Champagne—White Port

    Coffee, Crème de Mocco, Cigarettes.

The Artists were late—they had been over-~~gentile~~ [<] genteel [>] & imperielled [sic] the dinner. Clouds of roses ~~came~~ [<] had travelled [>] from the past summer or the summer to be & stayed in their clouds of cinnamon & rose-redness on the table.

Of course Ricketts protested he was of the Nineteenth Century & always wd. be—the Wonderful Century of Keats, of French literature, of Beethoven & Wagner. He had nothing to do with the 20th Century. He is an undiscovered master of the 19th. In vain we protest that we trust to unite two centuries in our work & Shannon asserts that he belongs to the new century & savours the opportunities it gives him: the Fairyman[2] declares he remains with Beethoven.

Of course we all believe we are celebrating the first birthday of

---

1 Bradley and Cooper, and Ricketts and Shannon.
2 Ricketts.

the century, not its birth. We hold with Cellini[1] & Napoleon, & laugh at clerics & men of science.

As the feast proceeds & two servings becomes pleasure's law Ricketts cries to his fellow "Shannon, do you think I shall live into the ~~next~~ [<] 20th [>] century if I eat any more cream?"

The pine he regards as scarcely a fruit—a thing of fragrance, like one of King Solomon's woods.

After glasses have touched, Shannon's plate begins to dance. I watch him at his ratiocination—so stolidly reasonable. He thinks there must be a joint in the table that he has sprung, so he moves the plate; & when it still feebly lifts[,] places his thumb on the edge. Really I am pumping air into a little bladder under it that is reached by a long tube under the table cloth. The trick has driven a doctor away from a dinner-party, convinced of evil spirits—but Shannon[,] after an instant's astonishment[,] considered & acted.

Ricketts confessed he wd. have thought it was the champagne, & striking a finger-point against his cheek imitated the complacency with wh: Yeats would have received the attention spirits showed him.[2]

Michael spoke of the "god like hardship" we prepare for ourselves. Then Ricketts tells a delicious story of Beerbohm Tree.[3] The actor is with his scene-painter & explains that every play by Shakspere [sic] has its ~~its~~ keynote. "I am sure you will agree with me the keynote to be expressed in the scenery of <u>The Tempest</u> is [R]omance; then in Midsummer Night's <u>Dream</u> of course it is <u>Poesie</u>; & with <u>Twelfth Night</u>, I am sure you will agree with me, it is <u>Joy</u>..... with economy." The practical terror that the exuberant keynote should run away with the scene-painter & drain <u>Her Majesty's</u> coffers, is simply all one could desire. So instead of "Godlike Hardship"—it is to be "Joy—with economy"!

The Coming Man of the 20th Cen. is Sturge Moore—his words have quality in themselves apart from what they express—this is virtue in a writer. Yeats may have some quality of metrical movement, but his words are hollow.

My wreath of forest-holly round Ricketts' mirror is a triumph. It is stood up to—the Painter fixes it for moments together as most beautiful & coloured against the white panelling. We must always twine wreaths for the mirror—oak or pine or forget-me-not.

---

1 Italian artist (1500–71).
2 Yeats was very interested in spiritualism and occultism.
3 Sir Herbert Beerbohm-Tree (1852–1917), an English actor.

We have the new leaves of the year—honeysuckle-wings from Petersham Common & roses on our table; tuberose on our mantel-shelf.

The old Crême de Mocco is savoured. I describe it as essence of coffee that has reached Heaven from faith in Hartshorne as its creed.

We handle the great Cellini (Vol. I)[1] just arrived—The [<] Morris [>] Chaucer of the Vale Press. The two Michaels (<u>Race of Leaves</u>, & <u>Julia Domna</u>),[2] the two Solomons[3] (<u>The Song</u> & <u>Ecclesiastes</u>), The Parables of Christ & Sturge Moore <u>Danaë</u> are all to be issued in the same type. For <u>The King's Quhair</u>[4] & other royal books ~~in~~ special type is preparing.

The Artists open their minds, uncertain & divided on the subject of my pendant—is it to be <u>Music</u>[5]—the Basset hanging from a lyre, his feet rolled over sapphires & his eye a ruby—or the bird plucking green grapes among the leaves of the vine at Spring Terrace? After an hour's talk on jewels & designs we agree that it shall be <u>Music</u> now & <u>The Vine</u> perhaps later.

We just note, Michael & I [<] to one another [>] that it is enviable to have Artists to provide us with our books, our jewels & our pictures.

When they leave they drop 2 packets of Jap. water-transparencies[6] on the table, that we may see what happens.

---

1 Benvenuto Cellini, *The Life of Benvenuto Cellini*. Trans. John Addington Symonds. London: The Vale Press, 1900. 2 Vols.

2 The Vale Press was the publisher of their Roman Trilogy *The World at Auction* (1898), *The Race of Leaves* (1901), and *Julia Domna* (1903).

3 Biblical texts: the *Song of Solomon* and *Ecclesiastes*, which was also ascribed to Solomon.

4 A misspelling of *The King's Quair*: the book King James I of Scotland wrote while a prisoner in England.

5 The women's pet basset hound. As well as being a painter and an engraver, Ricketts also designed jewellery. His most famous pieces are those designed for Michael Field. This particular piece took its name from their hound, Music.

6 Presumably Japanese decorations, to be put in water-bowls on the table.

[K.B.]
>   Our beloved Queen dies
>   January 22nd 1901

We are seated at our modest game of Khan-hoo.[1] The long day of suspense has been sickening, & the sweetness of hope destroyed—I am touching with pleasure the rose-cards—when I hear the soft, tear-quavering voice of our little choir-boy, come to say that our great Queen is dead. I—I have no tears. She sweeps away with her into the locked land my life, my youth, my breathing. I have no allegiance to any other. I love her. She is as simply my Queen as God is my God.

[E.C., c. 6 April]
A Kingfisher-flash! Ricketts is pouring out the jewels for Music on the Sun-Room table. A little pincer in his hand, he picks up one [?]dartling scrap after another & drops it in its hole. The jewel lies gorgeous with its jewels. And April itself comes & plays with them. Ricketts is absolutely absorbed before his work.

He has brought us Act III & half Act IV of the The Race of Leaves.[2]

Its poetry—what there is of it—is wholly Latin—it is brief, balanced, with a felicity of manner among the words; it attains the bull's eye of its conception.

Bank Holiday [8 April]
The river & breeze at horse-play—the little boats sharing it, the people delighted. The sun making leaves all over the ~~trees~~ boughs.

At night we read the 1st Edition of Underneath the Bough. Scarcely two dozen poems stand before our more perfect judgment.

The Poems like "Mortal, if thou art beloved" of our early dramatic period mostly stand—Those written under the Elizabethan impulse given by Bullen's Collection[3] have very precarious foothold: those under Bernhard's influence nearly all slip into the

---

1   The women were keen players of this Chinese card game, which was introduced to England in 1891 by the British consul in China and Korea, William Henry Wilkinson.

2   The women's 1901 Roman play.

3   Arthur Henry Bullen (1857–1920), editor of Old English lyrics. He became famous for his edition of *Lyrics from the Song Books of the Elizabethan Age* (1887), which was reprinted and expanded in numerous editions.

gulf. Lyric poetry is too often content with a [<] mere [>] personal emotion: whereas in all great poetry the object is the source of the emotion. This is why women cannot write love-poetry—they write of their own feelings, not of the power of the beloved as it reaches & envelopes [sic] ~~them~~ & draws ~~them~~ [<] back [>] into its depth. Women are nearly always frothy when they sing love. Sappho is not, because she sings Aphrodite ~~herself~~ & the passions with wh: she [?]lures mortals to herself.

We were not, in <u>Long Ago</u> because we sang Sappho, sang from the heart of her words. In all the gt. sonnets Michael has written she has been gained by the passion of the object. Wherever we are perishable we have sung an impression or feeling that is sporadically ours, just sown by chance in our sensibility. Bernard says now all Art is a Dream. It is a floating into a great passion other than our own; We are half-asleep with its power, we see & hear wonderful things, impossible if we stay at home with our own heart-beats.

[E.C., 30 June. Berenson visits Michael Field.][1]
I am bending over the new flame when he comes down alone. I rise & our hands join. He shakes mine Hamlet-wise up & down & says "Dear Field, it is delicious to see you again & just the same"—"and to see you again, the same Bernhard." I sit down by the wall ~~again~~ & he draws up his ~~chairs~~.

"And did you think I should not be the same Bernhard?" A shrug—"Who could tell—friends [<] do [>] change ~~sto~~ sometimes."—"Ah, there may come a cleft all through life; but that is very rare. It is beautiful to find you so at peace." [...]

Michael & Mary come down & we go into the Gold Room for tea, while Mary convinces [sic] him of flirting with Italian ladies, much to his ~~ag~~ anger—of holding the hands of one lady "Because I am very fond of her."

I don't care—none of the thrusts come near me. Bernhard & I are ~~just~~ one & the same to each other, & I dont [sic] want to be anything more or other. The Italian ladies may hold his hands & welcome—just as Mary has her wife's demands on him.

We part in the hall, touching ~~ey~~ each other by our eyes rather than our hands. It is deeply, peaceably goodbye.

---

1 This was their first face-to-face meeting in six years.

1902

[K.B.]
Tuesday January 7th.

[...] In the evening, Henry & I, left quite to ourselves, read madly the deep love-poems of Long Ago: read of the great poet who answered back our love in Asolando.[1]

[E.C., 18 January]
"I think Mr. Ricketts is there" she [Lillias, their servant] says stiffly. I go in to find the beautiful ring—my Love's Birthday Ring—lying on the table—a large lapis-lazuli & a chrysopraise surmounting it—with a ridged hoop & clasps of fleur-de-luce [sic] volutes—three little gold balls set triangularly on the green stone. So lovely![2]

[K.B.]
 Monday May 5th
I break in [<] here [>] to give their last state visit—knocks, as we were drinking tea last night—I rise hastily & leave Henry to receive them.... When I return I find Henry talking pompously of "a sacrifice to the poets," & dragging my attention to the lovely, China bowl that, during the Richmond period, has held the artists' sugar.—They all seem to me to be behaving like pompous fools! Then Fay gives me a M.S.[3] (typed) of John Gray's. They have been looking over their papers—It may amuse me to look at it. I need not return it. "Oh," I retort "that is what you will do with Michael Field's sonnets—come across them when you are looking over some rubbish, & toss them to a friend for a moment's amusement"—He makes no defence.[4] Talk begins. [...]
[...]
~~He~~ [<] Fay also [>] takes the base modern view that Shakespeare has not an attractive personality. If he were to enter the

---

1 Robert Browning's 1888–89 poem.
2 The ring was given by "Michael" to "Henry" as a present for her fortieth birthday.
3 Manuscript.
4 Though Ricketts admired Bradley, there were tensions in their relationship.

room, he would not feel towards him—the awe—he wd. feel if Michael Angelo, or even Milton came in.

Shakespeare is a creature made of plenty of exquisite [?]fur—a quantity of stuff cut to waste—it is what his work is perpetually that enchants—With regard to <u>Much Ado</u> he agrees with me it is disgusting in its issue, & he speaks much of Shakespeare's injustice to the male. He hates [<] Hal & [>] Orlando & Claudius &c. He quotes from the sonnet—"No longer mourn for me when I am dead"—& then—after regretting it is so defaced by reference to the worms—goes on to speak of the poem Christina [Rossetti] stole from it, making of it something even more exquisite. Henry thinks he alludes to "When I am dead, my dearest." If he does, that poem in its oppressive earthiness & rather bitter spite—"I haply shall remember, & haply shall forget"—is not worthy for an instant to be compared with the noble passion of—"No longer mourn for me when I am dead." That is what is finest in a man—sparing a woman, or, at all events sparing his friend—pain—better forgetfulness than suffering,—Christina's work is—it is all-dust & mortal & a chance—the <u>what does it matter</u> of despair.

[E.C.]
<u>Thursday</u> June 5th
We train our pomegranate & smilax asper on the balcony.
We wait—
Yeats & Tommy[1] come.

The first motion of Yeats is to seize a book for bread & support in his shyness.. it is Ricketts' <u>Hero & Leander,</u> ... And there is not another book in sight. We leave him to recover: then Michael shows him the river & the pendant.[2] The miniature he finds most lovely but does not know which of us it is.

His shyness makes Tommy more familiar. The stranger manifests that ~~were~~ [<] we [>] are somewhat intimate after a year's friendship. It is an easeful truth.

At dinner Yeats is fearfully shy at first, doctrinaire & "causy," but he gradually becomes warm & vivid in his monologuing. He is dark with a Dantesque face—only not cut in Italian marble! His hair dribbles in a Postlethwaite manner on to his brow. I wanted to give the order to Lillias to bring grape-scissors & cut

---

1   Thomas Sturge Moore (1870–1944).
2   The Pegasus pendant. It contains a miniature of Cooper by Charles Ricketts.

the locks. His eyes are abstract & fervid: when he speaks of spiritual things, & shakes back his forelock, there is a smile like an atmosphere on his eyes & brow. The mouth is for speech, speech—the hands ~~are like~~ flap like flower-heads that grow on each side a stem & are shaken by the wind. At first the gesture spells one; then it irritates, because it is a gesture & is not varied.

We put on our smilax-wreaths. Tommy looks like a primaeval forest-God—terrible, the source of panic & of [<] the [>] cruel laughter of simplicity.

Yeats feels he is wearing spectacles— ~~but~~ [<] & [>] the twine looks conventionally poetic on his hair. Then we cast the wreaths on to Whym Chow's neck.

Yeats is not of us—as Tommy & the Artists & Bernhard[1] are: he is a preacher. He preaches some excellent things & some foolish things.

He knows our plays well & seems to care for them with insight. I was not prepared for this:—but Dowden[2] fired him with them in youth when he was at Dublin University. His wit is rhetorical—not the instinctive mischief & drollery, the moment's wild happiness in some contrast, that is so engaging in Tommy.

He is an evangelist—quite sincere in his exposition & persuasion.

We have some amusing glimpses at George Moore—calling in a policeman to know if the law requires him to eat his landlady's omelette, or gazing at the amateur Dublin actors of the Clerk fraternity & pronouncing "Well, you are a seedy lot."

Yeats reads a little prayer to the psaltery—a most charming poem.

All the Archangels appear in it, with shoes of the [?]7 metals. Also he entoned [sic] as if to the psaltery Keats' Bacchic Ode.

A note comes from Ricketts who will have the "fatted bun" ready tomorrow & the lift strewn with roses.

Tommy lifts his hands in mock horror "Why, Shannon will not be there[.]"

The rogue!

"But Ricketts will" says Michael, profoundly hoping it will not rain, so that Tommy & Shannon may "bike" & we have the horrible bliss of Fay by himself. Yeats says that in his first review of

---

1 Thomas Sturge Moore, Ricketts and Shannon, and Bernard Berenson.
2 Edward Dowden (1843–1913), Irish critic and poet who was elected professor in English literature at Dublin University in 1867.

us, written when a college youth[,] he remarked we did not dream or saunter enough.

Poor George Moore, who wails over the way in wh: characters become faint under Yeats' handling, wd. find in this lack our safeguard.

We have been saying we envy men their conversation with each other. "Men don't talk well to each other—they talk well to women—there must be sex i[n] good talk" says Yeats. Tommy, lying Panlike on the settee echoes this with fervour, "a man has no ideas among men—but he goes home to ~~his~~ [<] a [>] cook or a countess, & he is all right" sings Yeats. Therefore he is a believer in many flirtations & believes Göethe's wisdom was born to him of woman.

[E.C.]
Oct. 7th—
We have just read that Lionel Johnson died on Sat. in St. Ba[r]tholomew's Hospital, of paralysis, at the age of 35. It is terrible.

One by one these young men who were about our way, when we began at Michael, have drifted down the hollow gusts of Fate to piteous graves.[1] My ears feel to hear nothing but the fluting of reeds shaken by the wind. And this little creature, with his face of a decoyed angel & his ominous fragility, was the man who alone ever wrote words about our work that our souls countersigned..

1903

[E.C. July]
Tommy comes to talk over our wills & what we are to do with this Book.[2] We do not want it to do harm—we do not want its vitality, ~~the~~ its real confession ~~that it is~~ injured. We have to leave the problem—but I think Tommy will "execute" us in respect to all other M.S.S.—even if Works & Days is not left to him. He is too intimately close to Fay: we fear influence.

---

1 W.B. Yeats's 1922 essay "The Tragic Generation" mythologized the tragic lives of the poets of the 1890s, and renamed the movement.

2 Their diaries, *Works and Days*.

Probably Fay's own terribly indiscreet Diary (now discontinued) will come to Tommy.[1] The years will not be without interest to him!

1904

[K.B.]
February 3rd
[...] Rossetti's comp[le]te edition of Christina arrives.[2] It gives the love episodes of her life. How this unhappy brother[3] has blurred the images of his great ones! One of the purest creatures he has known; but pure-blank, like a yard of calico.

Apparently religion was a deteriorating influence on her humanity & on her art. She is the creature who could have given us a cradle-song.

Woe to the gods that ruined her.

For she is essential poet—the female-dove.

She has neither out-look or inlook; she knows nothing: she has music & fragrance & flight; she passes among us a singing-bird, & her song drops spices—

Never shall she [have] written what does not float or fall, or pass as a mourner.

Movement always—& a stirring of feet that are happy.

Take her anywhere—she is the poet.

[E.C., c. 4 June]
We have had a letter too from Sturge Moore, about publishers— the all too necessary evil we have to face. It is helpful—but, ma foi, how it exasperates by a slip in taste! He tells us publishers regard us as the French tried to regard the Dreyfus case as a "chose jugée."[4] ["]No doubt you will come up again as the

---

1 In the end, the women left the diary to Tommy (Thomas Sturge Moore). Charles Ricketts's "indiscreet" *Diary* is held at the British Library.

2 *The Poetical Works of Christina Georgina Rossetti. With Memoir and Notes, & c., by William Michael Rossetti*. London: Macmillan & Co., 1904.

3 William Michael Rossetti.

4 Loosely translated as a "done deal" (French).

Dreyfus case has."[1] This from a younger poet to one of Les Vieux—It is cruelly strange, now the noble shelter of the Vale Press is lost, to have to meet publishing as if we were young things of eighteen—we who have lived & suffered such experiences to give man a few more emotions.[2]

1906

[End of January 1906. Whym Chow, the women's adored pet Chow dog is ill with meningitis.]

[K.B.]
[<] <u>Chow</u> [>] What an entry I have now to make! On Wednesday [Jan. 24]—I am asked to the Palace[3] to meet John Gray. It is a day of rising misfortune. Gas & water pipes go wrong, there is threat of a dog fight—Henry prepares me a stately costume. I go to the Palace. [<] On my return: [>] "I have rather bad news—meningitis [sic] is threatened"—& the face of Hennie one [?]throbby tear. —Instantly all the conditions of life are changed. My little green sofa becomes my evening couch. Chow roves & I stare at his wondrous circles in a marvel that first night. Far on the verge, as a rosy ruin, my visit to the Palace—formal, appreciating rosy John Gray: inscrutable & kindly—the Painter [Charles Ricketts] a little mocking, a little bored, very intimate.

There paces my Chow in mortal peril—wandering witlessly— & above me lies Henry of the broken heart.

<u>Friday</u> [26 January]
Yesterday—a specialist[,] Sewell—"I am sorry, it is a [blot of ink] bad case—I cannot say he will recover"—Yet if Chow were his dog, he would "give him a month"—there is chance, though it is vague chance, for life.

---

1 In 1894 Alfred Dreyfus, a captain of the French Army, who was Jewish, was wrongly accused of providing secret information to the German government. The case became a *cause célèbre* and highlighted the anti-Semitism of French society. Émile Zola's denunciation of the cover-up in a newspaper article "J'Accuse" opened the case. Dreyfus was pardoned in 1899 but only exonerated of the charges and restored to his military rank in 1906.
2 The Vale Press was closed down in 1904.
3 Home of Ricketts and Shannon, who arranged the meeting between Bradley and John Gray.

[E.C. 28 January]

Sunday—how terrible Sundays are! Milestones of doom to us as a family. Today I have had the worst loss of my life—yes, worse than that of beloved Mother or the tragic father ... My Whym Chow, my little Chow-Chow, my Flame of Love is dead & has died—O cruel God!—by our will![1]

[E.C. February]

~~Tuesday~~ Wednesday 14th

Sun—our South Sun! How immediate the sun! That is why Chow is with us—flash after flash we see him; & all his living zeal is round our spirits.

Our dearest name for him was & is the little Now-now—He was [<]—he is [>] always the moment Eternal of the Bacchic God—the inspirer of Life. Our Sunbeam, our instant torch—our Now-Now.

1907

[E.C.]

Friday—April 19th-(Month of the Holy Spirit, the Sanctifier) Good English Elphage [sic][2] being the saint to watch over "Edytha"[3]—

I am reconciled with the only True Church, which [<] guards [>] the perfect Symbol of Life ~~abides~~ forever present & [?]active on its altars—so that each one may converse with Divinity each day of Times.

---

1 Bradley put the dog down with morphine to end his suffering.
2 Elphege was an Anglo-Saxon Archbishop of Canterbury who was put to death by the Danes on 19 April 1012 for refusing to pay a ransom. He was buried in St. Paul's Cathedral, but his body was removed by King Canute to Canterbury in 1023. Feast day 19 April.
3 Old English for "Edith." Cooper is linking herself literally and histori- cally to the Catholic Queen Edith of Scotland (c.1080–1118), who changed her name to Matilde when she married Henry I of England (brother of William Rufus). She was a learned queen and a patroness of literature and the arts.

[K.B.]
Saturday morning April 27th.
—My way begins. It must be the way of Hope! I will not quit Edinburgh save as a member of the Catholic Church.[1] Pulsanti aperietur.[2]
—I am under the guard of S. Michael the cleaving angel[3]—wholly & forever beneath his divine protection—
—Invoked so carelessly[,] he has given me of his power—my judgment is a terror—my wrath shatters—

Unawares, I have laid hold of the most awful power of the Universe. "Which is Michael & which is Field asked little Arthur [Symons]" in 1884—
"Oh I don't know, <u>I am Michael</u>." And I am.

[E.C., still 27 April]
At Low Mass the Celebrant, the author of <u>Silverpoints</u>:[4] in one row Michael, Field & Raffalowich [sic], who thought he was writing to a boy of his own age when he wrote to the author of <u>Callirrhöe</u> more than 20 years ago.[5] Think of it!—And all of us before a Roman altar in adoration.

[E.C. 7 May]
[T]here is a revelation that turns the converted marrow in our veins right over—The sonnet by <u>Anno Domini</u>, Father Gray says is by the Seducer of Oscar[6] "He was the wicked man!" bursts out the vehement little priest—but the little Priest only laughs like a school-boy at the thought it is 'Boosy'[7] who has reviewed & be-sonnetted us. "He can write well-enough!"
God works by strange instruments—but in the cruel mood of

---

1 The women travelled to Edinburgh to be converted to Catholicism by Father [John] Gray, the poet.
2 Matthew 7:8: "To him that knocketh, it shall be opened."
3 St. Michael, The Archangel. The leader of the army of God during the Lucifer uprising. His name was the war cry of good angels in the battle.
4 Father (John) Gray, the poet.
5 André Raffalovich (1864-1934).
6 Alfred Douglas's sonnet "To a Silent Poet" was published under the signature A.D. Douglas wrote a favourable report of *Wild Honey* for T. Fisher Unwin, who accepted it for publication.
7 Bosey Douglas—Alfred's nickname.

rebellion now assailing me the Demon of Cynicism rises up like a mist-cloud, that our lives should be touched by the one infamous Creature—baleful to Genius[,] baleful to literature for a decade, the originator of <u>De Profundis</u>, the unrepentant Infamy whose recent deeds were recently uncovered to the shuddering Michael.

And <u>he</u> writes the words that make Fisher Unwin hope to be our publisher & he writes a lovely Sonnet—as if he stood, as St. Peter does, at the Gate of Paradise—not the Soul's, but the Poet's.

We have been abjuring the nineties, & all their spirit, in the Church John Gray of <u>Silverpoints</u> has raised for the Divine Presence, beautiful, austere, consecrated—& Alfred Douglas' is the voice that calls to the world to receive us as we come forth of the Church.

[Here E.C. pastes in a copy of "To a Silent Poet," by A.D.]

1908

[E.C., 3 September 1908: both women are now exploring theology, and its relationship with their art.]

I go on now to the afternoon of Sep. 3rd. I am waiting in a parlour with old black chairs & portraits made into old portraits by time, not their own mellowness. Through the window I catch the ~~square~~ [<] garden [>] enclosure of the monastery buildings, torn with the rains—yet full of the daisied flowerliness of autumn, bossed with French marigolds. And I am waiting for Vincent.[1]

He enters—a white suddenness of motion ... yes, his entrance is like Mephisto's, not in calm, like Gabriel's. We shake hands & as usual sit on each side the little Table. There is no shyness between us—any more than between the powers of colloquy in one's own mind. So strange! Before this Dominican I feel nothing of the hedge of personality that forbids one in another person—& forgetting one's own as a familiar thing one reaches a condition universal & abstract & exhilarating as the action & re-action of elements.

I tell him I am ~~happy~~ happier since my Confirmation, for I feel more urgently the call of the old Vocation to be made the new one. And I explain about the many mellow plays in the old spirit

---

1 Vincent McNabb.

of inspiration awaiting the press, & how we feel they are out of date to ourselves now & must therefore be printed anonymously. This seems to give pain to the historic bias of his mind; but, being assured that ultimately they will be brought back to their author, he is less opposed, & sees [<] how [>] they confuse present history beyond recognition. Then he speaks of our work—of how he prays that the things of the faith that have never been sung before may be sung by us ... "Oh, Father!" "Yes—it seems almost sacrilege to pray for it ... & perhaps it cannot be done here on earth" & with a low laugh he buries his head in the folds of his sleeves—then raises it & goes on with audacity that pleads to God "The dramas that lie in the Summa ... if they could be expressed in song—the subsistence in the one nature of God[,] of His Persons; or The Incarnation—the dramatic movement of God into death & sorrow for His Love's sake. But perhaps it cannot be done ... or were a great song if it could."

This word of the Incarnation brings me to the point of our interview & I ask if there is not error, mental sin in my contempt for fact in the supernatural scheme of Religion. I always see the whole of our faith, as a conception of God's perfectly supernatural, independent of scientific truth—having the truth of inherently creative revelations. To be quite honest, it would not interrupt my faith if Christ did not rise in phenomenal earnest, de facto, using fact scientifically. If a supernatural truth could not be believed as a phenomenal event I should not forsake the supernatural conception & its eternal validity.

"I understand ... I have felt like you; our minds work in just the same way. I see the whole reality of God's scheme that it has attained perfect self-expression in a sublime symbolism. But you are right—there is great danger in this. You have been saying what would shock many to the depths. I who understand your soul know you are sincerely putting forward the tendency that biases your mind as mine. We have to remember that a symbol is a relation—it is that wh: shows itself forth something by being other & yet resembling. A symbol to enter into relation with the supernatural must have a fundamentum.

There is the Res, the signum & the fundamentum.[1]

The Incarnation of God has made fact the fundamentum of our symbolic relation to the supernatural, & this fundamentum we must not dare to ignore. That there should be scientific accuracy in the account of the fact is not necessary—the number of

---

1 The thing or object, the sign and the foundation.

the loaves & fishes in the miracle of loaves & fishes, the number of people who partook &c.—But the fact that the miracle took place, is the possibility of its relation to supernatural Truth as manifesting the Blessed Sacrament.

So Vincent advices [sic] that as on the side of fact my mind lies open to scepticism, I should not read any works of criticism, or consider the question of discrepancies &c, but humbly dwell on the record of Christ's incarnate life. It will grow more & more essential & unfold new & striking symbolic suggestion. He specifies St. John leaving it to St. Peter to be chief witness of what had taken place in Christ's Tomb, & noting when he entered that the head piece of Christ's garment—the visible church, was laid away by itself.

Then Vincent speaks of St. John.

["]He was an idealist—a son of Thunder. How the Boanerges[1] in him swoops down on the world with the Logos" ... Vincent stretches his long white-sleeved arms & bows as if over a universe ... "Think of that beginning—the world that was before Creation making descent on men! But John knew that it was [<] to be [>] with men. He pulled himself together, & he made his gospel a record of discussion & discourse & for every event he chose the salient detail that marked it out. None of the other gospels have the ~~the~~ wealth of detail given relentlessly by John. And the teaching of the eternal Word is always brought down to practice. "He that loveth me keepeth my Commandment." We must seek to be like St. John, & not let the zeal we have for God's scheme make us contemptuous of its realization among men. We must quietly follow the records of the Incarnation & obey the commands of our divine Lover who came down to earth for us.

Then, speaking of this dread of the material side of our Faith, an impulse seizes me to speak of myself to this Comprehending Spirit, so soon to become in the Priory Church my confessor. I have long suffered under the sense he has esteemed me to be what I never have been [—] good. I tell him I do not want to make a general confession—indeed a holy saint [?]bound me never to make one of my life before I was a Catholic—even in the hour of death—but he must know broadly the truth if he is to be of help to me.

As I speak of the ancient wrong, of the wild sinning & wild penances-in-vain[,] the face opposite mine fixes with the gravity

---

1   Mark 3:17. Jesus gave James and John, sons of Zebedee, the name of Boanerges, which literally means the sons of thunder.

of the sacrament of penance as the late hours of the day with evening. I shall always see it in its sombre element abstraction. My own face felt like texture with a wind beating it to & fro. I did not cry, but every nerve flapped.

"You have known Christ's Redeeming Love—Thank God, Thank God!"

My relief he no longer misjudges me to my advantage! And he fully sees the necessity of candour. Immediately he speaks of all the apostles—sinners, traitors to their Lord, chosen to reveal Him. And he brings out what a good & sincere confession St. Peter must have made, that each lie & the circumstance of each lie is so poignantly sharp.

A cab comes for me....

"Father, tell the man to go away—I will pay him at the hotel. Ask him to send another in a quarter of an hour"—& I murmur of confession.

He seems to think I shall have endless penance in the suffering my art will give me.

We speak further of symbolism. He tells me of how St. Thomas writes the Elements symbolically with the emotions, most specifically the Host with the sense of strength, the Cup with Joy, & his is almost startled that I have prayed at the Elevation to have strength to be humble, pure, & loving & far to have 'joy in' humility, chastity & Love: He quotes

"Dedit fragi[li]bus corporis ferculum,
Dedit et tristibus sanguinis poculum"[1]

I feel I must rise. He says it is a temptation to talk of these things with me—He & Fr. Norbert talk of them for too long.

He gives me a long, [?]heart-shadowing time of preparation in the church. I am not sure if he has entered his box at the bottom of the church. Twice my voice startles me by asking 'are you there, Father'—and there is silence—as if "God did not say a word" to my claim for his sacrament of death. When he comes my confession is short—his words of homily briefer "you must love, till you forget everything else, forget your sins; till you are what the Holy Ghost Himself is[:] a subsisting, personal Loving"[.]

With a fine sense that he is dealing with the terrible things of sin he says "Go in peace—Pray for ~~you~~ me" in English, not in

---

1 "He gave to the weak the food of his body / He gave to the downcast and sad the cup of his blood." This celebration of the Eucharist is from the hymn *Sacris Solemniis* ("At This Our Solemn Feast"), which is part of the Office of Corpus Christi, composed by Thomas Aquinas.

Latin as to Michael. It might seem "et tous le reste est litterature"[1] ~~not to speak~~ [<] had he spoken [>] the phrases in [<] anything but the [>] vernacular in the neighbourhood of old mortal sins.

Almost as soon as I get back to the Wyvern, he comes—in black skull cap. Michael having provided cakes, wishes ascettically [sic] to bar him from a cake "I shall take a cake he says firmly.["]

How converse moves along with the oil of gladness—that unity when people understand each other's minds! He ~~takes~~ [<] talks [>] of Bently who made his cathedral far bigger inside than out—of the sisters of ~~naz~~ Bethany ... How he laughs when speaking of Martha he says "the church honours her." I reply "as a Semi-Double" ... of St. Joseph holy reticence under the husband's typical tragedy ... what thunder there must have been in that silence—the sound of its own awfulness!

He talks on till he has to run ... we are "so tempting to talk to of these things"—he could talk on & on.

We kneel for his brief blessing, look farewell into the crucified face—He is gone, beginning to pray for his nonconformists. At Benediction he says the glorious mysteries & reads a Homily on Poverty of Spirit. He does not give, but with us receives the Benediction.

1910

[E.C., mid November]
I must not forget a visit on ~~the~~ a Saturday before ~~this when~~ the Retreat when Fay came drunk with wrath against the Post-Impressionists—a school or rather an epidemic, that belongs to 20 years ago in France, but ~~in England~~ has been imported into present England by Roger Fry.[2] In torrents of disgust he brings

---

1 "And all the rest is literature." Cooper seems pleased to have been addressed in English rather than Latin because it connects the two people as humans rather than placing them in a ritualised and formalised relationship to each other, as a Latin utterance would have done.

2 The term Post-Impressionism was coined by Roger Fry when he named his exhibition "Manet and the Post Impressionists" at the Grafton Gallery, London, which included works by painters working in 1880s France: Cézanne, Gaugin, Van Gogh, and Matisse. It has been suggested that this exhibition, which ran from 8 November 1910 to 15 January 1911, symbolised the beginning of modernism.

before us the Artists & their works ... then breaks away into quotation of his letter to the Morning Post against them ... then gloats on the hope that his words have had a Damascus blade to shed Fry's blood & the Lamb's blood & ~~the~~ to make [?]Holmes' trickle. His eyes have a hectic, sleuth-hound light in them—his voice is high—his thoughts about his letter too high. Disgust, & vengeance make Italian havoc with the true Artist's condemnation of false method. He is so unlike himself, he tell[s] a story from under his handkerchief that is grossly bad. "I believe Michael is shocked" he says unhandkerchiefed. "Yes, Painter, I am"—"and you?["] he asks of me ... "Yes, I am" & I change the subject, while that sense of hot pain, he has never caused by a single word before, courses about—& his eyes have a queer sorrow in them. [...]

He leaves us, made sad & made anxious. Two days after the letter is got from the office of the Paper—it is not vindictive or malicious as he had [?]vomited it—too much in it to appear; while Ross's bon-bon ~~articale~~ article is really effective......

To return to the visit after my week of agony: we find he comes no more for the attack on Post-Impressionism—the subject is trite now, & to be dropped into a well. But, as I say, he makes a few remarks on himself & his miscalculations, we have broadly seen, but thought were undivined by him.

"In fact I have no sense of the Moment. I am logical—& logic has nothing to do with the moment—so I find I have always gone wrong, done the wrong thing—the reasonable thing & missed my aim. I don't know what will succeed or fail at the time. What is good & bad in itself I know—what will be successful is an enigma I don't solve." He thinks his entrance into the wretched Post-Impressionist quarrel was a mistake.

1911

[E.C., February 1911]
...... I am going back, though I write in the present, after a fortnight, the greatest in experience of my life.
~~Jan~~ Feb. 6th
We had been reading the office of St. Agatha,[1] that wail round the tortured breasts like birds round ravined nests, intolerable—

---

1 A martyr: St. Agatha suffered sexual assault on account of her faith. She
   had her breasts cut off.

beyond all beauty, beyond almost the submission of sanctity. The wail gave me a sickened sense of fear—the physical lamentation in it set ~~my imagination~~ me imaginatively on a way of panic.

I had not been well, & had told the Doctor of certain symptoms, he had examined into—& then had been silent about. On the Friday he had asked me if I were thinner.... He comes on this Monday & asks for Michael. As she is at the Vineyard, he comes in & talks burly cheerfulness to me. But I face him, tell him we are Catholics & must face reality & conjure him on this ground to tell me the truth. "You think I am suffering from something serious?"—"Well, as you have put it to me the way you have, I am bound to say I do." "With cancer?"—"I believe so. It is my opinion."—"And it will be fatal?"—"Yes."

All ~~I think~~ this length of short time I feel like a marble temple in ruined & immovable cold. Yet a breath slips round the cold— of God's will.

I am immovable, but there is motion from the high sky about me. And I learn more & more about this internal cancer, about its terrible indecisions & every way of it[s] horror & disgrace. I am undone before my own face as death undoes one after He has covered one's face from earthly life. There can be no removal— only a hideous operation of alleviation from what has to come. And I am to see a specialist tomorrow & learn his opinion. The Doctor, generally Scottish & kind & fond of me, is hard & speaks intemperately. Hard he is as an executioner, & he goes soon.

It was like this when the vet left me with the news Whym was struck with menangitis [sic]—only then the tears came with a whole firmament's descent.

Now I am too cold for abundant weeping—drifts of bitter rain—then I think of the terrible doom, & then of my Beloved who has again to enter the door of little Paragon, & hear of death to the Creature of her love.

A ring—she comes, & her voice is of Dominican & Apostolic joy—she has got an old Convert, who had grown negligent in his religious duties, to ask for the cleansing of penance .... . I cannot speak—she sees my speechlessness as an awful vision, far beyond anything heard; & her questions rive it. To tell her, "The Doctor says I have cancer!" To see her grow deadly fixed—& then the fixity break up in a moaning of negation. The dove moans over a nestful, the ~~doves~~ dove moans with springtime in labour, the dove affirms the pangs of living—the moan I ~~heard~~ ~~was~~ [<] is [>]— "no, no"—it ~~was~~ [<] is [>] of the abrogation of life, it ~~was~~ [<] is [>] the moan of agony that we must be severed—we, who are flesh of one flesh in our imaginations—bone of one bone in our common life. While she moans, I realise how infinitely distant from the love I have for her, are all, even the tenderest other loves. I wonder the blow lets her heart go on beating—the moans come between its crannies. O my little Love! I am cold no more—the fear of death made me cold—but the thought of losing my life on earth with my beloved, brings warmth, & tears more like those I poured over Whymmie. At last we eat, & make a comedy of life's attempt at nutrition. We read [?] Camphine & break into a passion of weeping together as I ask for a blessing, & she gives me the words "noctem quietam et finem perfectum concedat nos Dominus omnipotens."[1] So tenderly we weep from the Source [<] of the Divine Office. [>]

She goes to the Doctor's—

I move about in the strange rooms and I pray before my beloved Crucifix—I pray & I wonder & am astonished in my own Sun Room.

The Doctor will let us know tonight—when we are to see the specialist. He is still hard.

Together we go up to the Church. [...]

We return to weep & weep & weep against each other—we are close, close ... & the storm of parting breaks over us in deluges, through which we pray & kisses & then sever, only to unite in reading the Divine Office, & in plans to dominate this sorrow, & to bring to the measure of faith & hope & divine love. We will have a dog. We always told our little hound we should have to have another. We cannot gain any ring of cheer unless we all speak to a dog.

How I look at my Michael, & see in her our life of joy & sweet-ness—the violence of love one has for her quick smile, for the dapple on her brow of grief over her Hennie Boy. As the world appears hostile—the face of the Dearest becomes tenderer than could have ever been imagined. A transfiguration of the divinest union—that is glory of every look, that is a parting look of love's. O my little Master!

But I forget ... I send for [sic] in the afternoon for Gosscannon, with special urgency. He comes at five—the candles are lighted; as I enter he says briefly but with interest, "Well, what is it?" My throat tangles—at last I untangle it enough to say "I have

---

1 "May the Lord God Almighty grant us a peaceful night and a perfect end."

had a great shock." I do not see so much as feel a dense anxiety settle over my confessor, & I sob out the terrible doom—everything I know—everything that tonelessly he asks to know.

"I did not imagine your desire to see me had anything to do with you or I wd have come at once"—His words ~~come~~ [<] ooze [>] out like thick blood from a wound. His parchment colour recalls me to pity for him—& the nerves that have been so broken. He shelters himself under hope—the way my sight was spared last year.

No, no! I cannot bear hope—it weakens me ...

So he shelters me with his trust that I shall have peace at the end. He is sure I shall be blessed & have peace.

In his sorrow he is like a boy—or like an animal with delectable eyes. His man's sorrow has none of the expressions of completeness belonging to maturity—yet the holy self-control & priestly remoteness make the face in its sweet pain venerable. He blesses me lingeringly—then I call Michael—who finds him still more blank & boyish—only able to say the words of the Beloved in agony "if it is possible, may this cup pass from me. Nevertheless not my will but thine be done."

It is so strange after the passage of only one year to lie down at night again, as if the nightfall were not the end of the day, but the end of sorrow.

1912

[E.C. October 1912. *Poems of Adoration* and *Mystic Trees* were written separately, by Cooper and Bradley respectively, and together formed the final Catholic poetic statement of Michael Field.]

Words about 'Poems of Adoration' from Gordon Bottomley, that make light shine about the heart:

"I wanted to read 'Poems of Adoration' before I wrote; too many weeks are gone since then, but often I could not write at all! Michael bade me like 'The Dance of Death,' & I do think it beautiful with the strangeness that is to me the root of beauty. But I love more the first fourteen poems in the book, & the poems from 'Venit Jesus' to the end. 'Real Presence' seems to me one of the supreme things in its order; & in many of the poems again & again there is a wild (in the sense that an anemone is wild) pure energy, a startling closeness of expression to sensation wh: go past Patmore & F. Thompson right to Crashaw's side.[1] But it is a book of rapture & purgation ... Oh, 'Macrinus against Trees' is delightful, & true in more ways than one.

And the cover! O Michael & Henri to be envied! How happy I was to see the lovely lines playing together in crystal-clear chimings again, as I first saw them when I was a boy & thought there never was such a master of lines—& indeed, there never was, & there is not!

O don't think me naughty if I say how delighted I was to read in the colophon that one of the poems had appeared in The Universe. That is where we should all like our poems to appear."

1913

[E.C.]

Monday Jan. 13. All the sunshine gone! A deep, melancholy fog lies over the day. We hear that Bishop Brindle of Nottingham[,] coming across the line, "Pearl of gt. [great] price, within the monstrance set[,]" asked Soeur Marie du St. Sacrament who wrote it. Hearing of Michael Field he gave the military command, "Write & tell them I want a complete set of their works. The bill to be sent in to me." Of course the Bishop is supplied at once with "Wild Honey," as the turning-point from Paganism to the gt. [great] "Ecce, Agnus Dei"[2] vision of St. John the Baptist—& "Poems of Adoration" as the first-fruits of our Catholic life. I explained that as converts we wish our Pagan past to be left to itself. I speak of my illness & ask the prayers of a Shepherd of the Church for Field & Michael. Fancy even a soldier[-] Bishop with Attila, Stephania, The World at Auction, Julia Domna—not to mention Borgia & the works of the author Borgia![3]

---

1 Here the allusion is to the direct influence of the seventeenth-century poet Richard Crashaw (1613–49), rather than the seventeenth century as it is mediated through Victorian writers such as Coventry Patmore (1823–96) and Francis Thompson (1859–1907).

2 "Behold, the Lamb of God."

3 The play Borgia and the series of texts to which it belongs were disowned by Bradley and Cooper, after their conversion, and no longer considered works by Michael Field.

[E.C. still January]
I have forgotten to chronicle that on Monday 13th I had this exquisite letter from the cathedral, Nottingham.

"My dear child,
I am very grateful to you for the beautiful books: and yet—may I say it!—I regret that you were asked about them! I might, perhaps, have obtained them through some of the book-sellers, who send me their catalogues. .[.] I am not too proud to accept a gift; but "Wild Honey" has been used: it has little words here & there wh: show that it has been a friend to whom you talked: & I feel like the thief, who has robbed you of the companionship! So please forgive me! What compensation is in my power I will gladly make: on Thursday I will offer my mass for you both; & you shall have daily a memento. Most of my fifty years of priestly life have been spent where pain & sorrow had their home; & I have learned to see how God purifies the lives of His saints. Good-bye, child, & may God bless you both.
                    Yours in J. C.,
                    Robert, Bp: [Bishop] of Nottingham."

The Soldier Bishop is very gentle & exquisitely intimate in refinement of touch. He "roars us like a suckling dove."
    What a happy error to have given, unknown to me, that marked copy of 'Wild Honey,' that [illegible, deleted] [<] was [>] the the [sic] last in the difficult depths of the soldier's kit-box under our Bed—sought out by Josephine. And that little gossip of the Poet with his poems has brought us an especial mass & a daily memento at the altar by a tender Shepherd of Christ's flock.

[E.C. September]
In the evening comes the faithful Francis.[1] He was with us just before we went to Hampstead, & now he comes at the passing of that Melancholy Dream. Dear, faithful Francis!
And he found me so aged & in such weakness.
    Well, he has been with us the first week, coming from the Mansion Hotel at noon for a chat, lunching, drinking coffee in my Sun Room, resting at the Hotel, & coming back to dinner. Gradually I have passed from the death-in-life of the effects of Hampstead & the journey home. Still, though we have had much of the peaceful, gently humorous talk that wins welcome to

1 Francis Brookes, Bradley and Cooper's cousin.

François we have had no touch of the great days of old. Well, on Friday evening it is moved that I read from <u>Wild Honey</u> ... The great days begin—glorious things are spoken by that bee-circled Book. And I am moved to read to Francis (I believe it is only to him I could read what is so thrilling and sacred to my heart) I am moved to read Michael's poems to me[:] "Old Ivories"—"The dear Temptations of her Face" with "Atthis, my darling" of <u>Long Ago</u> added—the loveliest nocturne of Love ever created, <u>Palimpsest</u>—to say by heart "A girl

Her soul a deep-wave pearl."[1]

I am moved to show him my triumph & joy in this lovely praise, & in showing him my so often shaded mood before my glory I also let my Beloved realise what her poet's gift has been to me—her poet-lover's gift. Think of it! She has often read these lovely poems to me; she has not heard them, tender but high-voiced, from my lips. It is paradise between us. When we're together eternally, our spirits will be interpenetrated with our love & our art under the benison of the Vision of God.

For it wants <u>another</u>. There was need of Francis to listen to <u>Wild Honey</u>: there will be need of God to assure the immortal oneness of Love with Love, of praise & being praised & the response of the praised casting all joy unto union with the poet-lover. God [?]drive the time along! It was an evening of such infinite promises. The rarest evening of a life-time.

Francis dazzled & mystified[,] bade me good-night with a face under an ancient spell, & the impress on it of ancient acknowledgement of Power.

I have felt culminating illness in me all day: the malady is as a stone-chest on my hip; the ulsers [sic] tingle & declare their sharp-pointed agony, & internal bleeding breaks out, a strong attack of the whole night bringing relief from the crisis of pain the journey prepared for.

[K.B. September]
It is Francis' last night—How spend it? I find I am listening to Henry's voice—Hennie reading my love poems to her, aloud to Francis. Of course I have never listened to them before—she read the famous sonnet—'A window full of ancient things'—& also "Atthis" ... & others.

For a little while I am in Paradise. It is infinitely soft between

---

1 See poems in the Poetry section.

us. Warm buds open. I feel at least I have "merited" with these years of passionate love.

And Francis, who has loved me so well, listens to the singing amid the boughs, that is not for him—listening as he would listen to a nightingale overhead.

It is an intense moment.
A moment not of memory—but of creation.
A moment never to be forgotten of Francis, or of me.

[E.C. 4 December; Cooper's last entry in *Works and Days*.]
Father Prior has just been in to help & strengthen me. Before, he helped me against the rebellion that through my <u>own</u> Order I should have been restricted in the help given by the Blessèd Sacrament. Now it is a much more central rebellion he has to meet—against the Prince, the Bridegroom Himself—spaces of temptation far more dangerous—"<u>far more</u>." It is a rebellion of far deeper weakness & can only be met by elements of strength— sheer strength: by the Frontal Attack.

How is this to be done?

1st. By Giving thanks. You cannot have an insecure moment when you give active thanks. Why, & how give thanks <u>now</u> in my present case? That all through my time of special prayer for clear- ness of mind up to the End—all through my little sacrifice of the help of poppy,[1] that I might not be shattered in will like poor Francis Thompson; I had received already such marked & amazing response.

2nd. That I had learnt a tremendous secret of the spiritual life that I must offer during the hours of strength what in hours of weakness I could not. The hours capable of offering beforehand must be sacerdotal. [...]

3rd. Then again, I must remember that I am setting up a little gift of my own to be rewarded, & that this is not a spiritual motion of the soul.

The wonderful thing to realise is that Christ may give me at the End something of His own Holy End, "My God, My God &c," of Calvary & the previous joy: "I have longed for this hour"

---

1 Cooper refused to take drugs (opium) to alleviate the pain.

in the Supper-Room of the Blessed Sacrament. Never till Fr. Prior & I have had this talk has he realised the place of the Eucharist in the death & immortality of the Lord.

Again, we pray we may love God with all our heart and <u>mind</u>. Sometimes we have to give that mind wholly to Him—as we give [<] Him [>] the heart to do what He likes with. We must remember we don't give to dictatate [sic] but to delight. The dry Sacrament of Thanksgiving precedes in His precious death the blood-drenched weaknesses & merely mortal atmosphere of dereliction that God Himself endured when dying.

[K.B.]
Christmas Eve. 1913.[1]

O Hennie, Hennie, but a little blue nun has been with me in the river-room, dressing a wound in my breast—cancer.

O Hennie, my blue Bird, my Beloved—& this woe was shown to me in the octave of Corpus Christi.

I have been a bad nurse. This little extra offering I have been able to make clean for thee.

Two days after thou wert gone, bleeding came—God's quiet sign that I must open my secret.

[K.B.]
Such winter—such morning frost!

The dressing, & Divine Office, & a drive—Flowers—carefully chosen as for her, Gentle Miss Harding, hovering over the threshold of my home—

Then Salter to speak to me of "<u>Dedication</u>[<]<u>ed</u>[>]." Through thrills of business, I tell him of my love[.] We open Dedicated.

How eager is the young Scholar!

I read to him Jason. He hears in my Voice the intonations of her Voice—I hear the Silver Voice. I sob for her. And from all this high-excitement, I turn to the little Blue Sister, the dressing of a cancer-wound. Yet so tender is the Beloved—she dresses me swiftly with soothing hand, I am soon in a heavenly sleep.

---

1 Bradley's entry follows Cooper's directly; Cooper died 13 December.

[K.B. Final page and entry of the diary. 16 September 1914.]

We have been here[1] a month; & I have greatly learnt & profited

I must be true to my little Blues to the end and I must be true to my own soul.

Supposing God wishes me to leave all these Holy active Dominicans, & to find my rest at Wincanton Convent

St Theresa, I call on you to help.

Oh my Beloved come & comfort me

My intercessors stand round me & bless me!

Paragon Cottage.[2] Thank God. Sept. 18th.

All night Sister Carmel says I lay smiling[.] This morning I was [?]~~craved~~ [<] saved [>] the cruel torture of being carried & tossed, wheeled into church, receiving the immense charity—though so much ashamed of myself—I must offer the Mass in thanksgiving. And I am striving now to write a bit. The Fathers are in retreat which makes it so hard for me. They are merciful & charitable[.]

God take my offering.

---

1 Hawksyard Priory, where she moved to be near Father Vincent McNabb.
2 This was how Bradley christened the cottage to which she eventually moved, near Hawksyard Priory, just before her death. "Thank God" is her expression of relief at finally moving in to the new place.

2. Letters

[The correspondence between Michael Field and others charts more directly than the diaries the women's interaction with the literary and cultural world of the *fin de siècle*, defining their position in relation to characters whose importance to this scene is now better known. While there are in existence literally thousands of letters (carefully archived, primarily in the Bodleian library, the British Library, and the National Library of Scotland), the letters transcribed here have been chosen to represent, as best we can in so short a space, both the overall contours of this body of communication, as well as some of its highlights.

Without a doubt the bulk of the letters that survive relate to their relationship with just a few important friends and literary mentors. First, of course, is the correspondence between the two women themselves, and that with their families, which displays the most intimate, and often therefore cryptic, style of communication. Historical priority should then be given to the communication with John Ruskin, their (and more specifically Bradley's) first major mentor figure, whose powerful presence was eventually rejected by Bradley as too controlling and stifling of her creativity. Next, Robert Browning, another father-mentor figure, who to some extent replaced Ruskin in their lives after he wrote to congratulate them on the publication of the first Michael Field text: *Callirrhoë*. Browning was to remain a much loved friend and advocate until he died. The two John Grays occupied a special place in the women's affections. John Miller Gray—curator of the Scottish National Portrait Gallery, art critic, and literary reviewer—was another mentor from the first half of Michael Field's career and his advice was sought, and trusted, on matters of great literary importance.

The women got to know Bernard Berenson in the first half of the 1890s. Berenson was initially a mentor in the realm of the visual arts, but the relationship quickly developed into a much more highly charged personal liaison that did not mix well with Berenson's growing relationship with Mary Costelloe. Cooper's physical sickness was induced by what was, by 1892 certainly, an unrequited love[1] that resulted in a heady triangle of passion that led to a long break in their friendship. Nonetheless, both Bernard and Mary were enormously influential aesthetically. Later in their

---

1 See "Diaries" Section, p. 254.

lives, Bradley and Cooper seemed to find friends with whom they forged more equal and lasting friendships. Their relationship with Charles Ricketts and Charles Shannon is clear evidence of this. The two artists first published a piece by Michael Field in their journal *The Dial*, but a professional mutual interest was soon supplemented by a deep friendship, that lessened only towards the very end when Bradley and Cooper retreated into the Catholic community. At this point the women's friendship with the second John Gray—the decadent poet (and possible model for Wilde's *The Picture of Dorian Gray*) turned priest—flourished. With Gray they tried to reconcile their life and work with their new-found faith.

In addition to these core relationships, this selection aims to give a few representative examples of the myriad of other literary correspondents with whom Bradley and Cooper engaged. The women's search for patronage (as well as their own inclination) often seemed to take them to close relationships with male figures, but they did nonetheless have some exchange with well-known female contemporaries.]

a. Katharine Bradley and Edith Cooper to Each Other and to Family, 1885

1. K.B. to E.C.: 13 April 1885

The Stock Dove's Lament.

I sing thee with the stock-dove's throat,
   Warm, crooning, superstitious note,
      That on its dearie so doth dote
         It falls to sorrow,
And from the fair white swans afloat
         A dirge must borrow.

II
In thee I have such deep content
   I can but murmur a lament;
      It is as though my heart were rent
         By thy perfection
      And all my passion's torrent spent
         In recollection.

April 13th 1885. Sidmouth.

And see, my bonnie love, here is a branch of whortle-berry for our meeting—as the almond blossom meant desertion & farewell.[1]

Mother[2] must have a heart of stone if after this she keeps you from me. What is it to me to be in the woods without my Pretty swinging on the Bough? It was sweet to watch the boy's pleasure picking anemones among the dried "acorn leaves," & our own dead beech-leaves. I wrote the Dove-Song a few days ago, but when you spoke of returning the French passage, delayed to see if I could add a touch ...

Coo. Coooooo says the old Fowl—till his throat vibrates.

V. [K.B.]

Coo   Cooooooooo

2. E.C. to K.B.: no date [April 1885]

My own Deare, my Stock-Dove,

Sweet, very sweet is your call to me, I love it dearly & it does not coo in vain for me. I will come &, heaven favouring, we will indeed be happy! We will talk of Lucrece[3] & Loyalty[4] & the white book & feel the warm folding arms of nature round us both. But wait a little for our dear little Pussie's sake.[5] She is getting better & parents want her to have a full week at Weston now this lovely weather is given to us. Let her have this [<] full [>] week & then I will come. They promise that. If we could but set her up for the Spring!

Kisses for the darling coral blossoms. My Dearie[6] & I have plucked them at Ludlow & Tintern. They seem a rosy pledge that we shall meet. I shall always keep them folded between the wings of my Stock-Dove's Lament (what a sweet voice she has!) I still send the lovely passage on the Dove's voice for the thought-book.

Your Pussy was taken with melancholy yesterday when it wrote. In the evening it worked all right & happily at the prose scene between Margarito & the arch bishop.[7] I think it is very

---

1   While separated, Bradley and Cooper express their feelings for each other through an idiosyncratic language of love based around flowers, birds, nicknames (see the "Key to Names"), and baby-talk.
2   Emma Harris Cooper: Edith's mother, Katharine's sister.
3   Lucretia of their play *Brutus Ultor*.
4   Their drama *Loyalty or Love?*, published 1885.
5   Throughout, E.C. talks of herself in the third person.
6   Amy, her sister.
7   A scene from *Loyalty or Love?*

nice now. You will judge. The rest I still send. I think you can work at it more felicitously & you can think about the young priest. When I join you I will bring all the <u>Loyalty</u> m.s.[1] in the rough. Send back the scenes as soon as they are done. It will be a little rest from Spurius Lucretius.[2] I believe he has nearly killed you. The motto is not yet found. The Mother came in with these words "Patriotism is god's birth-mark on His child man" She read them as if from Pattison, but they were her own, bless her! I have looked through Dante, Mazzinni, Landor, Plato & endless others! It seems as if no-one had written about [?]Cambry.

I like so much what you wrote about the old woman twisting the threads of life.

Shan't you be glad when we reach the 5th Act of <u>William</u>?[3] I am getting so tired of proofs & revises. The nervous young men in the master's absence keep ~~seem~~ sending revises over & over again (as Kegan Paul did with <u>Bel</u>.[4])

"Coo, coo" is answered by "mew, mew"! Its little heart beats for you. Your own P. P.

3. E.C. to K.B.: no date [April 1885]

My own Deare,
May the Pussy be a little worthy of your sovereign love! The mild eyes are almost misty with delicious wonder & tremulous joy at being so richly loved. The tender morning dew-drops of Song are safe in the bosom of <u>Aganippe</u>.[5] It did not think, when yesterday it sighed for a song, that two such were flying [<] to [>] it, from the great, triumphing wings of the A. W. F. How dear & mighty you are & how your Pussy loves you deeper than anything but art!

Here is a proof—a good one & nearly the last. Your Pussy is purring with the great dead mouse of Kant between its little paws—not yet certain if it is a first class mouse or if that Tabby Davis has caught a better.

With love from the deepest well of my heart. Thine own Pussy

---

1 Manuscript.
2 A character from *Brutus Ultor*.
3 This is a complaint about the proofs of *William Rufus* (published in June 1885 together with *The Father's Tragedy* and *Loyalty or Love?*).
4 *Bellerophôn* (published by Kegan Paul).
5 *Drops of Aganippe*: a book of poems E.C. was working on.

4. K.B. to E.C.: April 1885

"Two of Us"

"If two of you"
"Are ye able to drink of the cup that I drink of?
they say unto Him: we are able."

Our God, though thou didst not indite
      In law or psalm
The things concerning us, so we resign
      Ourselves to thee,
Thou wilt accomplish in us blessedly
      All thy design;
And our poor aid
  Go to the glorious project thou hast made
    to travail for our immortalitie.
Our best ambition thou dost overshade
      With thy great Hope;
Work out in us thy full conception's scope
      Even to Calvary!
  Thus it behoves
The Christ in us to suffer; we grow calm:
  When God speaks by a man, the token
      Is a heart broken.
We take [<] ~~we cry~~ [>] humanity's most bitter shame
          [<] ~~deserted in the olive groves~~, [>]
    Weakness, & blame—
    [<] We cry, deserted in the olive groves [>]
    Even that nameless land,
      From which the sun is banned,
Loathing & fearful we ~~will~~ [<] must [>] penetrate:
  Yea, alienate
    From goodness, famish for thy Face obscured
      In cavern of sin's seamless sepulchre,
        Till all that thou dost write
      We have endured,—
        thy word's interpreter;
And thou at last empower us, without slur
      On thy dear Fame,
Unto our mortal signature
        To add thy Name.

               V. [K.B.]

["Tarquin"[1] written in margin next to the word "Loathing" above]

P.—it is very beautiful to see you standing up on your hind legs, pleading for the moral law! We will be loyal to that, while we love Browning. Tell Mother[2] she is a real scamp,—a scoundrel of the blackest dye—to write to me so comfortably of Swanwick, & Browning—as Simeon, & seem to regard it a settled thing we were to experience that high joy—& then turn round, & turn you; & say, I scarcely think it can be done. Tell her to beware: her hand is on a lion's mane. | Now P. this is what we will do. We will just wait, get out vol. II—see in what temper Browning replies to you (– it might be impossible to meet him) & if he is enthusiastic, we will somehow get seven days in London. Blackheath I decline: it would be infradig. But if I told Scott we wd. stay with her one week, & go out on the Friday afternoon she always receives, she wd. do just what I told her; & simply trot with us to new art galleries; & leave us to go alone to the British—I should say for study; & not allow her to accompany us. Mother wd. be happy about you if you were at Kensington: & I should not attempt any theatres or night excitement. But we will wait. Meanwhile prepare for Weston many warm clothes; for next week I mean to have you; indeed I shall not come home till they send you to fetch me. That will bring parents to their senses. Of course Michael bears the expense of all Michael's self if he goes to London to see the Flight into Egypt—the Demetia of the British Museum,—& the old gentleman himself![3] (I shall write to Swanwick holding out hope of June visit: nothing definitive).

I have got the invocation right in my bed this morning.
Re-Read.[4]

Now put down its moral paws: & love me. P.P. come to me: it is not natural for us to live apart.

Your own,
V.

---

1 A reference to Sextus Tarquinius of *Brutus Ultor*, one of the plays they were writing at this time (and also a reference to the Tarquin of Shakespeare's *The Rape of Lucrece*).

2 Emma Harris Cooper.

3 The three things in London are: a painting by Holman Hunt; a sculpture of Demeter; and Robert Browning himself.

4 Referring to the poem "Two of Us." (There is another, cleaned-up, copy of this poem included in the letter on a separate folio—we do not reproduce this here.)

5. K.B. to E.C.: no date [August 1885]

Friday morning

Sweet Wife, the hardships of early married life are beginning: let us bear them together bravely, & grow all the dearer to each other for the derision of the world. There has nothing happened to us; but what is common to all poets: let us rejoice to share their bitter herbs of adversity. Ah P. there is nothing at these times like psalms. David & his fellow-singers had the Eternal with them at all times—not only sin times—as is too much the case with Christians. There is no comfort like a past spent with the Eternal. "Remember the word unto thy servant upon which thou hast caused me to hope." "Thou hast established the earth & it abideth. They continue this day according to thine ordinances for all are thy servants" cxix.[1] The condition of permanence for dramatist & starry heaven is obedience to law. In subjection to Divine Law our work has been wrought, & it will abide. The time when I received the Pall-Mall[2] could scarcely have been more inopportune. After a long day's yachting, & no food [<] ~~safe~~ [>] (save a cup of tea & tartine at Acle Bridge) since two, we reached Runham at nearly eight—the Sim [K.B.] more than half asleep. Amy had discretion to stay upstairs; & we have kept the review a profound secret. I have torn it up to small fragments this morning that if Nellie asks "Have we received any more reviews"—I may say "yes there was one in the Pall-Mall for wh. I had no respect, & I destroyed it." I shall not mention it to the Brookses or anyone. Now with reference to it, dearie, I want to say some grave words to you. Do not desert Shakespeare & the Elizabethans. These with the sobering influences of the great Greek dramatists, whom you ought to resolve at once to study, are the only masters for us. Every dramatic writer must be full of his Shakespeare, as every religious writer must be full of his Bible. We must give up the tricks, the externalities, the archaisms, to ~~imitate~~ [<] copy [>] these is imitation, but we must seek to study & touch life as he [<] Shakespeare [>] studied & touched it, & our speech must always be utterly different from ordinary speech: because ordinary speech is not transfigured by emotions, & the ordinary speech of an age like ours is base with the exceeding vulgarity of materialism. God shall give our thought a body as it pleaseth him.

---

1 Psalm 119.

2 *Pall-Mall Gazette*, which included a review of their 1885 collection of verse dramas, by William Archer, on 22 August.

2nd Make no harsh resolve to abstain from metaphor. Remember all our finest passages—the Athenaeum's—are in metaphor. "All the long cruel blade is still to cut." My ruined ears. Is there no death in you. &c. &c. The murderer's speech was absolutely right & my Harold's speech absolutely: the unimmortal might have been altered & a few of the expressions in The Father's Tragedy.[1] But do not begin correcting or altering, & work freely. In Loyalty I was determined to avoid the cumbersomeness of Bellerophon & make way with the action, & the consequence was—an imperfect, not fully developed work. What really saddened me was that article on Matthew Arnold in the Athenaeum: "a classic to the finger tips"—"distinction & dignity of manners." But then you see P. he was not a dramatist: we have determined by Heaven's grace to give the English people plays full of poetry & religion, & humour, & thought. They will not like this. . [.] They will kick against the pricks, but ultimately they will thankfully accept us. Ah P. I had a dream that I was going with you to receive a music lesson from the old gentleman.[2] I very naturally objected that you should remain to listen to me, but you wd. When we arrived somehow the talk was all on the review, & he said he would never take in the Pall-Mall again, & also something about looking at the proofs in future. | I think by the way, we must get some one to do that. Or will the loving mud[3] undertake our grammar? What I am a little dreading is a sharp nasty notice in The Times, now Parliament has done sitting. The Times is sent on here; but I will promise to be quite calm.

And now P. oh let me tell thee that no yachting, or beauty or joy in heaven or earth, can hinder me from mourning long & bitterly over our separation. It will take so long to knit us up into one piece again. And you are so far on the horizon—you might be a tower or a stump, or anything. Far far away is the P. & can write no little word to its love. My heart aches for it. I will try to learn to day when we are expected to leave. It will be nice to have some little time at home before the new journey; but if yachting expeditions are planned, I must wait.

Kind Alf leaves tomorrow—I hope he will someday visit us.

---

1 The reviews they are responding to are of the single volume that included *The Father's Tragedy*, *William Rufus*, and *Loyalty or Love?* (London: George Bell and Sons, 1885).
2 Robert Browning.
3 Mother.

The father would love him. He will repeat the traditions of the good uncle. One great embrace.

Thine own forever,
Sim

b. From John Ruskin, December 1877

6. John Ruskin to K.B.: 25 December 1877

Corpus Christi College
Oxford

25 Dec

Christmas - 77

Dear Katharine,

Your letter telling me you have lost God and found a Skye Terrier is a great grief & amazement to me—I thought so far [<] much [>] better of you.—What do you mean? That you are resolved to receive only good at God's hands and not evil? Send me word clearly what has happened to you—then perhaps I'll let you talk of your dogs and books.

Ever faithfully yours,
JR.

[the following text is squeezed into bottom margin, and then continues up the left-hand margin of the page] "Be sure it is <u>bitter</u> enough"[1]—you say—nonsense—I don't care how bitter it is to you—but it's so ineffably ridiculous!—that anybody should be a fool from their birth—is too common a phenomenon—but to make a fool of themselves in a year is rare.

7. John Ruskin to K.B.: 28 December 1877

(28 Dec. 77)

Corpus Christi College
Oxford

My dear Catharine,[2]

I will be perfectly gentle with you—but you <u>must</u> be called a goose—because you are one; and you must be called a false dis-

---

1 A quotation taken from a letter Bradley previously wrote to him.
2 Here a capital "K" was changed into a capital "C."

ciple—because you are one. When you called me master—I understood that if in any thing you would obey me it would be in choice of books.—and you had your books indicated for you in Fors,[1] enough—to serve—Bible—Dante—Scott—Shakespeare—Goldsmith. You choose instead—without telling me a word—to read those miserable modern wretches—I call them wretches for their bad English—their impudence, and their ignorance—not their impiety.   I reverence Voltaire! But Voltaire is a grand and thoughtful man—Harrison & Clifford—paltry puppies whom I simply don't chastise as they deserve in pity to them—Knowles (of the 19th century) begged off Clifford, because he was in a [?]consumption—or he would have had it [?]hot before now—

For yourself, I scarcely know how to deal with you—you are too stupid!—saying I don't care for your grief—you double-feathered little goose!! Suppose a child whom I had sent on a perfectly safe road, deliberately jumped off into the ditch—wallowed then with the pigs without telling me—got torn by their tusks—and then came to me all over dung & blood, saying 'I [?]doubt I care'. What could I do—or say.

I have no time today to write more—and am really too scornful of you—and of the egotism and shallowness which can be converted by the love of a dog, and by an entirely lying jingle of a song about fairies.

In this love of a God! [<] to write what could be of use to you [>]
[<] Yea [>] I love dogs fifty times better than you do—that's another of your stupid misunderstandings.

—I don't believe you have read your Fors at all only dipped into it—or you could not—dared not—have thought or said that to —your disappointed & disobeyed Master.

---

1 Ruskin's *Fors Clavigera: Letters to the Workmen and Labourers of Great Britain* (published in instalments starting in 1871).

8. John Ruskin to K.B.: 30 December 1877

(30 Dec. 77)

Corpus Christi College
Oxford

My dear Miss Bradley,

The first sentence of your letter, that my "words are wild and whirling" is as true—as it was of the words of the person ~~of~~ to whom the sentence is first spoken.

You simply do not understand any of my words, or ways.

– nor can I explain ~~to~~ them to you. ~~It is not wonderful to [?]seek that~~ [<] I see how even [>] You [?]~~misread~~ [<] [?]~~maybe~~ [>] could not but misread that "I do not care how bitter it is"—which was spoken precisely in the sense of a surgeon, who— ~~u~~ looking [?]suddenly at the wounds of a soldier moaning in pain,—would say to him—"yes—yes—I don't care how much ~~they~~ [<] the wounds [>] hurt you—but is there any place where they <u>don't</u> hurt you—it is <u>there</u> where Death is."

Now—exactly in the same way—I say to you, I don't care how much pain you are in—but that you should be such a fool as coolly to write to me that you had ceased to believe in God—and had found some comfort in a dog—<u>this</u> is <u>deadly</u>. And of course I have at once to put you out of the St. George's Guild[1]—which <u>primarily</u> refuses atheists—not because they are wicked, but because they are fools. "The Fool hath said in his heart [?]etc["].[2]

You go on from folly to folly in your present letter—chiefly in thinking that when I talk of 'chastising' a [?]man I mean only to abuse him—When did you know me abuse <u>any</u> one? You think <u>yourself</u> abused indeed [?]just here—but that is simply because you thought yourself very clever—and are astonished that I think nothing of your poetry—and less than nothing of your power of thought. Reread every word of my letter—Read also the story of St. Theodore in Fors[3]—and tell me if you ever read it before.—
—As for answering Harrison—I know Harrison—and challenged him in Fors—he declined the challenge—as you would have seen in Fors—had you read it.

---

1 Ruskin's philanthropic society.

2 "The fool hath said in his heart, *There is* no God. They are corrupt, they have done abominable works, *there is* none that doeth good." Psalm 14:1.

3 Ruskin's *Fors Clavigera*.

I tell you to read it half not expecting you to obey me—but most assuredly—I cease—if you do not—to consider you [?]as my friend—Companion you can of course be no more, but I am always faithfully yours, JR.

c. To and From Robert Browning, 1884–85

9. Robert Browning to E.C.: 28 May 1884

19 Warwick Crescent,
W.
May 28, '84

Dear Miss Cooper,

I should be glad to know,—since it is you whom I address and must thank,—how much of the book that is "partly yours" is indeed your own part, as the book and the letter concerning it came to me separately, and I happened to be much occupied at the time,—and moreover as other books of poetry arrived just before or after this one,—I was deceived by the "Michael Field" on the title-page,—and only read the plays last evening and just now: and it is long since I have been so thoroughly impressed by indubitable poetic genius,—a word I consider while I write, only to repeat it, "genius." The second play[1] is brimful of beauty; in thought and in feeling, admirably expressed: I think I see often enough the proof of youth and perhaps haste; but the great promise is not promise only; there is performance in an extraordinary degree. So with the first play;—it recalls, to its disadvantage in certain respects, the wonderful "Bacchae" of Euripides,[2]—and the deaths are dealt thickly about in hardly an artistic fashion,—but the scene between Machaon and the Faun would compensate for almost any amount of crudeness and incompleteness,—which probably will be not so observable when I read both poems again, as I mean to do. Meanwhile, accept my true congratulations and believe me

Yours sincerely
Robert Browning

---

1 This was written on receipt of *Callirrhöe* and *Fair Rosamund*, bound in one volume.

2 A tragedy by the ancient Greek poet Euripides.

10. E.C. to Robert Browning: envelope dated 30 May 1884

Stoke Green,
Stoke Bishop,
Bristol

Dear Mr. Browning,

I cannot thank you for the words you have written. I have all Duncan's sense of the poverty & slenderness of thanks. You must forgive "the sin of my ingratitude" which is heavy on me. Such words as yours give more abundant life: to expend it in higher, more reverent effort is the only true gratitude possible.

As to myself & my part in the book—to make all clear to you I must ask for strict secrecy. My Aunt & I work together after the fashion of Beaumont & Fletcher.[1] She is my senior by but 15 yrs. She has lived with me, taught me, encouraged me & joined me to her poetic life. She was the enthusiastic student of the Bacchae. Some of the scenes of our plays are like mosaic-work—the mingled, various product of our two brains. The faun scene is mine. At I was just nineteen when with joy, mixed with a dreamy sense of woe, the conception came to me. Emathion also is almost wholly mine & much of Margery. I think if our contributions were disentangled & [<] one [>] subtracted [<] from the other [>], the amount would be nearly even. This happy union of two in work & aspiration is sheltered & expressed by "Michael Field." Please regard him as the author.

If we are united in our poetic work, so are we also in our true admiration & earnest study of your works. The book was really sent by both. Though a kind letter of last year from you to me gave me, it was judged, the privilege of writing to you.

Still hoping, doubting, that I can make you feel what your letter has been to me, I remain, dear Mr. Browning,

Yours, with deep respect,

Edith Cooper.

---

1 Francis Beaumont and John Fletcher were well-known collaborative dramatists who wrote during the early part of the reign of James I.

11. K.B. to Robert Browning: 23 November 1884

Sunday even.
Nov 23rd

Stoke Green,
Stoke Bishop,
Bristol

Spinoza, with his fine grasp of unity, says: "If two ~~natures~~ [<] individuals of exactly the same nature [>] are joined together, they make up a single individual, doubly stronger than each alone," i.e. Edith & I make <u>veritable Michael</u>.

And we humbly fear you are destroying this philosophic truth: it is said <u>The Athenaeum</u> was taught by you to use the feminine pronoun. Again some one named André Raffalovich, whose earnest young praise & frank criticism gave me genuine pleasure, now writes in ruffled distress he "thought he was writing to a boy— a young man ... he has learnt on the best authority it is not so." I am writing to him to assure him the best authority is my work. But I write to you to beg you to set the critics on a wrong track. We each know that you mean <u>good</u> to us; & are persuaded you thought by "our secret" we meant the dual authorship. The revelation of that would indeed be utter ruin to us; but the report of lady-authorship will dwarf & enfeeble our work at every turn. Like the poet Gray (M. Arnold) we shall never "speak out." And we have many things to say the world will not tolerate from a woman's lips. We must be free as dramatists to work out in the open air of nature— exposed to her vicissitudes, witnessing her terrors: we cannot be stifled in drawing-room conventionalities. In Clifton we have made a desperate fight for the freedom of our privacy; &, to my joy, yesterday Edith was asked by a friend to read a sonnet in <u>The spectator</u> I wrote a fortnight ago on Fawcett—"by Michael Field—a Bristol man"!! That is victory here ... meanwhile in London? Oh, with a word you can persuade the critics you have been tricking them: the heart of the mystery is not plucked out!

Besides, you are robbing us of real criticism—such as man gives man. The gods learn little from the stupid words addressed to them at shrines: they disguise; meet mortals unsuspecting in the market place, & enjoy wholesome intercourse.

We want to listen like that old poet of yours who sat quite still, & knew all that happened.

But you will divine all this & more. As women we trust to lead a quiet life, deepening in seclusion as the years roll on.

That deep nook in Michael's nature where the Faun plays—you, our Father Poet, will help us to keep free of tourists' prying feet?

In respectful entreaty
    I am,
        Faithfully yours,
            Katharine H. Bradley.

12. K.B. to Robert Browning: 27 November 1884

Stoke Green,
Stoke Bishop,

Nov. 27

Dear Mr. Browning,

I seem to remember that I wrote to you in my own name—as a woman. I trust you overlooked that in your reply.

I do not care to speak to you again of our relations to our work:—on one point however your mis-apprehension is so serious that I cannot keep silent.

I did not speak of combating "social conventions." It is not in our power or desire to treat irreverently customs or beliefs that have been, or are, sacred to men. We hold ourselves bound in life & literature to reveal—as far as maybe—the beauty of the high feminine standard of <u>the ought to be</u>.

What I wrote was:
"we cannot be stifled in drawing-room conventionalities." By that I meant we could not be scared away as ladies from the tragic elements of life.

I am sorry I should have to explain this to you.
    Faithfully yours,
        Katharine H. Bradley.

13. E.C. to Robert Browning: 1885

> Christchurch Vicarage,
> Westcombe Park,
> Blackheath,
> S. E.

Dear Mr. Browning,

We ask leave to tell you—for we could not speak at all on Saturday—of the happiness it gave us to be with you. Your belief in us will go on literally all our days through, goading us & yet keeping us patient in our labour. We shall always 'remember & understand'. If you should find any tricks of style, any individual mannerisms that break the unity of our work, will you be a critic as stern as you have been disinterested? We love our work too earnestly to be hurt by any educating severity. This you will know.

Hoping that we may some day meet again,

> Very sincerely yours,
> Edith Cooper

d. To John Miller Gray, 1893

14. K.B. to John Miller Gray: 1893

> Private
> Durdans

Monday
1893

> Dear Mr. Gray
> No word of response even this morning to my note—addressed Sunday—you must therefore be home again at Gayfield[1]—I am very sorry.

This morning I have been to my publisher discussing the "decreased" edition.[2]

—The publisher is loath to begin before a single review has appeared.[3] So—if you care that the "gnomic verse" shd. not dis-

---

1 Gayfield Square.
2 The second edition of *Underneath the Bough*.
3 Of the first edition.

appear suddenly as it appeared—write whatever notice you purpose writing I beseech you <u>at once</u>.

I cannot understand why Michael's friends thus withhold aid. The silence of the <u>Athenaeum</u> & <u>Academy</u> is simply <u>ruining</u> Michael's worldly prospects, dwarfing his hopes of Italy & embittering his heart. Remember neither <u>Athenaeum</u> nor <u>Academy</u> have even alluded to the existence of <u>Stephania</u>—I wish you could find out <u>why</u> Cotton has suffered this to be.[1]

—I have a terribly hard single-handed fight before me with <u>Rufus</u>[2]—now that the people have the lyrics flung to them they profess to care for so much, surely they might break from their dumbness.

═════

We are thinking of including in our new Bough 60 poems instead of 112. We shall like to send you our list, or if you wd. mark 60 in yr. copy—<u>the</u> 60 you wd. select we will return it [a line is drawn connecting this word back to "copy"] to you none the worse—indeed perhaps the better for our inscription.

—The things praised by my art-friends fill me with amazement.

Will you tell me whether there is obscurity in the last poem— "drunk with that ~~filling~~ [<] [?]Brimming [>] the ~~vine~~ [<] wine [>] that fills thy autumn vat"[3] What is the "that"? [a line is drawn from this word connecting it to the same third word in the preceding quotation] Does one have to pause & scratch one's head? My friends wd. have the poem omitted on the score of obscurity. Again, how does the poem affect you for good or evil beginning "Great violets in a weedy tangle."

Do, <u>please</u>, answer quite frankly, & try to suggest some reason for the <u>Academy's</u> sort of lockjaw silence.

I have such faith in the nice feeling of the Academy—it <u>must</u> be suffering from lockjaw.

Sincerely yours,

Michael

---

1 This paragraph berates two key review journals of the time for not publishing notices about Michael Field's recent publications, and blames, particularly, James Sutherland Cotton (1869–1916), who became editor of the *Academy* in 1881.

2 *William Rufus*, the play published in 1885.

3 In the first edition of *Underneath the Bough* the line is actually printed "... drunk with that / Kindling the wine that brims thy autumn vat!"

My brother[1] is writing to you about Scotland. I do hope you will
be able to assure him you can join him. Amy can hardly walk at
all; he is looking forward to yr. companionship.

M.

e. To and From Bernard Berenson, 1891–?1912

15. E.C. to Bernard Berenson: no date [c. 1891]

Dear Mr Berenson,

I have copied what I scribbled by <u>Der Traum</u>[2] that you may
have the fun I have had in seeing how similar was the impression
made on us both by the picture. We each seized on the frogs as
the acme of fancy in the conception—but I envy you that exqui-
site ~~verb~~ participle "apostrophising." In one detail you are cer-
tainly wrong: the cock does not <u>strut</u>—he sits as if he never meant
to move. I went to see him after reading your Article, & he was
vigorously at roost.

Now as to the Article—it is delightful; the reading of it greatly
enlarged our pleasure before the Corriggios [sic].[3] I have read it
three or four times, and always with clearer interest as I mastered
the handwriting of the end. Here & there I have taken the per-
mitted liberty of putting down a suggestion in pencil, where it
seemed to me that the English required to be sharper or the fall
of the sentence more gracious.

As to its publication—I am sure you should not lose time. I see
that a translation of Morelli is announced, & although your
article is movingly original in its treatment of the influence of
Dosso[4] on Corriggio [sic]—the portions where it coincides with
Morelli[5] would be fresher, if they appeared before the English
translation of of [sic] his first vol.

I suppose <u>The Art Journal</u> would be the place for it—or
<u>Harper</u>, with an excellent reproduction of the "Madonna of the

---

1 Amy's husband: John Ryan (technically Cooper's brother-in-law, but not
   Bradley's).
2 Battista Dossi's 1544 Canvas, *Il Sogno* (*The Dream*). Titled here in
   German because it was held in the Dresden gallery.
3 Correggio: Italian mannerist painter (c.1489–1534).
4 Dosso Dossi (1490–1542). Italian Renaissance painter, and Battista's
   more famous brother.
5 Probably the Italian art historian Giovani Morelli, known for his con-
   noisseurship (1816–91).

Holy Francis."[1] You would put your lip out in scorn, if I suggested The Hobby Horse. But do not delay.[2]

Your description of the "Madonna of the Holy Francis" is charming in its grace & reserve; especially the sentence: "Above, just under the Arch, two little angels are poised in the air, as if it were water in wh: they floated, deliciously at their ease." I should love to see the Circe of Dosso—it would be a picture to write about. For a year and a half we have been striving to find the real poems contained in several pictures we love—not what we dream of it them individually, but what the lines and colours sing in themselves.[3] You laugh, and Morelli feels uncomfortable in his grave—but the self-willed poets watch their pictures, receive of them, and write.

I think your aphorism is ~~right~~ true. Imagination is a very intense fresh seeing: it is always this in all the Arts. And so it comes to pass that Wagner has accomplished the miracle of giving visibility to Sound. The best poems always have in them something definitely & beautifully seen.

Artistic form in all the arts tends towards music;[4] artistic matter in all of them towards painting. It is pictures alone in which the technique is harmonious as a musician's score that lend themselves to poetry.

The Frankfurt Gallery delighted me beyond all prose-Expression. I am still weariable, but full of refreshment—which sounds a contradiction, but is not one. Though I can walk little and must sleep much, I enjoy a kind of early childhood—everything is new, & strikes my brain definitively. We are as quiet here as in the

---

1 A well-established and important American periodical published both in America and in England, *Harper's New Monthly Magazine* was well known among English late-Victorian literary circles for the quality of its pieces and for paying well.

2 *The Hobby Horse*, as its predecessor, the *Century Guild Hobby Horse*, was an expensive and beautifully produced art magazine, which ran from 1884 to 1892, and promoted the Arts and Crafts movement.

3 This volume was published in 1892 under the title *Sight and Song*. In the Preface (see section on *Sight and Song*, p. 85) they noted "The aim of this little volume is ... to translate into verse what the lines and colours of certain chosen pictures sing in themselves."

4 Edith is, of course, paraphrasing here Pater's declaration in "The School of Giorgione," "*All art constantly aspires towards the condition of music*," one of the key literary statements of the British *fin-de-siècle* (*The Renaissance*, 106). Pater's statement concurs with Wagner's views on literature and music.

Krankenhaus[1]—I cannot yet reach London—& we spend all the days together in our pretty work-room spinning poems, reading Morelli & evoking the impressions of the Summer...

> With kindest regards & congratulations on the restored Lotto,
> Very sincerely yours,

Edith Cooper.

Der Traum.

A woman lies (from right to left) on a black rock; she wears a grass-green, crenulated cloak, a dress of luminous indigo, and a hood of bright ochre-yellow. Her arms, great as those of a daughter of the Titans, are heavily folded; her face has no charm of youth in the healthful features. She sleeps on a white pillow—she sleeps and dreams. Beside her on the black stone sits a vigilant cock...but, bless my soul!—he is sitting just like a hen on the nest & his eye amid the corals of his comb is maternal in its fixity.

Above her head is a grey, moon-eyed owl, & through a rift of blue clouds, dire and formal, the moon is blown out like a bubble. Behind her & to the left is grasped the nightmare—energetic and yet stationary. A dog-fish stands on webbed feet & drags along the head of a sword-fish, that ends in a noble volute from wh: hangs a ~~noble~~ lighted Roman lamp. Then comes a basket, over which two heads are ranged—one like Sesostris in his boyhood (Could there be anything more terrible than an ancient Egyptian King "im werden"?[2])—the other a negro's, with a tongue that hangs like that of a hot dog's. On the basket is a white bird, its eyes gouged out, & a streamer of plumes a 'top. Then two falcons sit together, ~~like~~ the King and Queen of Carnage, one red, one pale, both shaggy with incurved tails & wings. Above them a litter of tiny stalks. A wee chap of a lobster on a small tortoise tilts with a mousy apparition in the midst.

From the right advances another band—a larma, virulently sentimental; a creature that grows out of a shell & has the head of a little old lion; a long-legged bird that waddles forward; a bird of long nose & fascinated eye, like an ancient miner—his pointed bonnet spirts up two thin feathers on his brow: beyond him frogs

---

1 "Hospital" (German). This suggests the letter must have been written on Michael Field's return from Dresden (where Cooper was hospitalised) in 1891.

2 "In the making."

stretch their throats and sit in the cool of a conflagration, for the blue, devouring rays of the distance have no heat. A white burst of non-flame comes from a house over the river & smoke from a tower. Behind the woman's head is an assiduous old man—very, very kind—(only his beard is stormy & there is [?]rime over his eyes) so kind that he would fan the air—that still aggregation of air & many animals—with a feathered-brush. His arm is mighty under his red cloak: but the air remains motionless, it is populous & its people stand. O gods, it is pleasure that fleets—while pain stands, & stares, & keeps company!

16. Dictated notes sent by Bernard Berenson to K.B. and E.C.: 25 January 1892

[marked] Doctrine[1] on à Rebours

"Huysmanns' A Rebours" has interested me more than any novel I have read for a long time. The story takes up only a small part of the book. Nothing of consequence happens. A man at the end of his youth retires to a place near Paris to be alone. He wishes to be within easy enough reach of the world not to be tempted to go back to it. He hates it, hates all its interests, hates people, & beyond endurance he loathes everything that is sordid, commonplace. He is well born, has plenty of money, & has had every opportunity to satisfy his tastes. He has tried everything, & now he shuts himself up in a little house, to live his real life utterly untrammelled by contact with other people's lives. But he is in bad health. Frail & bloodless at the start, a life of experiments with his own sensations has brought him to the brink of the grave. His stomach & his nerves are exhausted. He had forced his sensations to do such feats that they ended by breaking down their natural banks & spreading into one [?]common stagnant marsh. At last he has to choose between death & a return to normal existence. The less interesting part of the novel describes the hero's life à Rebours. He turns night into day & day into night, finds bitter sweet & salt insipid. Everything that gives us ordinary mortals pleasure nauseates him. But there is a logic to all this monstrosity, & that is why the description of it is entertaining. The hero is so perfectly clear in the analysis of his own sensations, wh. to him are as sharply defined as rectangles are to

---

1 A pet name for Berenson.

the rest of us. He is cathartic to the utmost. He has cultivated all his senses equally, & in his retirement he confines life entirely to them, giving each one course in turn. But having exhausted most forms of sensation before shutting himself up, he finds each sense capable of giving him very little pleasure indeed.

The real interest of the book lies in the history, nay, the biography of each of his senses. This Huysmans writes with a precision, a discrimination, a subtlety that makes even the de Goncourts seem crude, heavy, & with a sincerity that even Tolstoi might envy. When you have read through the biography of each sense, you perceive that the hero, des Esseintes, has simply taken Pater literally. He gets as many pulsations as possible into a given time. He is Marius the Epicurean living at the end of the XIX century. But he is French & therefore more logical with himself than an English mind could imagine. À Rebours is therefore "La Confession d'un Enfant de la Fin du Siècle."[1]

Brought up by Jesuits, des Esseintes has never been taught to think, & has of course been discouraged from exploring his mind, & discovering what an immense pleasure there is in some cerebration. So he was shut up to his senses, & they end by refusing to serve him. He proves conclusively in his own person that no life of mere sensation can possibly be satisfactory. Sensation is butter & intellectual activity is bread. You can easily limit life to your own sensations, but on the condition that your mind always remains on the perpendicular, so to speak, to your senses.

In reality, however, À Rebours is a series of criticisms upon literature and art, but criticisms wh. have nothing official about them, nothing to do with professors or reviewers. Des Esseintes is very representative in the way he took literature. It was to him a sensation on a level with other sensations, & he knew just as well whether a page of writing gave him supreme pleasure as he knew whether a certain wine or a certain meal satisfied his palate. Tolerating only what gave him positive pleasure, & having passed the age when one reads for sympathy, or for finding one's own experiences or sensations well described, he read only for the ring of the phrase or for the vividness of the image, & he ends by finding very little left worth reading—that is—worth re-reading. He goes over the list of great books in Latin & French, & the criticism of each is startling in its decision & in its originality. He ends by finding only a few pages in Baudelaire, Goncourt, Flaubert, & Zola. This seems to me a logical conclusion. A person

---

1 "The Confession of a child of the fin de siècle."

who reads for the pure aesthetic pleasure of the sensation must end by finding next to nothing to read, literature being so very much more limited a sensation than painting, or music, or natural landscape.

The upshot of <u>A Rebours</u> is that no matter what the art is, you soon exhaust it aesthetically, & that a merely aesthetical devotion to the arts leads to insanity. Art cannot be separated from life, and still less from thought."

17. Bernard Berenson to K.B. and E.C.: 30 May 1892

3, Rue Bara, Paris.
May Tues 30th, 1892

Dear Michaels, I received "Sight & Song" this day week, but I have been very busy since, & I trust you will excuse me for having delayed my thanks. The fact is I did not want to thank for this daintily bound, prettily printed book. I wanted to see what was inside. Now I have read thro' the poems several times, have turned them over on my palate, & the taste is decidedly good. Personally I prefer the Tura St. Jerome[1] to all the others. I do not say this as criticism. I have a notion that there are two poetries: one of which is always interpretive in the first place, & the other decorative. I happen much to prefer the interpretive, & of that kind I find your poem on Tura's Jerome has caught something of the adamantine strength of Tura's own work. After the St Jerome I like the poem on Procris[2] best. It makes me see the whole [?]scene vividly, & [?]fall in [?]love. Your description in that poem is exquisite in precision & quality. I find your description capital thro'out.

I was interested also in your interpretation of Watteau. It is not the French interpretation that Verlaine has given us—& how wonderfully!—in his <u>Fêtes Galantes</u>, which you must know, I am sure.[3]

Your versification is very clever, & as a whole very smart. <u>Vous enjambez un peut trop</u>.[4] That is the worst I have to say about it.

I am sincere in congratulating you over this fascinating little volume. I shall read it thro' more than once during the warm days

---

1 Cosimo Tura's *Saint Jerome in the Desert* (*Sight and Song*, 53–57).
2 Piero di Cosimo's *Death of Procris* (*Sight and Song*, 47–52).
3 Verlaine's collection of poems, *Fêtes Galantes* (1869), was inspired by Watteau's paintings that were grouped under the same heading.
4 "You use enjambement a bit too much."

of the coming summer—my especial thanks for the green book-
mark.

   à bientôt,
      Bernhard Berenson

18. E.C. to Bernard Berenson: 26 February [1894]

Durdans
Reigate Feb. 26

Dear Doctrine,
   It's more paralising [sic] to me to sit down before a sheet of
letter-paper than before a sheet of foolscap on which I must trace
the scenario of a new drama or the beginning of a Croquis.[1] A
letter isn't one of my forms of expression. I don't know where to
begin, or how to handle my own personality, or approach that of
my correspondent. Nevertheless I must make an effort to save
you from the "temptation" of thinking your words of friendship
were not welcome. I don't much believe in the reality of the temp-
tation; because I fancy we both know we are friends, in so far as
two people so much alike can be friends. Still if you want my
assurance—in answer to all you said about pictures & what our
fellow-enjoyment of them could do for you, I have only to confess
that I don't write Croquis as I did in the summer after being with
you. My sensations were at their highest power then. Now they
are lazy, & don't vibrate, & don't draw the right words to them
magnetically. Like kindles fire in like; & though we're not quite
two flints (I hope) we influence each other on the same principle.
   It's quite a different thing with drama—that doesn't want sen-
sational alertness: indeed a power to realise other peoples' [sic]
actions & passions is almost incompatible with interest in the
record of one's own senses—& now Croquis languish, I am
absorbed in my characters as I have scarcely ever been before.
   Then there's another thing that makes it impossible we
shouldn't come to be friends—we are contemporaries, in spite of
all the differences in our education & work: I mean that your atti-
tude toward life is the attitude I understand & have, broadly [sic]
speaking, held of my own accord.

---

1 Following the advice of Berenson, Cooper began to write short prose
   impressionistic pieces called *croquis*, a French form, which can be trans-
   lated into English as "sketch."

Furthermore, I think I know why we chafe each other almost as much as we animate: I'll [<] tell [>] you. I'm sure that a man agrees best with a woman who is his opposite, who gives him the <u>full</u> advantage of a different sex, or else with one in whom his ideas charm him spontaneously as instincts—& much the same holds good of a woman's friendships with men. But, you see, I naturally think what I feel, & feel with the same self-consciousness as you—with the same acuteness—& there's all the trouble!

If I don't like letter-writing at most times I like it less than ever when I'm in the midst of conflict & all winter I've been in the state of Keat's <u>Lamia</u>, when she was changing from a serpent into a human being—a state of torrid transition. I don't know what I am or what I shall become. <u>The Modern</u>
"has spoilt my silver mail & golden brede,
Eclipsed my crescents & licked up my stars"
and as I feel all I think as well as thinking all I feel you won't be surprised if I continue the quotation—
        "of all these bereft
nothing but <u>pain</u> & <u>ugliness</u> were left"[1]
Yes, these two words have had significance for me of late. I wish I could get my change over, for it's not pleasant, or more positively speaking, it's almost unendurable…a mortal strife. And you who can discover the "Genesis of the Work of Art"—is it true you think your interests are so remote from us artists? Have you no help? Even Plato saw what pitiable wretches we are, wondering between reality & illusion forever, & finding no rest.

I analyse modern plays, watch life whenever I can, greet the spring as it creeps out of the hedges & the evening sky, eat my own heart like a civilised canabal [sic],[2] try to imagine that Discontent is a leader in whom to have confidence, work ~~to~~ till my head reels & I cry aloud for amusement, [<] which I [>] get where I don't want it—in books. Now I'm studying Tourguénef.[3] I find much of myself set down in some of the male-characters,

---

1 Keats's "Lamia" reads: "And, as the lava ravishes the mead, / Spoilt all her silver mail, and golden brede; / Made gloom of all her frecklings, streaks and bars, / Eclipsed her crescents, and licked up her stars. / So that, in moments few, she was undressed / Of all her sapphires, greens, and amethyst, / And rubious-argent; of all these bereft, / Nothing but pain and ugliness were left." As in the previous letter, Edith uses an art form to talk to Berenson about her feelings for him.

2 i.e., cannibal.

3 Probably a reference to Ivan Turgenev, a famous Russian novelist and playwright of the nineteenth century.

& one of them, at least, makes me laugh & perhaps shiver a little at his points of likeness to you.

Hegel's <u>Aesthetic</u> belongs to me, though Michael rightfully claimed it, as all mine is his; but the tiresome marks on every page are by me, in early youth. Try to ignore them.

Is this an affectionate reply?

Yours out of debt,

Field.

19. Bernard Berenson to K.B.: 1 February 1908

Febr. 1, 1908

I Tatti,
Settignano,
Florence.

My dear Michael,

Honey of any kind, wild or otherwise, is not to be gulped down in gallon-measure by any person of my years. So I have read of your last volume[1] but a little daily, & I have found it delicious. I truly congratulate you & tell you frankly it is far above what I expected. There is much poetical stuff throughout, & not at all infrequently real poetry, if not of the highest, all but the highest kind. The chief, perhaps, the only drawback is that you occassionaly [sic] fall into a certain Donne-ishness,[2] a certain obscurity while you do not quite inspire the confidence that one must delve for sense. I like too many of these poems to tell you which I prefer. On the whole those which are most Greek in theme, & most impersonal in address. And those few Greek lines— they are from Oedippus [sic] Coloneus[3] are they not?—that preface "The Longer Allegiance,"[4] they are ideally placed.

Well, I have read & shall read again, sip this wild honey. It is real bee's work & no compound of glycerine & God knows what.

---

1   *Wild Honey from Various Thyme.*
2   He likens Michael Field's poetry here to the metaphysical verse of the seventeenth-century poet John Donne.
3   *Oedipus Coloneus* is an ancient Greek tragedy by Sophocles.
4   A section of poems in *Wild Honey.*

I am working hard at my lists, & reading zo- & bi- & physiology, & Goethe. At this minute a most delightful volume of German letters addressed to Fritz v. Stein[1] which bring up most vividly a century ago. Mary, is, for her, still not very well, but getting better.

With much love to you both

Bernhard

20. E.C. to Bernard Berenson: 10 March 1911

1, The Paragon,
Richmond, Surrey

March 10th. 1911

Beloved Bernhard,

You have shared so much of our lives, Michael's & mine, that I can't keep secret from you what is happening to me now. I have to become used to the thought that I have a mortal disease; I have to become used to travelling a country of quite new features. The Doctors have found out I have Cancer of the bowels—which accounts for my constant ill-health—worse for the last half-year. There can be no operation of removal & the Doctors abandon all hope. However, when praying to our Lady, an intimation was given to me that I should seek a newspaper-cutting, I made 10 years ago, in wh: cures of Cancer by the use of violet-leaves were chronicled. I drank the violet-leaves & pain certainly was lessened. I have nights of heavenly sleep. So I have sundered myself from the Doctors & live thankfully on the violet-bed mercy that answered my praying. My will is entirely bowed to the Holy Will—whether I am to tread the royal Road of the Cross, or to be lead back slowly to life through a wood of violets "covered up in leaves."

The shock of all the horrible circumstances of my doom, the Doctors made so brutally manifest, was very great & whelming: only I had a shield they did not know of thrown round me & absolutely impervious by despair or rebellion.

---

1 Fritz was the son of Charlotte von Stein, the woman with whom Goethe (the German writer, 1749–1832) exchanged hundreds of letters and who was a huge influence on his life and work. Goethe's letters to Frau von Stein constitute a much better known volume of correspondence.

But I cried two days the tears of parting—tears Michael & I mingled. The thought of our great union here on the sweet Earth of the Sacraments, of human love & friendship, of man's lovely creativeness, of the beauty of ~~of~~ God's Book of Genesis, of the light, the stars, & seas, of the Seasons with their flowers or bare boughs; of living creatures, so loveable—we faced my severance from all these things. Then we turned to our peace in the Blessed Will—"in sua voluntate."[1]

Such love has been shown to me, Bernhard dear—such prayers have been rising for me singly or in chorus! Such changes too have made me clearer in my very self, that I can now call my Woe my Mercy.

Very happily I am awaiting my Shroud—the white wool habit of St Dominic, to wh: as a novice of his penitential Order I have the right. Before the month is over, I shall be a dedicated Tertiary: I, a raw convert, I, so unworthy, shall be in the same Order as St. Catherine of Sienna—still in the world, but, like her, dedicated. Though I am awaiting my shroud, it may be I shall stay among the violet-beds some years yet.

Dear Bernhard, I know you will realise all we have been passing through—your Michael & Field—in our sorrow. You are very close to us, & you have certainly adorned life for us, you dear Faun! Yes, & beyond the Conditions of life here, I have always loved you, & that deep friendship continues through all struggle & suffering.

Would you could so fulfil the Circle of the years that you could come back to the Splendid Reality you grasped too early! Prayer & love are a single devotion when I am thinking of you—every-day.

So lovingly Your
Field.

21. K.B. to Bernard Berenson: no date [c. 1912]

Dear Bernhard—
But you must know what you ask is impossible—the Book[2] when I die will be sealed from all eyes for a term of years—this will remove your special pain.

1　"In his will."
2　Most probably their diary, *Works and Days*.

But your request, dear Bernhard is <u>inconceivable</u>. You will see this, if you imagine others making it—
—Henry you must know forbids it—You have Field with you in her letters, in her spirit, in her work—& in her prayers[.] <u>Follow these</u>—then indeed, dear, dear Bernhard you will draw close to her.

I have been learning rather hard news—this week—the Doctor says I am out of danger—so sweet to be in!—& his prophecy is for, as <u>minimum,</u> 2 years more of life—

The malady is to go on—indeed it is already [<]re-[>] beginning.[1] Nevertheless I have won great relief [<] from operation [>], & been supernaturally carried along. So <u>I shall be to the end.</u>

I have always held that Sacramental Life with God is blessed. Reluctantly, I go from hospital to take to the field again. *[2] I trusted I was going to be ordered home as a permanent invalid or Contemplative!!!—Instead!

But all is well.

And to-morrow will be radiant.

Corpus Christi is at hand

Michael.

* I thought I was going home to rest & long sleep, & all that sweet life Pater speaks of in one of his Essays—when the [?]Jury, disgraced soldier, slept out his sleeps in his child's bedroom[3]

      —Oh Michael!!!

f. To Mary Costelloe, later Mary Berenson, 1892–?1912

22. K.B. to Mary Costelloe: 2 February 1892

Feb 2. 1892
Durdans

Dear Mrs. Costelloe.

Can you tell me whether Giorgione's Venus is a noontide picture? It seems to M.F. it is; but out on seeming! "the male con-

---

1 The letter shows that both Edith and Katharine were dying of cancer.
2 Bradley's own asterisk.
3 Bradley's handwriting, usually difficult to read, was even more indecipherable at the end of her life. The asterisked part of this letter is one such example.

science"—exclusion of fancy & all sentiment not as truly of the picture as the drop of honey oozing from a plum—this is our aim.

We have now finished the Giorgione Venus. Scarcely a bit that has not been over painted—I mean scarcely a verse that is not quite other than it was in its first form. This has been a full month for poems, & one of peculiarly happy work. M.F. was determined to get in the angel's scarlet shoes in the Giovanni Bellini—as the painter has got them in, painting them with great joy—& not feeling them incongruous in the midst of that tragedy & passion. The scarlet shoes are in the poem: indeed I do not think a detail of that Bellini is shirked.

Then we have had immense joy over the Apollo & Marsyas (Perugino) of the Louvre—such joy over "the [<] doom of the [>] brown, inferior man, & the removal of bad work from the world["].[1] But I must not give you, as it were, an interview with <u>Sight & Song</u>, before it is lawfully in Society. I now want to plague you about the Lorenzo Credi of the ~~Louvre~~ Burlington. Edith came back & told me she had found a Madonna with an arbutus tree for a throne. I could hardly speak for pleasure, because in my childhood the two really exquisite & decorative flowers I had seen in growth about my home were the cistus & the arbutus. I had never seen the arbutus in art. But again, no <u>enthusiasm</u>—probably to use Mr. Berenson's ruthless phrase "this is not an arbutus at all." I do not know Italian flowers. In the same picture, the whole foreground as you will remember is full of the loveliest strong bunches of cream coloured flowers. That might be strawberry flowers, or anemones of tougher make than our wind flowers. I wonder if you Botanist could be made to recollect. If not, we shall have to decide what they are & you all, by devout exercises must bring yourselves to receive the faith when it is delivered to you.

Thank you so much for the papers & the literary criticism. I do not think you can understand how we desire you should excel in literature. You know how often the notes to a book may be of quite rare value. Think what it would be to make perfect guide-books.

---

1 This painting by Perugino (c. 1450–1523; Italy) shows the musical chal-
lenge between Marsyas (here shown as a shepherd, of ruddy complexion
and cropped hair) and the god Apollo (with flowing locks and paler
skin). As a result of losing the challenge Marsyas was flayed by Apollo.
Bradley and Cooper's delight seems harsh and is tinged with disdain for
the uncouth shepherd.

The lives I should begin as simply as a fairy-tale "—once upon a time"—only I should set the student down in the time. I should quietly state what were the religious, & political influences of the painter's youth, & what the character of the scenery in wh. he lived, if <u>his pictures bear trace</u> of susceptibility to outdoor impressions.—I should never say "of <u>course</u> such an[d] such person bears trace of Giorgione's influence" such a remark makes the poor student hot with shame & angry at his ignorance—tell the poor novice who were the artist's masters, & give the names of his most receptive & sensitive pupils. I also think as a matter of art it would be well to reserve the [<] ~~detailed~~ re-production in detail, [>] & criticism of the typical masterpiece to the end. I know & respect your abhorrence of fine writing; but you have powers of re-creating a picture, & then of making one enjoy what is worthiest in it. Take Dosso Dossi's Circe. Write & write—always from life—I mean before the picture—then go home & transfuse into art. At present I feel at the end of one of your studies you leave off thankful it is over. <u>This must not be.</u> The impression must be that you are brimfull of your subject (as you are) but that you leave your student to look & think for himself, having taught him the use of his eyes.

The criticism on <u>A Rebours</u> is far better than any of the work on painters. One feels by it brought in contact with the book.
—The sentence—"the hero is so perfectly clear in the analysis of his own sensations, wh. to him are as sharply defined as rectangles are to the rest of us["]—saves pages. Not to be diffuse & prune; but thus from the first to be thrifty of thought & time is the true method.

"With stuffs that tickle the eye & yet rest it" is a phrase in the Bonifazio paper—that gives one the very artist. You can give the artists so that the reader won't recognise them by the signs in their hands, as St Barbara's tower, or wh. is little less wooden, by the [?]lop[1] of their figures' ears, but by <u>their way of taking pleasure</u>, whether they liked the <u>feel</u> of a stuff, as well as its hue, & how it seemed to them nicest the folds shd. fall.

Oh I end. I grow tedious. But indeed something must be done. "Crivelli[2] is always <u>so funny</u>" someone remarked ~~to~~ [<] near [>] me the other day whilst I was studying his passionate & terrible pietà.
—The more you can tell us of your Florence life the better.

---

1 Perhaps this was meant to be "loop."
2 Carlo Crivelli (c. 1430–c. 1495), an Italian Renaissance painter.

—Whenever your mood serves; but be free. Even when we [?]hurry you with questions, keep us waiting, if you are in the midst of the Florentines.

Affectionately yours
K.H. Bradley

PS. I like to hear about Ray[1]—dear little soul—& to learn what Italy seems to a child.

23. K.B. to Mary Costelloe: no date [1894]

Friday
    I have the Yellow—Book Fever—I must speak.
    Mary, I was about to scold you for not goading yourself on to recognise something or to discover it—in that blue play bill of Beardsley's.[2] I was about to use a simile to you—& say the modern is the line of débris left by the last wave; & the truly contemporaneous person is to be found on the scurf-rim of the beach, poking about with an umbrella among the decayed seaweed &—possible?—rare shells.
    But everything has got mixed & disabled, & in my wretchedness I came to the conclusion that we—immortal 4, Faun, Our Lady of Prose, & that Cloud that moves together,[3] if it move at all—are all of us nice people—hunting—seeking is the word—for pearls... & being rewarded for our search by horrid swine troughs...
    The Yellow Book was born on Monday.[4] I went with young joy in my heart to hail it. Behold the whole window of the Bodley Head was one rank yellow. And then—& then!!—but Mary I will not write about the text of the Yellow Book—all the people who write in it are my literary cousins—I will merely call the attention

---

1   Ray Costelloe, later Strachey, was Mary Costelloe's daughter.

2   Aubrey Beardsley, the infamous illustrator and art editor of the *Yellow Book*.

3   The "immortal 4" are Bernard, Mary, "Henry," and "Michael." The Faun is Bernard, Mary is "Our Lady of Prose," and the "Cloud that moves together" is "Michael Field."

4   The Bodley Head published the first number of the highly anticipated and quintessential magazine of the 1890s *The Yellow Book* (1894–97) on 16 April 1894. It is important to note that Oscar Wilde openly despised the publication.

of the Doctrine to the poem by Le Galienne,—[<] Le Galienne [>] whom he for one moment hoped was the coming poet. But this age has no poet—cannot have—it is going down quick into hell. Write to me about the text—you have no cousins there; &— Oh, I must speak out concerning George Egerton—that shameless creature—whose pages are really "the sweepings of a Pentonville omnibus.["]¹—The vile, yellow pest has doubtless spread to Florence, & you will be reading it—so do glance through <u>A Lost Masterpiece</u>—& note the expression "a chunk of genius." There ought to be in letters an outcast class to whom we can relegate such offenders. They should never be admitted into the society of good books—who sin such sins. I am sick & ashamed of belonging to the corruptors of my own language. These dreadful Georges—George Fleming, George Egerton &c—a new Hanoverian curse. I shall in future write frankly as Messalina Garden.² (Henry says this is <u>his</u> jest! dear boy![)]

The a̶r̶t̶ [<] art [>] of the Yellow Book—well, I can speak of that. Let the Doctrine prepare to say "Good Lord"! & bury his face, as he sees what Beardsley has made of Mrs. Campbell's rich, human beauty. What a fool the woman must be to sit for him!

Concerning other of these illustrations I feel with Henry they are not fit for the eye to rest on.

Tell the Doctrine I God-bless him for his modesty & sense; & propose to him to write a chapter on the connection between affectation & foulness. I wish he could spare time to write to Michael a letter on Japanese art, & its legitimate use by Western nations.

---

1 "Michael" is quoting here Ruskin's essay "George Eliot." Ruskin rejected Eliot's narrative technique in particular and her fiction in general arguing that "the persons of George Eliot's novels suggested nothing so much as the sweepings of a Pentonville omnibus." John Ruskin, "George Eliot," in *The Literary Criticism of John Ruskin*, ed. Harold Bloom (New York: Da Capo Press, 1965), 384–85. George Egerton's piece for the first volume of the *Yellow Book* was "A Lost Masterpiece. A City Mood, Aug. '93." In Egerton's piece the narrator travels by omnibus in search of a "masterpiece."

2 George Fleming was the pseudonym of Julia Constance Fletcher (1858–1938). She was born in America, though she lived most of her life in Europe. Among her best-known novels are *Mirage*, *The Truth about Clement Ker*, and *For Plain Women Only*. Oscar Wilde dedicated to her his poem "Ravenna." George Egerton was the pseudonym of Mary Chavelita Dunne (1859–1945). In 1887 she eloped to Norway with Henry Higginson.

Its misuse—is shown in the Yellow Book. I am really dreadfully bothered by this.—In my haste—I am tempted to ~~say~~ feel that Eastern art is unwholesome for Western nations; but I want to listen & learn.

Poor Michael will be—only a shred of him—in the second Yellow Book.[1] Oh, that some angel would deliver him from that prison!!!!

Send Maeterlinck[2] [<] can't spell [>]— without fail—I mean Doctrine on him, & add printed Doctrine on George Egerton. We must not let these women go rampant.

[here the letter continues: there follows an excerpt transcribed from the diaries recording the women's response to the first issue of the *Yellow Book*; this is reproduced in the selection from the diaries given in this volume]

24. K.B. to Mary Costelloe: no date [1895]

Dear Mary,

There was a p. c.[3] about a sore-throat with your letter, & since no books & silence, Mary, you are not ill?

As for me, yesterday brought me news of Oscar's Two Years,[4] & do what I will, there they lie on my heart.—If you hear of any friend who has clung to him, of any one who has turned to him a human side, let me know. Meanwhile I wake in the cell, & wonder what the gruel will be like, & touch the prison-clothes & feel for my long hair—& think what [<] a fool [>] I was when I was out at bail at Torquay—not to bathe, & get out of my depth, accidentally, & drown in the big, cleansing sea. Henry remarks this is not making for life. Truly: but I can't bear to think of an affectionate creature shut up, & hearing nothing but howls.—The more I think about his wife, the more sorry I am she has cast him off. If her boys have a shameful father, well, she can't help that— why does she not give them a splendid mother, one who through

---

1 "Michael Field" withdrew their prose-poem from the *Yellow Book*.
2 Maurice Maeterlinck (1862–1949), Belgian symbolist poet and play-wright. Perhaps his most famous work was *Pelléas et Mélisande* (1892).
3 Post card.
4 Oscar Wilde was sentenced to two years of hard labour for the crime of sodomy.

all infancy has clung to the man she loves. Mary, you once said that nothing, not murder, or any crime could make you love any one you loved less. <u>Then</u>, my hair rose; but at present I am in doubt.

[the letter continues]

25. K.B. to Mary Berenson: June [possibly 1912]

1, The Paragon,
Richmond,
Surrey.

Beloved Mary,

One writes June, & I remember it was in June you hoped that Ray's child would be born.

[...]

We suffer—that is all I can write of us, dear Mary.

We are together; we love being together, & Paragon clothes us round.

Henry writes & lives very acutely—& loves her flowers, her home, & Michael—also she is loved back.

—This is all our news.

By the way—Henry at Easter published a book of Catholic verse (Poems of Adoration all Henry's own) Sands: Edinburgh 5 shillings net. Rothenstein—is it not strange? cares for it <u>extremely</u>. To me it is a great joy,—I often go to it adoring. <u>Only some of the poems</u>:

—We shall not be angry—if you & Doctrine who love Henry so dear—do not love her catholic books. Perhaps you are lovers of the faun Henry. I do myself prefer the faun perhaps. But get the book, & write to me how it is to you.

A white passion flower looks in at my window: I cling on to the growing flowers: we cannot travel.

Bless you, dear Mary. Best come to England & see us. <u>Michael.</u>

g. To and From Charles Ricketts and Charles Shannon, 1895–1907

26. Ricketts and Shannon to K.B.: October 1895

31 Beaufort Street Chelsea.
S.W.

Cher Maître,

We are now completing a new Dial. Should you care to let us print your beautiful poem on the Tintoretto portrait, it would give [<] us [>] genuine pleasure.[1] We have to confess that the reward we offer contributors to the Dial is so small that we call it a present. It may, if you prefer it, take the shape of a ~~very small~~ [<] unworthy [>] crystal, a marvellous shell or an inconceivable piece of coral. This is for you to decide.

While staying near Birchington-on-Sea, we placed a pot of red lilies on the grave of Dante Gabriel Rossetti & stole from it two little tired rose leaves bitten by the sea air.

The Pageant[2] is at last finished & we can breathe again. Verlaine has written on one of the Rossetti pictures. Bridges has sent a long poem and we have a very short Swinburne. There is a capital story by W B Yates [sic], a possible poem by W E Henley, a good John Gray & one or two mistakes for which we are not answerable. We do not refer to dear ridiculous Cunninghame Graham, who has written his contribution in Spanish (quite obviously).

> Believe us
> Yours very truly,
> The Editors of the Dial

27. Ricketts and Shannon to K.B.: 26 February 1899

8 Spring Terrace,
Richmond

Dear Poet,

You mention more pieces of furniture than were ever designed by Sheraton. Our Happy Hunting places are however [?]Maivers

---

1 "On a Portrait by Tintoret in the Colonna Gallery": *The Dial* IV, 1896.
2 Published in 1896.

& Stephenson[,] Mr.[?]Lucens Elm Fulham Road. A small shop almost opposite the above called an Art Association or something. And the [?]Farmer's shop [<] in Richmond [>].

In colouring a house, see that the temper of ~~the~~ [<] each [>] rooms is kept.—When a room hides from the sun provide it with colours & hangings that love the shade: the green of green shadows in the heart of a wood, blue of that blue haunting a grot, the colours found <u>under</u> the sea. [<] Place also [>] mirrors [<] in it [>] that listen to you, that look like pools. In these cool rooms various objects may be hung or placed; shadow is kind to ugly but useful books.

In rooms that love the sun, use colours that love the sun also: white, ivory, gold, yellow, fawn, some shades of rose even. In ~~this~~ [<] these [>] rooms, the objects should be well-chosen[;] the sun is angry with ugly thick shapes, but loves the corners of delicate frames, and dainty furniture. Here the mirrors should be allowed to <u>talk</u>: provide them with subjects of conversation, carnations, roses, anemones, woodbine, rings on hands, fruit in a basket or on a silver dish, Chinese embroideries.

In a room given over to melancholy before or after ~~dinner~~ lunch, a blue (the colour of my dear books) may be combined with white and enlivened with bright pieces of china, sufficiently expensive to make their sudden destruction undesirable. In all these rooms strive to keep the furniture close to the walls, as in Persia. The air and light will love you for this; a rare carpet may then brood in ~~the~~ [<] an [>] open space, lady friends will not overset snowdrops in slender glasses or bump against things, & male friends [<] or relations [>] will not leave hot briars, or smouldering cigarettes upon satinwood, or [<] even [>] galoshes.

We beg you to kiss the Chow behind the left ear for our dear little cat. I think a mess of basset paws au Périgord might induce him to leave Durdans;[1] if not, there is [<] still [>] the river gate. We shall expect to see your roses in an ebony car drawn by zebras, you of course will arrive in a chariot of ivory drawn by pards. Please consider us in the matter of meals or other small matter of assistance your slaves on the date of your arrival.

Ever yours sincerely

CR & CS

I hope I've spelt Basset wrong.

---

1 Bradley and Cooper's old house in Reigate that they left in their move to Richmond on 16 May.

[written on an accompanying postcard]
Since writing the accompanying letter, I have repented—warm colours should pervade the home: warm blues warm greens warm whites warm everything! So that if you should get inundated you will still be dry. The little shop opposite Queens Elm with the preposterous name is the one to go to first[;] his goods are not priced but they are very very [illegible] & you can always knock him down considerably. In fact he prefers it.

CR&CS

28. Ricketts to K.B.: 9 April 1906

Lansdowne House,
Lansdowne Road,
Holland Park, W.

Dear Poet,
I am quite unable to face an interview with this excessive and dolorous lamentation[1] still in your ways of speech, and [<] also [>] these countless refferences [sic] and reminiscences of an event, unpleasant & distressing in itself, but which in common decency should have been relegated to ~~y~~ a volume of your diary which could afterwards be suppressed.—When you're in a mood to talk about Salome,[2] or to say cruel things about Aphrodite & Artemis[3] ~~and~~ [<] or to make [>] eternal aphorisms on the ways and manners of your friends, I shall be pleased to call; not till then.—So please by Palm Sunday or the festivals in commemoration of the ~~p~~ Passing of Adonis, I forget the date! be you crowned with violets like the chorus in Moore's play and with a washed and smiling face, & I shall talk in immortal cadences about the inconveniences of my travels, and about the house of the Tragic poet in Pompeii, about the flight of the Berensons on my arrival at Florence, about the greek marbles which I purchased in Paris, and the [<] too [>] short tunic of Theseus in Moore's play; about the headdress of [?]~~Herodias~~ [<] Herod [>] which is to be played ~~as an~~ [<] as a recognisable [>] imitation of you upon the stage; all this I promise if you are both well and lure

---

1. This letter was written to chastise Bradley for the longevity of her grief over the chow dog that died much earlier in the year.
2. Wilde's play, which Ricketts had a hand in designing.
3. A play by Thomas Sturge Moore recently performed in London.

me with choice sandwiches. / The Palace[1] is fearful, we are in the hands of the house-painters!—Please order yesterdays [<] Saturday's [>] <u>Tribune</u> as I there issue forth to destroy W. Archer and the day after tomorrow I shall in all probability destroy Max.[2] Ross is also about to attack Archer in an article entitled W. Archer versus Artemis & another.[3]—During the performance I nearly died with laughter; and both Theseus and Hippolytus have since banished themselves to the provinces out of sorrow.

So be you ~~not~~ [<] no longer [>] mossy and autumnal, but in a new frock and full of malice[<]ious[>] ~~and of~~ news about the Oxford Widdow [sic].[4]

Please ponder over these events and realise how tragic it would have been had I died on Sunday with a pocket handkerchief stuck down my mouth, with the coroner's verdict ~~as~~ "found dead by strangulation, [<] ~~from~~ [>] ~~cause only too well &~~ whilst in [?]~~as ever~~ [<] a [>] sound frame of mind."—So, dear Poet, be wise, banish this mildew from your self and slay the fatted mufin [sic] in anticipation of my return; be [<] very [>] explicit in time and dates & places. Be good or is[5] shall praise Stephen Phillips' Nero[6] to you or more terrible still not call for ever, or at least six weeks & out-Bernard Bernard Berenson.[7]

Yours ever

The Sage

P.S. This is all quite serious, I won't listen to any more laments.

[written on envelope] Find today is Palm S not at home Friday, could call on Wednesday if invited.

---

1 The name given to Ricketts's new home.
2 William Archer and Max Beerbohm, who had both failed to praise Sturge Moore's play.
3 Robbie Ross, art critic and friend of Oscar Wilde.
4 Alice Grenfell, a friend of Bradley and Cooper.
5 Presumably meant to be "I."
6 A poetic drama.
7 Bradley and Cooper's break with Bernard Berenson was spectacular and long lasting, although eventually they did see each other again.

29. K.B. to Charles Ricketts: no date [1907]

The Royal Hotel,
Princes Street,
Edinburgh

Dear Painter,

I am telling you some-thing, I would far rather crept to you secretly as the dawn—I am telling you that I have become a Catholic, & by baptism I am Michael now.

Being a serpent & so wise, I trust this news will not startle you; for you must have seen how "the Ruddy Mass Book" has been with us all the winter.

And you will be glad of this great plunge I have taken into the universal, so that the sun of furthest Ind[1] burns close; & I invoke your Catholic mother of the many lovely manners to plead with you to be glad.

Michael.

h. To and From John Gray, 1907–?1912

30. K.B. to John Gray: no date [April 1907]

Dear Father Gray,

I want you very much to help me—as of the Power given you of God.—You did help me—answering my fears by that confidence—by an experience.

Indeed it is our [<] one [>] hope—"He will have none of our [?]terms—nor dare I ask to make terms with Love. My terror is to <u>deny Him in my past years</u>. I have received Him in communion—He has sought me from a child—and again & again I have forsaken Him, & broken away on the great wave of "modernism"[2] that swept over us in the eighties—sometimes deliberately I have turned my lamp upside down to be sure not a drop of oil was left in it—& lo—mysteriously it has been fed for me again—and this is my praise—and this keeps me weeping for joy.

---

1 An abbreviation for India.
2 This refers to theological modernism.

Prince Charles once said to us—of our Bacchic worship—(a worship that abides)—"you are enthusiasts & not worshippers"—no word has ever struck more chill on my heart—It was profoundly true—and new in the Blessèd Sacrament we worship.

Very slowly—indeed only the last day or two—I have come to be able <u>myself</u> to offer the sacrifice to the Father.

Bear with me while I make you understand how ignorant I have been. I knew no more—heeded no more than—was it not Philip—who said he did not know whether there was a Holy Ghost or not? I did not know there was a Church ..... (I have learned so many of His new names <u>Rex Israel</u>, <u>Imperator</u>—when He is infinite in condescension—<u>Domine</u>.

My dear Fellow has asked one of the priests Rev. G. FitzGibbon to "let her in"—She could no longer stand against the great appeals of Easter, being, as Father FitzGibbon found she was—already full & entire Catholic on the central Doctrine of the Blessèd Sacrament.

It cost much for us—who are one poet—thus to break in twain. For me, I must wait, till you know whether you can open the door.

With me it is quite simple, I will be thankful to be re-baptized—& glad to be led to make true confession. I adore the Blessed Trinity—as Crevelli's [sic] Francis[1]—I am at the foot of the crucifix—where the blood drops from the Blessèd Feet—&—but I am <u>still I see</u> very dull in this—every day I am learning a little more [<] of the sacrifice [>]—that is all. | And my poor Fellow is to be examined in the penny catechism[2] this afternoon—Oh, but this holds good only for Wales & England—<u>not</u> Scotland!!!!! Gloria tibi, Domine![3] [Added in margin as a commentary alongside these last two sentences:] no fault in the gentle & good priest. Henry won't read theology—& the catechism has to be .. in England

Doubtless I am too wild for the Fold. And I love all that is pagan in the Church so dearly. I love the Paschal Candle with a great hugging love. I want to sing the bees who make the wax. I love all about the lights. It is "Lumen Christi"[4] that set my heart on fire. Is it that once I was a torch-bearer on the hills?

Michael.

---

1 Reference to a painting by the fifteenth-century artist Carlo Crivelli.
2 Adopted by the bishops of England and Wales, this was the best-known Catholic catechism for many years.
3 Glory to you, Lord!
4 "The light of Christ."

I must [?]play[1] a little—It is grief to me to read of Felicitas & Perpetua.[2] Perpetua is the name I choose for my Fellow in my book of sonnets to her—& Felicity is my name—willy-nilly. And lo—they were not virgins—And quite rude to their husbands, & monstrous to their little ones. But so many thanks to you for the Golden Legend. I want to read the great story of [?]your intercessors—the [?]40. I cannot find it. Will you give me a heading?
M.

31. K.B. to John Gray: no date [Spring 1907]
[This postscript has become separated from the main body of the letter in the archive.]

P. S.
If any wisdom is given to you, O let me have it on this theme.

———

"Let your writing be as frankly Christian as it has been frankly Pagan" says a correspondant,

———

& there are no frankly Christian poets?
Milton—only a poet when he forgets he is a Christian.
Wordsworth a worshipper of "In the Beginning"—somewhere one feels behind the altar to the Blessed Trinity—the ~~object~~ goal of his adoration.
Cowper[3]—Fie! and he sang the solfa![4]
Dante—of course telling all the other way—& so at his best in classic legend, & with centaurs, or medieval Romance.
    I fear Oscar is right—the real Catholic poet is Verlaine?

———

And might there be a fresh poetry—interpreting, painting the great mystery—we say Ave Maria stupidly—while we are far from our lips—if the lips could a little say the truth?

M.

---

1 Possibly "ply."
2 The story of Felicitas and Perpetua is from the martyrdom narratives of the early church. The women were arrested for being Christians and sentenced to death.
3 William Cowper, eighteenth-century poet.
4 The solfa is a system that uses syllables (do, re, me, etc.) to represent the notes of the diatonic scale.

32. K.B. to John Gray: no date [Spring 1907]

Dear Father Gray,

That is best—the search-light—in response—I will do all I can to aid—And now I am sending to you a little picture. It is a picture of our Bacchic altar—taken before we left our old home of Durdans, Reigate, in—I think, 1899. I said—we must have our Bacchic cub at the foot of the altar, & he obediently fell asleep there..... That day I met you at the Palace Jan. [<] Tuesday [>], 1906—I went home to learn my Chow was already in frenzy (stricken of same awful brain disease).[1] I nursed the little creature day & night—ready at once to part with him—[<] prevented—[>] vets said tonight to give him a chance, till on the Sunday—for the bright eyes were growing blind & the little feet wandering in circles—that no gentle caress wd. stop—I resolved to kill him. . It was in sacrifice—& indeed much for the sake of Love itself & then,—through blunderings as pitiful as Gosscannon's[2]—I was nearly 5 hours seeking to quieten that too sturdy life....

.And no prayer was listened to—and I heard the cries of my little Whym—when after chloroform—he was being driven by the vet for the final puncture—I <u>hoped</u> unconscious — —

Then I came home, & took down the candles from the altar of the Trinity—& was left for oh—<u>a very brief while</u>—without God. | Before Whymmie was brought home to be buried at the foot of the altar of Dionysus in the garden—we were able to pray & to ask God to accept that sacrifice—and presently—a month or two after—at Rottingdean—I was quietly told of Heaven; that we three Henry, Whymmie, & Michael were accepted—to reflect as in a dark pond—the Blessèd Trinity.

It is our mystery—<u>it is our secret</u>. In return for our blasphemy, Whymmie returned to us to be our guardian angel. (jube haec perferri per manus sancti angeli tui in sublime altare tuum[3]) & little living Flame of Love. He is my little Fellow, as Henry is my Fellow.

---

1 This letter describes the events covered in the diary entry; see p. 280.
2 A nickname for Gerald Fitzgibbon.
3 Order our offerings to be borne by the hands of your holy angel to your high altar (part of a prayer from the Latin Mass).

There! I have told you of my intercession, as simply & bravely as you confide[d] to me; & I shall never forget them—the story of yours.

—I knew nothing of sacrifice till I offered one. It has been accepted. To my dear Henry the pain was worse—for she loved him most.

And from this I have learnt all I know of the Sacrifice in the bosom of the Trinity. And the search light you must cast is on my blasphemy—and God rewarded that—so!

—There is nothing in my life worth talking about to God! I suppose it would be wrong to say—Would there were! | I have had so sweet & noble parents—my nature lies all at unity with itself—& away, as it seems to me (?) by happy instinct[,] from the Seven Deadly Sins. But there is deeply, heretic blood in me—and I pray by penance—by all that may help—that I may be cleansed to receive the mysteries.

Pray for me—for Michael.

33. K.B. to John Gray: no date [Spring 1907]
[We reproduce here only the postscript.]

P.S.
Our friendship is so very new (tho' older than the Ark) I feel perhaps an extract from our diary in [?]our my Fellow's hand-writing will help.

She speaks of how "we have been trained in the universal rituals of wheat & grape, & are, if anything, articulate ... we have been trained in Latin, & had the widest & most exacting disci-pline in the philosophic thought of the ages. The discovery of the Highest Life in the highest symbols, those that gather up creative Imagination from the beginning, & Imagination cannot tran-scend & therefore acknowledges her master-piece, comprehen-sive as the universe—this discovery has been like the sun falling its light on a dark world of complete knowledge".

This is not how it has happened with me. More than seven years ago I built a little altar to the Blessed Trinity; &, waxing strong in this worship—drew my Fellow in with me along—this is my worship, & my adoration—my joy has been to discover in the bosom of the Trinity—the sacrifice.

But I fear—the right place—will always be with the waves—
Do not mistake—I do <u>not apprehend</u> any of the great doctrines
of the Catholic church—save this of the Sacrifice—blood on the
wings of the Dove—the Gift of the Father—the offering of the
Son.

M.

34. K.B. to John Gray: no date [Spring 1907]

1, THE PARAGON,
RICHMOND,
SURREY

My dear Father,
    They told me to stand God-mother & I stood. I did
not realize at all what I was doing—nor how a whole, sweet new
relationship was breaking.
 "The new Michael"—but is that so? You make me feel
inclined to rush at Henry's throat. My meaning was Henry
should come under the Great Word (and Henry wd. choose S.
Michael)—however—unless unduly vitalized in mid-July—I can
learn to decrease & watch Henry[,] Michael's dear[,] increasing.
My [?]part to Henry—it seems to me –? . . is to [?]become a
mother's Godmother,[1] softness & indulgence—I am thankful to
say I am a little hard on myself now. But all round I am hard.
 It is disfiguring.

Now, very seriously, I ask your wisdom concerning the question
of my Godmother,
Henry? I know not
To me a relation is like this.
lover & loved
mother & child
server & served—
not mother <u>&</u> mother etc.

---

1   Bradley has very mixed feelings about Cooper becoming her God-
   mother, because she is already, in some sense, occupying the position of
   Cooper's mother.

But Henry shares with Heaven the great quality of jealousy, & no woman in the world may be allowed, I fear, except on the sly!! to pray for me. Would some dear little nun, the younger the better, give me her fresh young prayers—& by my God-mother.
Amy has a god-mother nun.

[...]¹

Postscript
Can I—yes I can—take a second name at confirmation? I want to take the name of John the Evangelist. John Baptist is most deeply reverenced—I must try to exclude him from the connotation. Everything St. John does or writes makes me happier: the beginning of his gospel is my life; I find no stumbling-block in his doctrine of sin—& in age one may hope for [?]Patmos² & the Vision. That he is not a martyr is a pity—childish & dramatic, he repeats his doctrine as a rose-bush her roses. And he has handled the Word of Life. Henry would like to take the names Michael Sylvester. But can she? I fear she cannot take 2 names. She did not take one at her baptism. | Sylvester—as reprover of the Fauns she has written a delightful little poem about. I find the word Sylvester in an old family Bible—I should think probably it was a name in my family.

Oh thank you, Father, for your most charming letter. It came this afternoon to me worn out with reading solemnly, not "very slowly," but with attempt at a rush. Matins & Lauds—with the Latinist. | I should not like to be preached to by a Dominican, or by any one at this time of year. | I sigh to open the Winter Breviary. | It will be of deepest interest to me to have the loan of your precious [?]loan book of hymns. You will tell me about the hymns when I come. You will have ready for me—poems & beginning of your own: you must not go shrimping about in the shallows of translation. I push myself into enchanted ground by the shoulders.
Michael

---

1 At least one sheet of the middle of the letter is missing.
2 This probably refers to the vision of St. John the Evangelist at Patmos, of Christ's Second Coming (detailed in the *Book of Revelation*).

35. K.B. to John Gray: no date [March 1908]

The Tumble Down Dick Inn
 Farnboro'
  Hants
[written on notepaper headed 1, The Paragon, Richmond, Surrey]
Friday

    My dear Father,
              Little Amy[1] is to be confirmed next Sunday, at 1, o'clock, in some church in Dublin. A mass, please, in her intention, as soon as, without inconvenience, you can say it.

Father, it is answered prayer. I have so desired to get sense of the majesty of God—here from midst of the noble music, the solemn rites, offered in adoration to God, I get so ashamed, I realize the Beatific Vision—& with something of a cry, ask for purgatory.

    As everywhere—so here they are kind: otherwise we could not bear— the arrested music—the silence of a whole community as to us, the sole communicants[2] (the other morning S. Joseph's Day) was borne the Blessed Sacrament—the sign of the light beside. I have spoken since to Father Prior—he says we may communicate on Saturday when there is Pontifical mass, before mass; but we were right to go up to the rails, & must every day. I knew it must be right—I had to bear the mortal peril of it for Henry.

    And out of all this what hot cheeks for the religious !! poems in Wild Honey. Is there nothing to erase them?—all, save the envoi. With lay hands they touch the things on the altar, they offend.

                                  Michael

36. John Gray to K.B.: 24 November 1908

24th November 1908
My dear Michael
    Your letter today is quite fit & twice welcome. The best is to send you vol. 1 of Lewis (the works having been found and secular dust removed with a clothes brush) which I do. [illegible, deleted] [illegible, deleted] [<] The life therein [>] is quite as simple as either of two Italian lives which I possess—this is the moment perhaps to acknowledge a packet of books directed in

---

1   Edith Cooper's sister.
2   Bradley and Cooper were the only members of the congregation to receive Holy Communion.

Henry's handwriting. I have invincible love of St John of the Cross because, I suppose, he made a hole in the covering which I had woven about myself to hide me from God. There was a random comparison made by a writer in the Edinburgh Review "like Aristophanes or St John of the Cross"; & so I came upon En una noche oscura[1] instead of Bekerekex Coax Coax:[2] and with that S:[3] Michael rammed his lance into the rock of Edinburgh and angels traced in black sand the lilies & mouldings upon the font & the dew of heaven filled it. Rorate caeli desuper.[4]

Detachment is good enough. . Do not fear, do not hurry. Avoid sin, pray.

Rhoda came from outside the Arthurian circle—from Liverpool or 'the north'.[5] She had intense admiration of her husband & brought her life in all details into line with it from devotion. She has not an easy time, but she played her part like a woman. Arthur never drank or misbehaved. He was however a faithful habitué of their mermaid.[6] The drinkers used not to go there when drunk: it was rather a place of refinement & women were of the company, among them a gentle person called Janet whom Image[7] married. Horne[8] used to go there too & Mrs Hacon[9] not Beardsley. Billy[10] was never there that I know.

John Gray

---

1 "Noche obscura del alma" ("The Dark Night of the Soul")—the best known work of St. John of the Cross.

2 This represents the croak of a frog, and is a reference to Aristophanes' play *Frogs*, in which these words form part of the chorus. Here Gray represents his fortunate intellectual trajectory towards the sublime rather than the comic.

3 Saint.

4 From the chorus of a hymn often used in the Mass and Divine Office during Advent: "Rorate caeli desuper, et nubes pluant iustum" ("Drop down dew, ye heavens, from above, and let the clouds rain the Just One"). Here the analogy is between Christ and the dew that comes to give moisture and life to the earth, but then evaporates back into the sky.

5 Rhoda Bowser, who married Arthur Symons in 1901.

6 "Mermaid" was a euphemism for prostitute.

7 Selwyn Image, the artist, designer, and poet.

8 Herbert Horne, the writer and art collector who published the poetry collection *Diversi Colores* in 1891.

9 Presumably Edith Bradshaw, wife of Llewelyn Hacon who notably collaborated with Charles Ricketts.

10 All the artists referred to here are *fin-de-siècle* decadent acquaintances of Gray and Bradley, but it is not clear who "Billy" might be.

37. K.B. to John Gray: no date [1909]

[We reproduce here only the final part of a letter written on 24 January, "Feast of St. John Chrysostom"; written from Grove House, Milltown.]

Then of S. John of the Cross! Oh that I could read him with quiet heart! I send you 2 or 3 lines of translation or thought-reading. | Will you—can you lend me his "Spiritual Canticle" & "Living Flame of Love." You know I cannot read Spanish. Can you tell me of any French translation—if you have no English one. Father, what St. John says about the substitution of Hope for Memory is vital to me—I cannot speak of the new life I am getting from St. John—perhaps this is best—not a drop of the precious emotion is wasted—it is all wanted for the Spirit's use. | I have written very foolishly, & at speed—forgive me.

From St. Peter's ("god pardon sin!") I cannot detach—I was giving thanks for the sacraments & my Restoration to them this morning—

Michael.

Aridity

O Soul, canst thou not understand
    thou art not left alone
    as a dog to howl & moan
His master's absence; thou art as a book
    Left in a room that He forsook,
    a book of His dear choice
    that, quiet, waiteth for His Hand,
    that, quiet, waiteth for His eye,
    that, quiet, waiteth for His voice.
M.

38. K.B. to John Gray: no date [1911-1912]

1, THE PARAGON,
RICHMOND,
SURREY.

My dear Father,

We have <u>never heard</u> of the Publisher's Note forming part of adoration[1]—the sentence condemns itself.

—But there are in me no [illegible]. My best & truest friends are carrying through this venture.

—Will you say to Sands[2] that M.F. cannot consent to the Publisher's note—or to any note of preface—being <u>in</u> the book adoration.

—We hear with pleasure that you, Father, have consented to write the "Note"—for the usual destination of such things—the Bookman etc. etc.

Our decision cannot be altered; & no time need be wasted about it so far for Sands.

Dear Father, if it were not <u>adoration</u> how we would prize your Note, & love to enclose it!

We are profoundly grateful you will consent to do this bit of work for the Press. Please let us just see it for technical purposes before you send to press.

None of the Borgia series ie. Borgia, Mariamne & the 2 yellow vols (I sent you?[)]—beginning with the accuser [—] are to be mentioned. These are not by Michael Field.

—Pass on from the last signed work—by Vale Press—Julia Domna(?)—to "Wild Honey."

Michael Field is always one. ["]This writer["]—& ["]he["] when a pronoun must come in—nothing "<u>laboured</u>"—the youth of the early nineties, turning new to the Visions of Age. Open allusion to the year of grace: [?]1997—"by [?]whom we men are men."

I made once a rhyme on a certain Puzzlehed [sic].

—something—Henry (?) Bradley

lexicographer

---

1 *Poems of Adoration*, Cooper's final collection of poems, published in 1912.

2 The publishers.

wandering at the Clarenden
is it him or her?"

Michael

I am full of interest in your Tertiaries & Faculties. I [illegible]
[?]bit of them.

M.

i. Other Interlocutors, 1884–90

39. A. Mary F. Robinson to "Michael Field Esqre," care of his publishers: 16 May 1884

May 16th 1884
20, Earl's Terrace,
Kensington. W.

My Dear Sir,
 I have waited several days to acknowledge the pretty volume
you sent me; because I wanted to finish reading it before I began
to thank you. Now I can do so, with sincerity & earnestness.

——————— ———————

Your two plays[1]—and especially Calirrhoë—seem to me of very
great promise; the motive is clear & not to [sic] prominent; the
style (which yet too often lacks distinction) is often wonderfully
expressive, vigorous & picturesque. Best of all, you show a rare
power of grasping true, unusual, pathetic character.... Especially
the delayed=immature, if I may say such a phrase.
 There is much truth & might be much pathos in your shock-
ing, ghastly, psychologically correct, & very moving picture of the
old Virgin priestess, never allowed to use & develop her soul,
which remains nineteen in a body of 90. Your sketch is strong; but
you might have made it more poignant & tragic, had you cared,
had you been less in a hurry, less eager for the goal ... It is a good
fault, to say yr ideas are so original you ought to make more of
them... This fault I find in the charming relation between the

---

1 The dramas *Callirrhöe* and *Fair Rosamund* were published in one volume
  in 1884.

unworldly quixotic old knight & the fallen girl, whose shamed maidenhood he does not discover. You should not touch such things too trivially.

Never be trivial: sometimes you have a beautiful gift of simplicity: as in Sir Thopaz' speech of the dead girl—who left his love only the night she died [?]at, also Margery's phrase "you came along so new & wonderful"[,] the faun's song: in fact the whole figure of the Faun . . & it happens that some times you trivialize (forgive the word) this simplicity, & send odious echoes of Gilbert & Sullivan among the echoes of Browning, & Fletcher, & Shakespeare, out of which, I hope, you are going to beat us a new music.

But beware of triviality. . you have already, here & there, a true psychologic insight. You easily can have a rich harmonious passionate style; so take care; be very jealous of these gifts & admit no inferior thing in their company.

Forgive my speaking in this monitor's fashion, I could no more write your plays than fly, yet I plead my love for our Art as a sufficient excuse for my warnings.

With thanks believe me, Very truly yours,
A. Mary F. Robinson

40. Havelock Ellis to K.B.: no date

Imperial Sanatorium
Harrogate
Sat.

My dear Miss Bradley,

It seems a long time since I had any news and I do not know how things are going with you. But I am sure you will let me tell you how much I have been enjoying 'Long Ago'—more, I think, than I expected, for I certainly think that blank verse is M. F.'s proper medium. The poems, I see, have not really much connection with Sappho's fragments & do not often suggest comparisons & this is quite as it should be. In reading them I divided those I liked into three classes—a X (positive) class, a XX (comparative) & XXX (superlative) class. I find in the X class nos. 7, 11, 14, 20, 25, 36, 37, 40, 42, 47, 50, 59, 66, 67. It is quite likely that in going through the volume again I should be inclined to add to this class. The XX [<] class [>] is of higher degree & only contains four poems—8, 48, 61, 62. The XXX is a very superlative & therefore very small class; it comprises 49 &

60—both, I think, very charming, though quite unlike each other, of course. The arrangement is one of personal taste; I do not know if anyone else would agree with me—though I feel pretty sure about the excellence of the XXX brand. I hope the book has been reviewed well; I do not see the reviews but I came across the pleasant notice in <u>Scottish Leader</u>.

In the Canterbury Series in Sept. will appear a volume of 'Selections from the Greek anthology', edited by Graham Tomson.[1] This ought to be worth seeing. She has, I believe, been helped by a number of the best people.

I have had some delightful excursions from here; have also done a fair amount of work—absorbed latterly in Tolstoi. (If you want any of his books they are <u>all</u> now being included in Scott's edition.)

With kindest regards to all,

Yours very sincerely

H. H. Ellis

41. E.C. and K.B. (as "Michael Field") to Pater: 11 June 1889—a letter in draft form

Dear Sir

Ever since the issue of my little volume <u>Long Ago</u>, I have had the intention of pleasing myself by offering a copy to you: circumstance alone has intervened. I feel I have a hope that you will understand the spirit of my lyrics—you who have sympathy with attempts to reconcile the old and the new, to live as in continuation the beautiful life of Greece. Renaissance is the condition of man's thought which seems to have for you the most exciting charm. What I have aspired to do from Sappho's fragments may therefore somewhat appeal to your sense of survival in human things—to your interest in the shoots and offspring of elder literature.

Sincerely yours,

Michael Field.

---

1   Graham R. Tomson was the poet otherwise known as Rosamund Marriott Watson.

42. Oscar Wilde to "Michael Field, Esq.": no date [c. 1890]

16, Tite Street,
Chelsea. S. W.

I have only just come back from France—and your lovely book[1] is the most gracious of welcomes. Thank you so much for it. Your Queen is a splendid creature—live woman to her finger tips—I feel the warmth of her breath as I listen to her—she is closer to flesh and blood than the Mary of Swinburne's Bothwell—who seems to me less real than the Mary of his Chasterlard[2]—indeed I thank you very much, though by comparison my own little gift of little Fairy Tales shows but poorly—yet I like such inequality—for it keeps me your debtor, and since I read Calirroe [sic] I have been that, without hope of repayment.

Sincerely and with gratitude
Yours Oscar Wilde

43. Arthur Symons to K.B.: 15 August 1890

9 Upper Terrace,
Hampstead,
NW.

Aug: 15: 90

Dear Miss Bradley

I am sending a copy of the delightful Indifférent.

I want MF. to meet Miss Mathilde Blind,[3] who wants to meet him. When can we arrange a meeting? Couldn't we all meet at Upper Terrace—that is, if there is room for four of us in my diminutive sitting-room. If you don't know it, I want you to know that part of the Heath, which is to me the most enchanting part of London—of London county. You must come & sit on Judges Walk, which is just outside my cottage. As you generally leave town rather early, & it is a long way to & from Hampstead, I would ask you to come & have lunch with me, & I will arrange for Miss Blind to come too. I don't know whether your first impression of her will be favourable, but when one gets to know

---

1 *The Tragic Mary.*
2 *Bothwell* (1874) and *Chastelard* (1865) were both closet-dramas by Swinburne on Mary Queen of Scots.
3 The poet (1841–96).

her she is singularly interesting. Let me know as soon as possible if you can both come, & when will suit best, & I will communicate with Miss Blind.

Cotton[1] comes back on Tuesday, & my three weeks will be up. I shall resign the editorial chair with regret & relief.

Ever truly yours,
Arthur Symons.

---

1   This possibly refers to James Sutherland Cotton (1869–1916), who became editor of the *Academy* in 1881.

Reviews

[If the reception of their first joint book of poems, *Bellerophôn* (published under the names Arran and Isla Leigh), was marked by a rejection of the classical theme and by a critique of their "trumpery pedantry," their first volume of lyrical dramas as Michael Field, *Callirrhoë: Fair Rosamund*, was praised precisely because of its strong classical origins. In general, during the 1880s, there was a sense of anticipation at the arrival of a new book by Michael Field, and their work, both lyric poetry and drama, received mostly good reviews. This was particularly the case with *Callirrhoë* and *Long Ago*. The publication of *The Tragic Mary* in 1890, when it became known that Michael Field was "two ladies," and later *Stephania* in 1892, altered the public perception of their work. And yet, despite the lukewarm response received by *Sight and Song*, the signed reviews are a testament to the highly controversial nature of Michael Field's aestheticism in the heyday of British decadence.

The second half of Michael Field's career is marked by a shift in reception. While in the early days it was the plays that were most praised, after the non-too-successful performance of *A Question of Memory* in 1893, the plays seemed to receive slightly less positive comment, while *Underneath the Bough* and *Wild Honey* elicited, generally, much more favourable notice. After *Wild Honey*, however, when the poetry becomes strictly a vehicle for Catholicism, it immediately disappears off the radar for mainstream literary reviews editors. *Poems of Adoration, Mystic Trees*, and *The Wattlefold* are pretty much ignored outside of Catholic periodicals, though the later volumes *A Selection* and *The Wattlefold* were reviewed by the chief literary magazine of the twentieth century, *The Times Literary Supplement*.

Michael Field's fortunes were chequered, to say the least. The high points (such as the call for Michael Field as Poet Laureate, in Higginson's *Harper's Bazar* piece) were high indeed, and there is certainly enough evidence to say that Michael Field was a well-known name in literary circles for the majority of their career. The low points in these reviews are quite crushingly awful, but nothing like as bad as being ignored, by the end of their career, as "quaint" and marginal Catholic writers, no longer a player in the literary marketplace of the twentieth century.]

1. Review of *Long Ago* by John M. Gray, *The Academy*, 8 June 1889

It is four years since Dr. H. T. Wharton, by his excellent little volume upon Sappho—"memoir, text, selected renderings, and a literal translation"—did all that care, scholarship, and tact could do to introduce the great Aeolian singer to English readers; and now a powerful English poetess has come to do much more—to extend the Sapphic fragments, that have been preserved for us by the quotations of grammarians and lexicographers, into original lyrics, embodying the aspirations, human and artistic, of her of Lesbos, and mirroring the surroundings of gracious land and goodly fellowship amid which these songs of piercing sweetness were sung so "Long Ago."

The poems of the volume, then, are no immediate and instinctive songs—like those of Burns, for instance—embodying the singer's own pressing and momentary feelings. To adopt a classification used by Mr. Browning regarding certain of his own pieces, while "lyric in expression" they are "dramatic in principle," "so many utterances of so many imaginary persons, not mine"; or, rather, they are the imagined utterances of that one greatest poetess of antiquity, who has been to some of us little more than a visionary presence, the dimmest shadow of a shade. Into this far-off personality, aided always by the surviving fragments of its utterance, the imagination of the latter-day singer has entered most effectively, the "life in her abolishing the death of things," her own most ardent poet- and woman-heart—"all air and fire"—throbbing in rhythm with that which has so long lain still, her mouth receiving its song as though direct from the lips which for thousands of years have ceased to curve and quiver.

The readers of Michael Field already know that she possesses much of lyrical power. The songs scattered through her dramas, as well as a few stray pieces published in various periodicals, some of them in the pages of the ACADEMY, were enough to prove her skill and aptitude in this direction. The snatches of wavering song that flit through her plays—the "Where winds about," of "The Cup of Water"; the "Who hath ever given," of the "The Father's Tragedy"—were lyrics of the most typical quality, similar in kind to the "It was a lover and his lass," and the "Sigh no more, ladies, sigh no more," of Shakspere [sic]; to the "O Sorrow, why dost borrow," of Keats; to the "My silks and fine array," and the "O Rose, thou art sick," of Blake—things of a clear, simple, insequent, bird-like note, in which we do not at all look for recognisably logical continuity of thought; in which sound, at least as much as sense, is the effective agent in the emotional effect produced. The lyric is, indeed, the most typically poetic of all poetic forms, that in which we find poetry in subtlest and purest quintessence, most "free from baser matter." And the lyric is most characteristically itself, is seen in its most typical form, in songs such as those we have named—songs in which it has reached its utmost possible height, and trembles on the border-line separating it from another form of art; in which it is ready to pass into music, to dispense altogether, for its effect, with the aid of words, and to employ sound alone as its minister.

But a *volume* of lyrics of this most typical, this doubly-refined and rarefied, sort is impossible: singer cannot long sing, listener cannot long breathe in air so thin and keen. Lyrics of this kind are the true "song of the dramatists," points of pause, or rather of sudden airy flight, amid the tamer or statelier diction of the dramatic form—a diction which, of all poetic forms, approaches most closely to the actualities of real life, to the mere recorded speech of veritable men; and which is, in consequence, of all poetic forms the least essentially poetic, that most apt to drop, in all hands but the very highest—sometimes, for a moment, in the hands of the highest himself—into the insensitiveness of prose.

The lyrics of the present book, then, are no fitful snatches of song, evolved by mere instinct, comparable in emotional effect, and in the mode by which that effect is reached, to the sounds of nature, to the murmuring of the brooklet, or to the sighing of the wind through autumn branches. More of conscious aim and effort, more of definite brain power, is required in lyrics which are meant to open and disclose the "red-leaved tables" of the heart of the perfect poet, the supreme lover of "Long Ago." The theme of the book is the loveliness of visible things—of nature, in that sweet Aeolian land, and of the fair humanity to which this nature was the fitting setting; the overmastering power of passion; and the struggles of the poet's soul, irresistibly impelled to seek perfect expression for both: surely a sufficiently ample gamut for the music of any poet. Here is a noble rendering of the singer's heart, striving to touch and kindle into sympathy the hearts of all its listeners, and then ready to sink back into the simplest longings for the warmth of most ordinary human bliss:

[Here the reviewer reproduces "I sang to women gathered round." See p. 64 of this book.]

Of even finer temper and higher pitch is the following, in which Sappho dedicates her mirror to Venus, and then—in her love for Phaon—recalls with splendid effect the story of how he ferried the disguised Aphrodite, and won her choicest gifts:

"Deep in my mirror's glossy plate
　　Sweet converse oft I had
With beauty's self, then turned, elate,
　　To make my lovers glad;
But now across the quivering glass
My lineaments shall never pass:
Let Aphrodite take the thing
My shadow is dishonouring.

"Ah, fond and foolish, thou has set
　　Aside the burnished gold,
But Phaon's eyes reflect thee yet
　　A woman somewhat old!
He watched thee come across the street
To-day in the clear summer heat;
And must he not perforce recall
How the sun limned thee on the wall?

"I sigh—no sigh her bosom smote
　　Who waited 'mid the crowd
Impatient for his ferry-boat,
　　An agèd woman bowed
And desolate, till Phaon saw,
Turned swiftly, and with tender awe
Rowed her across, his strength subdued
To service of decrepitude.

"Beneath a beggar's sorry guise,
　　O laughter-loving Queen,
Thy servant still must recognize
　　A goddess–pace and mien.
He loved thee in thy fading hair,
He felt thee great in thy despair,
Thy wide, blue, clouded eyes to him
Were beautiful, though stained and dim.

"Daughter of Cyprus, take the disk
　　That pride and folly feeds;

Like thee the glorious chance I risk,
  And in time's tattered weeds,
Bearing of many a care the trace,
Trusting the poet's nameless grace,
Stand unabashed, serene, and dumb,
For Love to worship, if he come."

Still more powerful is the succeeding lyric, No. lii, unfortunately too long for quotation, dealing with the story of how Tiresias slew the snake, and so unwittingly, changed his nature—a myth in this poet's hands, serving to illustrate, in singularly penetrative fashion, the bi-sexual make of the true poet, his

"Finer sense for bliss and dole
His receptivity of soul."

From strenuous work like this, from poems charged with gravest, profoundest thought, we have exquisite pause and relief in the leaping gaiety of such lyrics as the "Dear bridegroom, it is spring"; while, amid the ebb and flow of tumultuous passion which sweeps through so many of the pieces, the rich full notes of the two Epithalamia—"She comes, and youthful voices," and "O Hymen Hymenaeus"—strike with admirable effect, set as to the sound of organs and of trumpets, pulsing as to the measured tread of gravely-pacing, happy feet.

The quotations which we have been able to give are sufficient to indicate, what is confirmed by a careful perusal of the entire volume, that the art of Michael Field has been rapidly gaining in certainty of touch, in sense of proportion, in power of delicately artistic finish. Indeed, this book is enough to prove that she is no longer a "Prentice in the Divine Art of Poesie," but a "past master," with complete command over tools and material—entered upon that paradise which the artist attains when he can do "what he will with his own." From the first, her work has been informed with intensity and passion, has evinced sufficient native force and freshness to assure its reader that a new and original poetic personality had grasped the pen. But what she has hitherto done, amid all its splendour, was often marred by extravagance, by want of measure and of balance, and by want of finish; and these faults were fostered by the freedom of dramatic form in which most of her earlier work was embodied. She has been wise to turn to the finer, firmer, lyric measure, and to submit herself to the straighter discipline which it affords—to its more imperious demand for the utmost possible refinement of expression, rhythm, and melody; to the facilities for balance and rounded completion afforded by brief poems, each of which, from the first, can be clearly kept in view in its entirety—as a whole possessing a definite beginning, middle, and end, with mutual bearings one upon the other.

Accordingly, the present book is by far the most perfect and thoroughly satisfying that its author has yet produced. It shows all her old force and fire. One has only to turn its pages to cull, in plenty, examples of that vivid magic of unforgettable phrase which has been a characteristic of all this poet's work, to find lines like the following—

"To give us temper of eternal youth,"

or this other—

"Full of the sap and pressure of the year."

But, in addition to the old qualities that delighted us, we have here an artistic finish, we have an ease, precision, and restraint, such as has not hitherto been visible in the work of Michael Field.

To my mind, almost the only blemish in the book, the only point that calls—and it does call rather loudly—for revision, is its final poem, one distinctly unfortunate in the minor key in which it is set, and forming no satisfying or effectively dramatic culmination to the lyrical sequence which it closes. It does not leave one tingling with excitement; it is too quietly meditative in tone; neither in its measure nor in its words does it suggest the moment that preceded the wild flashing of the white form from the Leucadian cliff.

In spite, however, of this defect—this all but solitary defect, as I hold it—the volume is one for which we may well be right grateful, one to which many readers will turn, and turn again.

It becomes the wary critic to be sparing of prognostication—to avoid, as far as may be, "the gratuitous folly of prophesying"; for experience has taught him how blindly oblivion "scattereth her poppy," and how many lovely things have had but their moment of praise and now lie unregarded in the world. But there are times when even the most cautious must grow bold; and perhaps such a critic would not greatly err on the side of temerity if he were to assert his conviction that the present book will take a permanent place in our English literature, as one of the most exquisite lyrical productions of the latter half of the nineteenth century.

2. Review of *Sight and Song* by W.B. Yeats, *The Bookman*, July 1892

This interesting, suggestive, and thoroughly unsatisfactory book is a new instance of the growing tendency to make the critical faculty do the work of the creative. "The aim of this little volume is, as far as may be," says the preface, "to translate into verse what the lines and colours of certain chosen pictures sing in themselves; to express not so much what these pictures are to the poet, but rather what poetry they objectively incarnate." That is to say, the two ladies who hide themselves behind the pen-name of Michael Field have set to work to observe and interpret a number of pictures, instead of singing out of their own hearts and setting to music their own souls. They have poetic feeling and imagination in abundance, and yet they have preferred to work with the studious and interpretive side of the mind and write a guide-book to the picture galleries of Europe, instead of giving us a book full of the emotions and fancies which must be crowding in upon their minds perpetually. They seem to have thought it incumbent upon them to do something serious, something worthy of an age of text-books, something that would have uniformity and deliberate intention, and be in no wise given over to that unprincipled daughter of whim and desire whom we call imagination.

We open the book at a venture, and come to a poem on Benozzo Gozzoli's 'Treading the Press.'

> "From the trellis hang the grapes
>   Purple deep;
> Maidens with white, curving napes
>   And coiled hair backward leap,
> As they catch the fruit, mid laughter,
> Cut from every silvan rafter.
>
> Baskets, over-filled with fruit,
>   From their heads
> Down into the press they shoot
>   A white-clad peasant treads,

Firmly crimson circles smashing
Into must with his feet's thrashing.

Wild and rich the oozings pour
   From the press;
Leaner grows the tangled store
   Of vintage, ever less:
Wine that kindles and entrances
Thus is made by one who dances."

The last couplet has some faint shadow of poetry, perhaps, but as for the rest—well, it is neither more nor less than 'The Spanish Gypsey' again. It is impossible not to respect it, impossible not to admire the careful massing of detail, but no man will ever feel his eyes suffuse with tears or his heart leap with joy when he reads it. There are scores of other verses in the book which are as like it as one pea is to another. None of them have any sustained music, for music is the garment of emotion and passion, but all are well put together with carefully chosen rhymes, out of the way adjectives and phrases full of minute observation. Having looked in vain for anything conspicuously better or worse than the lines we have quoted, we open the book again at a venture, and find a poem on Cosimo Tura's 'St. Jerome.' We quote the first two stanzas:—

"Saint Jerome kneels within the wilderness;
Along the cavern's sandy channels press
The flowings of deep water. On one knee,
On one foot he rests his weight—
A foot that rather seems to be
The clawed base of a pillar past all date
Than prop of flesh and bone;
About his sallow, osseous frame
A cinder-coloured cloak is thrown
For ample emblem of his shame.

Grey are the hollowed rocks, grey is his head
And grey his beard, formal and as dread
As some Assyrian's on a monument,
From the chin is sloping down.
O'er his tonsure heaven has bent
A solid disc of unillumined brown;
His scarlet hat is flung

> Low on the pebbles by a shoot
> Of tiny nightshade that among
> The pebbles has maintained a root."

These stanzas do not contain a single commonplace simile or trite adjective, the authors even prefer "osseous" to "bony" in their search for the unexpected. There is intellectual agility in every sentence, and yet of what account are these verses, or any number like them? What new thing do they bring into the world? They are simply unmitigated guide-book.

One regrets the faults of this book the more because they are faults which have for some time been growing on "Michael Field." 'Callirhoë' [sic] had imagination and fancy in plenty, and we hoped its authors would in time get more music and less crudity and at last create a poem of genius. A few years later 'Brutus Ultor' came and almost crowned our hopes, but now we have watched and waited for a long time in vain. 'Sight and Song,' following as it does 'The Tragic Mary,' is enough to make us turn our eyes for ever from the "false dawn" we believed to be the coming day.

3. "Women and Men: Women Laureates" by T.W.H. [T.W. Higginson], *Harper's Bazar*: New York, 17 June 1893

The colleges for women have been discussing the vexed question who should be poet-laureate of England. It is a curious fact, which perhaps has not occurred to any of the fair disputants, that if the award were made on the ground of pure strength of genius, and what may be called the Elizabethan quality, it would doubtless go to a woman. Or it would go, more awkwardly, to two women—that unnamed aunt and niece who jointly hide themselves under the masculine title of Michael Field. This general recognition of their superiority does not rest with the present writer alone, but with the *Saturday Review*, which said of "Callirrhöe" [sic], "It is many years since we have read a new poem so instinct with the immutable attributes of poetry"; with the *Spectator*, which said, "It is the ring of a new voice, which is likely to be heard far and wide"; with the *Athenaeum*, which said of "The Father's Tragedy," "The dramatic expression not infrequently rises to almost the strength of the Elizabeth men"; with the *Academy*, which found in "Brutus Ultor" passages that "suggest the work of our old dramatists, and would not disgrace the greatest of them"; and with the *Nation*, which found in the same poem "a dramatic strength unsurpassed in this age."

Every succeeding dramatic poem by Michael Field has added to the proof of power. Amid the "debonair verse" which, in Stedman's phrase, now prevails in London, there is something extraordinary in this wielding of the sword of strength by two recluse women. There have been a few strong poems by living English poets. Swinburne wrote "A Song in Time of Order," and has been meekly apologizing for it ever since. Meredith wrote "The Burial of Attila," and it turned out to be caught at second hand, measure and all, from a mediaeval Latin poem. Morris wrote "The Death of Paris," and has been lavishing himself ever since in petty and occasional utterances. But Michael Field, meanwhile, has been issuing a series of dramas, borrowing their themes, in Shakespeare fashion, from the great periods of history, and never waning in strength. "Callirrhöe," "Fair Rosamond" [sic], "Brutus Ultor," "Canute the Great," "The Father's Tragedy," "William Rufus," "The Tragic Mary," all show the same essential qualities, marked at first by excess of wealth, and even by the occasional weakness which excess gives, but held together as with a frame-work of iron, full of an iron vigor. Joined with this is the power of discrimination between different shades of the same emotion, as in "Fair Rosamond," where the romantic passion of the king and his mistress is set off at each stage by the lower and baser seduction, by one of his knights, of Rosamond's half-child-ish sister. When both girls lie dead and the knight is dying, the king turns upon his coarser follower and exclaims:

> "What lips God sets
> To his chalice-cups of love! What drink
> He gives foul mouths! Is there comparison
> Betwixt our deeds? From this slain innocence
> I wince not, for I worshipped. You—I swear
> By the lost childhood of that cheek—defiled."

Fine as is this self-justification, it is fitly rebuked by the fearless answer of the mere cynic:

> "We had our pleasure the forbidden way
> Each after his own fashion. For the rest,
> I bleed to death; it's painless."

Meanwhile, in the background is the injured queen, who holds her own dignity of years:

> "Old age is heir
> Apparent to the majesty of Death;
> And thought of the impending majesty

Softens the manners, and should awe the heart
Of youth—that churl of nature!"

Everywhere in these dramas there are sentences of which, as Emerson said in another case, "Cut them and they will bleed." "Callirrhöe" is a picture of the last contest between the Greek Bacchic festivals and a dawning scepticism; the absolute line of transition between ancient and modern thought seems caught and imagined in it. In "Brutus Ultor" we have the whole strength of Rome; every man, every woman, good or vile, has the Roman quality in their veins; even the infamous Sextus Tarquinius is urged on, when he hesitates, by the tyrannical training of a Roman mother:

> "Tullia,
> Give me thy tiger-heart, that I may drive
> The steeds of my ambition past the spot
> They rear at in recoil! ...
> My mother, come, imperial, to my aid,
> Gibe me with cowardice: —'What, *Lord of Rome!*
> And shudder at a woman's chastity?'
> Thou knowst the trick; it spurred me as a boy.
> Why now 'tis dark—I cannot feel the door."

Never in literature did a pure woman's nature so pass among scenes of crime and shame as in this drama, depicting them with a touch of fearless strength, yet going through them innocent as Spenser's Una. There is scarcely a man who could have touched the story of "Brutus Ultor" so freely without coarsening it, and yet there is no man living who could have given to it added strength.

The longest dramatic poem by Michael Field is "The Tragic Mary," the phrase being borrowed from Walter Pater, who says, finely, in his volume of *Appreciations*: "Old Scotch history, perhaps beyond any other is strong in the matter of heroic and vehement hatreds and love, the tragic Mary herself being but the perfect blossom of them." The drama of course awakens immediate comparison with Tennyson's "Queen Mary" and with Swinburne's "Mary Stuart and Chastelard"; and it is impossible not to pronounce it the richest and strongest of the three. Michael Field has no lyric charm which can vie with the songs, especially the French songs, in "Chastelard"; but in all else the younger author, or double-author, is the victor in the comparison. The three characters, Mary, Darnley, and Bothwell, stand out before the imagination more vividly than they ever were portrayed before, except perhaps in one brief Imaginary Conversation by

Landor. The essential queenliness of Mary is broken by passion into a mere series of tumultuous impulses; she in turn governs Bothwell and is governed by him. As for Darnley, she reads him through and through.

> "O God! to see you scared and garrulous
> Who should lie stunned before me!"

That "scared and garrulous" tells the whole of Darnley in three words—a nature which danger belittles instead of elevating into dignity. To Mary religion itself is a battle and a march. When caught in a mesh of perils she bends, and writes in her Book of Hours:

> "*O Lord! avenge me of mine enemies.*
> I set it down; make Thou a bond with me!
> Have we not common cause? These hypocrites
> Pull down all holy things. My sturdy mood
> Bides not the click of rosaries: receive
> This sentence writ across the martial psalms,
> And levy for me from the ends of heaven
> Thy laggard legions; make me, in Thy stead,
> Victor and sovereign."

This is the tragic Mary indeed; since Milton's Beelzebub, "none higher sat." She and Bothwell meet and unite because no one else can match either of them in daring, in reckless defiance; no disguises can avail either of them. The strong Bothwell has to brace himself to his act of bold achievement:

> "The royal witch,
> She thought to disenchant me in the guise
> Of formal coldness, she the beauty, she
> The madding, unfoiled beauty."

But the very peril spurns him to carry her off by force:

> "Night's stinging moments spin
> And stir me to an act; the regicides
> With their dismaying weapons shall have done
> By far less intimate irreverence
> On majesty than I in person dare."

And she, on the other hand, has felt his power over her from their first meeting:

> "I have not dreamed so since I saw him first,
> A captain of the Scottish guard in France.
> How I remember! ...
>   My Maries then
> Could see no beauty in his resolute
> Gashed brow and hasty lips. I trusted him,

And turned me over many a night to dream
How he had dragged me from mine enemies.
Ah, then, what golden rills
Of youth coursed through me, sudden bounties, gifts
Of goodness, incommensurable joys
That never had an issue."

Then comes the waning of their passion, as merciless and vol-
canic as its waxing.

Many more dramas may yet be printed on the ever-fascinating
and still-perplexing theme of the Scottish queen, but it will be
long ere another is written so well deserving of its title as "The
Tragic Mary." The work done in literature by these two modern
English women, whose very names have not yet got into print, is
so closely welded that no criticism will distinguish the two
threads; and it is possible that they may go down to posthumous
fame simply as Michael Field.

T.W.H.

4. Review of *Underneath the Bough* (Anon.), *The Athenaeum*, 9 September 1893

Although many of the lyrics in "Underneath the Bough" have
long been well known in Michael Field's plays, they are welcome
thus reprinted; for the bringing them together in one volume, and
together with other lyrics not from the plays, besides making a
convenient collection of goodly verse, presents the reader with a
compact yet varied view of Michael Field's lyrical impulses and
combinations. The intellectual strength and originality—the
acquired mannerism—the rich condensed expression—the fine
intensity planned and dominatingly present, yet skilfully kept half
concealed—the splendid control of meter, coupled with the
inability, or more probably the want of wish, to fascinate by the
melody of balanced cadences and with the preference for the
grace of quaint and skilful mingled stiffness—are, while always
recognizable in any of Michael Field's songs and brief separate
lyrics, brought into still stronger prominence as essential charac-
teristics by the close kindred resemblance apparent when these
poems are grouped together.

The beauty of thought and phrase in the contents of "Under-
neath the Bough" is great. So is the beauty of their themes. The
two great thoughts, Death and Love—with Sorrow for the inner
name of both—are in fact almost the sole inspirations of the
whole, but there is no monotony. Michael Field is too masterly to

harp on recurrent ideas and jade sentiment to triteness, and the inspirational thoughts pass into new themes, themes with each a varied aspect, if with the same core of life. And while on a first quick perusal one receives the impression of unity—almost as if the poems were irregular stanzas of one work—afterwards, try to find any two poems to pair together as written from exactly the same point of view and you fail. Or if there be an exception to this, it is in the songs of the Third Book—where a supremely sympathetic affection repeats itself in poems which in other respects are diversified. It is in the conceptions of death that shades of difference are most frequent and most marked. In one poem we have death as a kindly annihilation:—

[Here the reviewer reproduces "Death, men say, is like a sea." See p. 116 of this book.]

In another poem the feeling is of death as a freedom and an expansion of soul:—

> Death, for all thy grasping stealth,
>   Thou dost convey
> Lands to us of broadest wealth,
>   That stretch away
> Where the sunshine hath no foil,
> Past the verge of our dark soil,
> Past the rim where clouds uncoil.
>
> Mourners, whom thine avarice dooms,
>   Once given a space
> In thy kingdom past the tombs,
>   With open face
> See the smallness of our skies,
> Large, until a mortal dies
> And shrinks them to created size.
>
> O the freedom, that doth spread,
>   When life is shown
> The great countries that the dead
>   Have open thrown;
> Where, at our best leisure, we
> With a spirit may walk free
> From terrestrial poverty.

Then here is a tender fancy of death's life—almost like a spiritual allegory:—

> Dream not no darkness bars
> Her world, who in the stars
>   Had such delight
> That jealously she turned to slumber;
> Her eyelids now sleep doth not cumber,
>   And she, awake all night,
>   Helps God to number
>   The shining stars.

And still in poem after poem death will be found appearing somewhat other than before—the treatment modified by the immediate theme. Love is set forth in sundry ways—sometimes in conceits, sometimes in utterances of grave poetic earnestness, as adoration, as reproach, as reminiscence—but almost always it is connected in some way with death, and always it is very near sadness or pain.

A peculiarity of these poems is that while they are of antique mould, ancestral not merely in form but in expression, they are in feeling distinctively modern. There may fitly be applied to them their author's words in "An Invitation,"

> all the songs I sing
> Welling, welling
> From Elizabethan spring:

But their waters have gathered in the breath of to-day. The sad heart of the nineteenth century speaks through this later Elizabethan. They were cheerier mortals in the era of the Elizabethan race of poets than we are now. They had perils and calamities from which we are exempt; rebellions, plots and rumours of plots, with their consequences of headings and hangings and imprisonments and confiscations—not to speak of religious persecutions and of other rough risks, legal and illegal—would bring sudden storms of misery into many a home, and kept everybody familiar with the thought of the direst tragedies as among the ills incident to human life: but they had more content with life than we have. They took their joys and sorrows separately; they knew the one kind from the other—which we scarcely do—and they understood their sorrow for the downright thing it was, and they were not wistful in their joy. Most likely it was because they lived face to face with troubles of so frankly unmitigated a kind and the contrasts between their fair-weather and their foul-weather experiences were so strenuously marked, they were less unsatisfied and questioning, less burdened by a sense of the pathos of mortal existence, than we who have fallen on stiller days: it is not a tussling period that trains to brooding and lassitude, it is a drifting one. But without searching in the causes of the difference, certain it is that a spiritual, deprecating melancholy, not found in sixteenth and seventeenth century literature has a deep and pervading influence in the thought, and especially in the poetical thought, of our time. And by this quality Michael Field, however markedly and ably of the school of the more ancient period, is unmistakably dated nineteenth century.

There is a portrait in the Third Book which, besides being of most gracious workmanship, is notably interesting for its statement of a strange poetic unison of two. This is it:—

[Here the reviewer reproduces "A girl." See p. 125 of this book.]

The concluding lines, those which describe the dear fulfilment of the older life in the young, are psychologically as well as in expression very beautiful and wise; but to most readers the peculiar interest of the stanza will lie in the suggestion of the two lives, not twin, but with one heart.

5. Review of *Wild Honey* (Anon.), *The Academy*, 8 February 1908

At last the heretofore inaccessible work of the two poets who write under the name of Michael Field has been published in England. "Wild Honey" is one of the most delightful books that the last ten years have given us, and should be read by every lover of poetry. In a time when a hundred writers have learnt the trick of a pseudo-poetic diction that seems as the voice of Apollo himself to all but the true enthusiast, it is very good to find verse with the unmistakable, indefinable thrill of ecstasy that distinguishes the singer by impulse from the singer by rule. Many of the poems in "Wild Honey" are inspired by the lovely myths of Greece, and it is in these that the mystical ardour burns most keenly. Tennyson can produce a piece of verse on a classical subject, degrading gods and heroes and fair women to empty names and dead dust in the process; one in a thousand can feel that the gods are not dead, but only changed and less joyful, and that the old myths lose no beauty, but attain a new gravity when seen by modern eyes, so that, as in "Wild Honey," Ixion forgets his torment in dreams of a cloud, and, if Persephone is sad, it [is] because she is homesick for Hades. A good example of this new interpretation of old allegories is a sonnet called "Silenus Sober":

As a man looking down from a hill-brow
I look down on all creatures that begin,
On night, on Saturn, on the heavy din,
Round Chaos when the Titans fight enow:
Sometimes a mortal, questioning me how
Life fareth smoothest some slight jest doth win,
Sometimes agape I watch the Fates that spin,
Or in my woodland track the snuffling sow.
Sometimes I watch the satyrs growing old
And call them the Sileni, but no fold
Is in my heart; my wisdom is to ride,
Benignant to a fair god at my side –
To drink, to drink with him, to sway his mood,
Then home, to fill myself with solitude.

The lyrics in the volume seem to vibrate with a passionate love for every aspect of life, its joy, and beauty, and pain; "the universe, so whole within my mind"—that is the keynote from which every one of these poems is derived:

O Love, O bitter, mortal journeying
    By ways that are not told!
I would not sing, no song is sweet to me
    Now thou art gone:
But would, ah! Would I were the halcyon,
That sky-blue bird of Spring,
    So should I bring
Fair sister companies of fleetest wing
    To bear thee on,
    Thou being old,
With an untroubled heart to carry thee
Safe o'er the ridges of the wearying sea.

Such a lyric emerges triumphantly from the only final test that can be applied to this form of poetry: it is a true cry from the heart.

Appendix: Index to Names of Major Artists and Literary Figures Appearing in the Life-Writing Section

Moore, George, 239, 245, 258, 277, 278.
Moore, Thomas Sturge, 271, 272, 276, 277, 278, 279, 335.
Morris, May and William, 245, 272.
Moreau, Gustave, 243.
Moulton, Louise Chandler, 239, 243, 244, 246.
Nietzsche, Friedrich, 264.
Pater, Walter, 234, 240-42, 258, 267, 316, 319, 326, 350.
Patmore, Coventry, 258, 292.
Plato, 301, 322.
Queen Victoria, 273.
Rabelais, François, 243.
Radford, Dollie and Ernest, 245.
Raffalovich, André, 282, 311.
Redon, Odilon, 243.
Ricketts, Charles, 246, 268, 269, 270-72, 273, 275, 276, 277,
    278-79, 280, 287-88, 333-37.
Robinson, A. Mary F., 244, 348-49.
Rodin, Auguste, 233, 243, 244.
Ross, Robert, 288, 336.
Rossetti, Dante Gabriel, 232, 238, 245, 246, 255, 333.
Rossetti, Christina, 238, 276, 279.
Rossetti, William Michael, 238, 279.
Rothenstein, William, 332.
Ruskin, John, 238, 266, 306-09, 330.
Russell, Bertrand, 263, 267.
Sand, George, 241.
Sappho, 233-34, 257, 274, 349, 350.
Shakespeare, William, 236, 244, 252, 271, 275, 276, 303, 304,
    307, 349.
Shannon, Charles, 246, 269, 270-71, 277, 280, 333-35.
Shelley, Percy Bysshe, 260, 262.
Spencer, Herbert, 236.
Smith, Alice and Logan Pearsall, 263, 267.
Spinoza, 311.
Swinburne, Algernon Charles, 333, 351.
Symons, Arthur, 243, 244, 245, 258, 260, 267, 268, 282, 345,
    351-52.
Symonds, John Addington, 272.
Tennyson, Lord Alfred, 242, 256.
Thackeray, William Makepeace, 241.
Thompson, Francis, 292, 295.
Tomson, Graham R., 350.
Tolstoi, Leo, 319, 350.

Bibliography of Bradley and Cooper's Major Published Volumes

For a complete list of works, published and unpublished, see Ivor C. Treby's *Michael Field Catalogue* [De Blackland Press, 1998] in which the major archival holdings of Michael Field manuscripts are described.

The Poetry

The New Minnesinger and Other Poems (London: Longmans, Green and Co, 1875) by Arran Leigh.

Long Ago (London: George Bell and Sons, 1889) by Michael Field.

Sight and Song (London: Elkin Mathews and John Lane, 1892) by Michael Field.

Underneath the Bough (London: George Bell and Sons, 1893) by Michael Field.

Underneath the Bough, revised and decreased edition (London: George Bell & Sons, 1893) by Michael Field.

Long Ago (Portland, Maine: Thomas B. Mosher, 1897) by Michael Field.

Underneath the Bough (Portland, Maine: Thomas B. Mosher 1898) by Michael Field.

Wild Honey from Various Thyme (London: T. Fisher Unwin, 1908) by Michael Field.

Poems of Adoration (London: Sands and Co., 1912) by Michael Field.

Mystic Trees (London: Everleigh Nash, 1913) by Michael Field.

Whym Chow (London: Eragny Press, 1914) by Michael Field.

Dedicated (London: George Bell and Sons, 1914) by Michael Field.

A Selection from the Poems of Michael Field (London: The Poetry Bookshop, 1923) ed. T. Sturge Moore.

The Wattlefold (Oxford: Basil Blackwell, 1930) unpublished later poetry of Michael Field, collected by Emily C. Fortey, with a preface by Vincent McNabb.

English Poetry, full-text database (Chadwyck-Healey), includes 565 of Michael Field's published poems.

There are unpublished poems to be found in draft form in the diaries, many of which have been published in Ivor C. Treby's three-volume collection of Michael Field verse: *In Leash to the Stranger. A Shorter Shîrazâd* (De Blackland Books, 1999), *Music and Silence* (De Blackland Books, 2000), and *Uncertain Rain* (De Blackland Books, 2002).

The Drama

Bellerophôn and Other Poems (London: C. Kegan Paul and Co., 1881) by Arran and Isla Leigh.

Callirrhoë and *Fair Rosamund* (London: George Bell and Sons, 1884) by Michael Field.

The Father's Tragedy, William Rufus, Loyalty or Love? (London: George Bell and Sons, 1885) by Michael Field.

Brutus Ultor (London: George Bell and Sons, 1886) by Michael Field.

Canute the Great, The Cup of Water (London: George Bell and Sons, 1887) by Michael Field.

The Tragic Mary (London: George Bell and Sons, 1890) by Michael Field.

Stephania. A Trialogue (London: Elkin Mathews and John Lane, 1892) by Michael Field.

A Question of Memory (London: Elkin Mathews and John Lane, 1893) by Michael Field.

Attila, My Attila! (London: Elkin Mathews, 1895) by Michael Field.

Fair Rosamund (London: Ballantyne Press, 1897) by Michael Field.

The World at Auction (London: Ballantyne Press, 1898) by Michael Field.

Anna Ruina (London: David Nutt, 1899) by Michael Field.

Noontide Branches (Oxford: Henry Daniel, 1899) by Michael Field.

The Race of Leaves (London: Ballantyne Press, 1901) by Michael Field.

Julia Domna (London: Ballantyne Press, 1903) by Michael Field.

Borgia (London: A.H. Bullen, 1905) published anonymously.

Queen Mariamne (London: Sidgwick and Jackson, 1908) by the author of *Borgia*.

The Tragedy of Pardon, and *Diane: A Fantasy* (London: Sidgwick and Jackson, 1911) by the author of *Borgia*.

The Accuser, Tristan De Léonois, A Messiah (London: Sidgwick and Jackson, 1911) by the author of *Borgia*.

Deirdre, A Question of Memory, Ras Byzance (London: The Poetry Bookshop, 1918) by Michael Field.

In the Name of Time (London: The Poetry Bookshop, 1919) by Michael Field.

Above Mount Alverna, Iphigenia in Arsacia, The Assumption (Oxford: Basil Blackwell, 1930) published anonymously.

English Verse Drama, full-text database (Chadwyck-Healey), includes 26 of Michael Field's plays.

The Diaries and Correspondence

The manuscript diaries and letters have been published in the following forms:

Works and Days: from the Journal of Michael Field (London: John Murray, 1933) ed. T. and D.C. Sturge Moore (with introduction by Sir William Rothenstein).

Michael Field and Fin-de-Siècle Culture and Society. The Diaries and Correspondence of Michael Field held in the British Library. Introduced by Marion Thain. Adam Matthew: 2003. (13 reels of microfilm.)

Binary Star. Leaves from the Journal and Letters of Michael Field 1846-1914. Ed. Ivor C. Treby. Bury St. Edmunds: De Blackland Press, 2006.

Journal Publications

For details of the many publications of verse and short prose pieces in journals we refer readers to Ivor C. Treby's *Michael Field Catalogue.* Here we list some that might be of particular interest to readers of this volume.

"An Old Couple" (*The Contemporary Review* 51, February 1887, pp. 220-25)

"Mid-Age" (*The Contemporary Review* 56, September 1889, pp. 431-32)

"A Lumber-Room" (*The Contemporary Review* 57, January 1890, pp. 98-102)

"Effigies" (*The Art Review*, vol. 1, no 3, March 1890)

Select Bibliography of Critical and Related Work

Andrews, Kit. "The Dialectics of Conversion: Marius and Michael Field." In Stetz and Wilson, 97-105.

Armstrong, Isobel. *Victorian Glassworlds: Glass Culture and the Imagination 1830-1880*. Oxford: Oxford UP, 2008.

Basant, Wendy. "Aesthetes and Queens: Michael Field, John Ruskin, and *Bellerophôn*." *Journal of Pre-Raphaelite Studies* 15 (2006): 74-94.

Bickle, Sharon. "Rethinking Michael Field: The Case for the Bodleian Letters." In Stetz and Wilson, 39-47.

Blain, Virginia. "'Michael Field, the Two-Headed Nightingale': Lesbian Text as Palimpsest." *Women's History Review* 5.2 (1996): 239-57.

Bristow, Joseph. "Michael Field's Lyrical Aestheticism: *Underneath the Bough*." In Stetz and Wilson, 49-62.

Cameron, Brooke. "'Where Twilight Touches Ripeness Amorously': The Gaze in Michael Field's *Sight and Song*." In Stetz and Wilson, 147-53.

Cauti, Camille. "Michael Field's Pagan Catholicism." In Stetz and Wilson, 181-89.

DeGuzmán, María. "Attributing the Substance of Collaboration as Michael Field." In Stetz and Wilson, 71-82.

Delaney, Paul. "Book Design: A Nineteenth-Century Revival." *The Connoisseur* (1978): 282-89.

Dellamora, Richard. "The Sapphic Culture of Michael Field and Radclyffe Hall." In Stetz and Wilson, 127-36.

Donoghue, Emma. *We Are Michael Field*. Bath: Absolute Press, 1998.

Ehnenn, Jill. "Looking Strategically: Feminist and Queer Aesthetics in Michael Field's *Sight and Song*." *Victorian Poetry* 43.1 (2005): 109-54.

Faderman, Lillian. *Surpassing the Love of Men*. London: Junction Books, 1981.

Fehlbaum, Valerie. "Sisters in Life, Sisters in Art: Ella and Marion Hepworth Dixon." In Stetz and Wilson, 107-15.

Fletcher, Robert P. "'I Leave a Page Half-Writ': Narrative Discoherence in Michael Field's *Underneath the Bough*." In *Women's Poetry, Late Romantic to Late Victorian: Gender and*

Genre, 1830-1900. Ed. Isobel Armstrong and Virginia Blain. Basingstoke: Macmillan, 1999. 164-82.

Frankel, Nicholas. "The Concrete Poetics of Michael Field's *Sight and Song.*" In Stetz and Wilson, 211-21.

Fraser, Hilary. "The Religious Poetry of Michael Field." In *Athena's Shuttle: Myth Religion Ideology from Romanticism to Modernism.* Ed. Franco Marucci and Emma Sdegno. Milan, Italy: Cisalpino, 2000. 127-42.

——. "A Visual Field: Michael Field and the Gaze." *Victorian Literature and Culture* 34.2 (2006): 553-71.

Hickok, Kathleen. *Representations of Women.* Westport, Connecticut, and London: Greenwood Press, 1984.

Hughes, Linda K. "Reluctant Lions: Michael Field and the Transatlantic Literary Salon of Louise Chandler Moulton." In Stetz and Wilson, 117-25.

Ireland, Kenneth R. "*Sight and Song:* A Study of the Interrelations between Painting and Poetry." *Victorian Poetry* 15 (1977): 9-20.

Laird, Holly. "The Coauthored Pseudonym: Two Women Named Michael Field." In *The Faces of Anonymity: Anonymous and Pseudonymous Publications from the Sixteenth to the Twentieth Century.* Ed. Robert Griffin. New York: Palgrave Macmillan, 2003. 193-209.

——. "Contradictory Legacies: Michael Field and Feminist Restoration." *Victorian Poetry* 33 (1995): 111-27.

——. *Women Coauthors.* Urbana: U of Illinois P, 2000.

——. "Michael Field as 'the Author of *Borgia*'." In Stetz and Wilson, 29-38.

Leighton, Angela. *Victorian Women Poets: Writing Against the Heart.* Hemel Hempstead: Harvester Wheatsheaf, 1992.

Locard, Henri. "Works and Days: The Journals of 'Michael Field.'" *Journal of the Eighteen Nineties Society* 10 (1979): 1-9.

Lysack, Krista. "Aesthetic Consumption and the Cultural Production of Michael Field's *Sight and Song.*" *SEL Studies in English Literature 1500-1900* 45.4 (2005): 935-60.

Madden, Ed. "Penetrating Matthew Arnold." In Stetz and Wilson, 83-95.

Maltz, Diana. "Katharine Bradley and Ethical Socialism." In Stetz and Wilson, 191-201.

McCormack, Jerusha. *The Man Who Was Dorian Gray.* Basingstoke: Palgrave, 2000.

McDonald, Jan. "'Disillusioned Bards and Despised Bohemi-
ans': Michael Field's *A Question of Memory* at the Indepen-
dent Theatre Society." *Theatre Notebook: A Journal of the
History and Technique of the British Theatre* 31.2 (1977): 18-29.

Moriarty, David J. "'Michael Field' and Their Male Critics." In
Nineteenth-Century Women Writers of the English-Speaking World.
Ed. Rhoda B. Nathan. New York: Greenwood Press, 1986.
121-42.

Morley, Rachel. "Constructing the Self, Composing the Other:
Auto/Fixation and the Case of Michael Field." *Colloquy: Text
Theory Critique* 8 (2004): no pagination:
<www.colloquy.monash.edu.au/issue008/morley.html>.

———. "Talking Collaboratively: Conversations with Michael
Field." In Stetz and Wilson, 13-21.

O'Gorman, Francis. "Michael Field and Sapphic Fame: 'My
Dark-Leaved Laurels Will Endure.'" *Victorian Literature and
Culture* 34.2 (2006): 649-61.

———. "Browning's Manuscript Revisions to Michael Field's
Long Ago (1889)." *Browning Society Notes* 25 (1998): 38-44.

Pionke, Katharine (JJ). "Michael Field: Gender Knot." In Stetz
and Wilson, 23-27.

Primamore, Elizabeth. "Michael Field as Dandy Poet." In Stetz
and Wilson, 137-46.

Prins, Yopie. "Greek Maenads, Victorian Spinsters." *Victorian
Sexual Dissidence*. Ed. Richard Dellamora. Chicago and
London: U of Chicago P, 1999. 43-81.

———. "A Metaphorical Field: Katherine Bradley and Edith
Cooper." *Victorian Poetry* 33 (1995): 129-48.

———. "Sappho Doubled: Michael Field." *Yale Journal of Criti-
cism* 8 (1995): 165-86.

———. *Victorian Sappho*. Princeton, NJ: Princeton UP, 1999.

Reynolds, Margaret. "'I Lived for Art, I Lived for Love': The
Woman Poet Sings Sappho's Last Song." In *Victorian Women
Poets: A Critical Reader*. Ed. Angela Leighton. Oxford: Black-
well, 1996. 277-306.

———. *The Sappho History*. Houndmills, Basingstoke: Palgrave,
2003.

Ricketts, Charles. *Letters from Charles Ricketts to "Michael Field"
(1903-1913)*. Ed. J.G. Paul Delaney. Edinburgh: The Tragara
Press, 1981.

———. *Michael Field*. Ed. J.G. Paul Delaney. Edinburgh: The
Tragara Press, 1976.

———. *Some Letters from Charles Ricketts and Charles Shannon to "Michael Field" (1894-1902)*. Ed. J.G. Paul Delaney. Edinburgh: The Tragara Press, 1979.

Roden, Frederick S. *Same-Sex Desire in Victorian Religious Culture*. Houndmills, Basingstoke: Palgrave, 2002.

———. "Michael Field and the Challenges of Writing a Lesbian Catholicism." In Stetz and Wilson, 155-62.

Saville, Julia F. "The Poetic Imaging of Michael Field." In *The Fin-de-Siècle Poem*. Ed. Joseph Bristow. Athens: Ohio UP, 2005. 178-206.

Snodgrass, Chris. "Keeping Faith: Consistency and Paradox in the World View of Michael Field." In Stetz and Wilson, 171-80.

Stetz, Margaret D., and Cheryl A. Wilson, eds. *Michael Field and their World*. High Wycombe: The Rivendale Press, 2007.

Sturgeon, Mary. *Michael Field*. London: Harrap and Co., 1921.

Taft, Vickie L. "The Tragic Mary: A Case Study in Michael Field's Understanding of Sexual Politics." *Nineteenth-Century Contexts* 23.2 (2001): 265-95.

Thain, Marion. "'Damnable Aestheticism' and the Turn to Rome: John Gray, Michael Field, and a Poetics of Conversion." In *The Fin-de-Siècle Poem*. Ed. Joseph Bristow. Athens: Ohio UP, 2005. 311-36.

———. "Apian Aestheticism: Michael Field and the Economics of the Aesthetic." In Stetz and Wilson, 223-36.

———. *Michael Field and Poetic Identity (with a Biography)*. London: Eighteen Nineties Society, 2000.

———. *Michael Field: Poetry, Aestheticism and the Fin de Siècle*. Cambridge: Cambridge UP, 2007.

Vadillo, Ana I. Parejo. "*Sight and Song*: Transparent Translations and a Manifesto for the Observer." *Victorian Poetry* 38 (2000): 15-34.

———. *Women Poets and Urban Aestheticism*. Houndmills, Basingstoke: Palgrave Macmillan, 2005.

———. "Outmoded Dramas: History and Modernity in Michael Field's Aesthetic Plays." In Stetz and Wilson, 237-49.

Vanita, Ruth. *Sappho and the Virgin Mary*. New York: Columbia UP, 1996.

Vicinus, Martha. "The Adolescent Boy: Fin de Siècle Femme Fatale?" *Journal of the History of Sexuality* 5 (1994-5): 90-114.

———. "'Sister Souls': Bernard Berenson and Michael Field

(Katharine Bradley and Edith Cooper)." *Nineteenth-Century Literature* 60.3 (2005): 326-54.

———. *Intimate Friends. Women Who Loved Women, 1778-1928.* Chicago: U of Chicago P, 2004.

Ward, Dinah. "Michael Field and Saint Sebastian." In Stetz and Wilson, 163-70.

White, Christine. "Flesh and Roses: Michael Field's Metaphors of Pleasure and Desire." *Women's Writing* 3.1 (1996): 47-62.

———. "'Poets and Lovers Evermore': Interpreting Female Love in the Poetry and Journals of Michael Field." *Textual Practice* 4.2 (1990): 197-212.

———. "The Tiresian Poet: Michael Field." In *Victorian Women Poets: A Critical Reader.* Ed. Angela Leighton. Oxford: Blackwell, 1996. 148-61.

Williams, Rhian E. "Michael Field's Shakespearean Community." In Stetz and Wilson, 63-70.

Wise, Julie. "Michael Field's Translations into Verse." In Stetz and Wilson, 203-10.